From the reviews of *Handy Hints on Legal Practice*

"It is redolent of robust common sense, humour and broad humanity . . . there is plenty of sound advice for practitioners young, tired or embattled. *Handy Hints on Legal Practice* is a book which a lawyer could profitably read on the afternoon of his or her admission to the bar, and then re-read on every anniversary of that admission."

Northern News

"Read this book! It will give you a practical foundation on which to build your skills as a lawyer."

Law Institute Journal

"A copy of this book ought to be given to every graduate upon his or her taking their first job; it ought to be an obligation to re-read it every fifth anniversary of that first job."

Law Society Journal (N.S.W.)

"Commonsense is largely acquired by experience, but a great deal of it can be obtained from the advice contained in this book."

Journal of Professional Legal Education

"All-in-all, a valuable text book, yet as entertaining to read as a novel."

Criminal Law Journal

"It seems unlikely that there is any situation in which a lawyer may find himself that is not referred to in this book."

Australian Law News

"This is a book which ought to be read from cover to cover by all young lawyers."

Lawyer

About the authors

GORDON D. LEWIS, LL.B. (Melb.), is a Judge of the County Court of Victoria. He has formerly held the positions of Executive Director of the Law Institute of Victoria, Victorian Commissioner for Corporate Affairs, Victorian Government Solicitor and Part-time Lecturer in Professional Conduct, University of Melbourne.

EMILIOS J. KYROU, LL.B. (Hons) (Melb.), B.Com. (Melb.), is a solicitor of the Supreme Court of New South Wales and a barrister and solicitor of the Supreme Courts of Victoria, South Australia, Western Australia and the Australian Capital Territory. He is a partner of Mallesons Stephen Jaques, Solicitors.

Lewis & Kyrou's

Handy Hints on Legal Practice

Sales Centres and Agents

Head Office: 44-50 Waterloo Road NORTH RYDE N.S.W. 2113
Tel: (02) 887 0177 Fax: (02) 888 2287

4th Floor 167 Phillip Street SYDNEY N.S.W. 2000
Tel: (02) 235 0766 Fax: (02) 221 4004

568 Lonsdale Street MELBOURNE Vic. 3000
Tel: (03) 670 7888 Fax: (03) 670 0138

1st Floor 40 Queen Street BRISBANE Qld 4000
Tel: (07) 221 6688 Fax: (07) 220 0084

9th Floor St George's Centre 81 St George's Terrace PERTH W.A. 6000
Tel: (09) 321 8583 Fax: (09) 324 1910

Sales Representative Keith Peterson GPO Box 384 ADELAIDE S.A. 5001
Tel/Fax: (08) 295 7644 Mobile: 018 84 3052

Preferred Stockist The Bookworld 30 Smith Street DARWIN N.T. 0800
Tel: (089) 81 5277 Fax: (089) 411 226

Sales Representative Peter Stewart CPO Box 3139 AUCKLAND N.Z.
Tel: (09) 366 7204 Fax: (09) 309 5336

CANADA AND U.S.A.

The Carswell Company Ltd
Agincourt, Ontario

HONG KONG

Bloomsbury Books Ltd

MALAYSIA

Malayan Law Journal Pte Ltd
Kuala Lumpur

SINGAPORE

Malayan Law Journal Pte Ltd

UNITED KINGDOM

Sweet & Maxwell Ltd
London

U.S.A.

Wm W. Gaunt & Sons, Inc.
Holmes Beach, Florida

Lewis & Kyrou's

Handy Hints on Legal Practice

by

GORDON D. LEWIS
LL.B. (Melb.)

and

EMILIOS J. KYROU
LL.B. (Hons) (Melb.), B.Com. (Melb.)

SECOND EDITION

Foreword by
SIR NINIAN STEPHEN

THE LAW BOOK COMPANY LIMITED
1993

Published in Sydney by

The Law Book Company Limited
44-50 Waterloo Road, North Ryde, N.S.W.
568 Lonsdale Street, Melbourne, Victoria
40 Queen Street, Brisbane, Queensland
81 St George's Terrace, Perth, W.A.

First edition 1985
second impression 1987
Second edition 1993

National Library of Australia
Cataloguing-in-Publication entry

Lewis, Gordon D. (Gordon David), 1934-
Handy hints on legal practice.

2nd edition.
Includes index.
ISBN 0 455 21201 5.

1. Practice of law. 2. Practice of law—Australia. 3. Law offices.
4. Law offices—Australia. I. Kyrou, Emilios J. II. Title.

340.068

Designed and edited by Tricia Hogan

Typeset in Garamond, 10 on 11 point, and in Omega, by
Mercier Typesetters Pty Ltd, Granville, N.S.W.
Printed by Ligare Pty Ltd, Riverwood, N.S.W.

Gordon Lewis dedicates this book to his wife Rhonda.

Emilios Kyrou dedicates this book to his wife Peris, his children, John, William, Stephen and Catherine and his parents, John and Stella.

Foreword to the Second Edition

THE RT HON. SIR NINIAN STEPHEN

For any young solicitor, for any junior at the bar, pitfalls abound, as do occasional, and compensating, days of triumph. Life as a young lawyer as I remember it was as stressful as it was exciting, constantly fluctuating between deep despondency and high exhilaration, depending on the fortunes of the day. Nor is all this confined to the tyro; even the veteran lawyer still occasionally experiences the angst of the unfamiliar and it will be a sad veteran who has wholly forgotten the savour of occasional high success.

What one soon learns in the law is that to know the relevant law, assuming that blessed state to be occasionally attainable, is not enough; there are innumerable practical questions to which legal studies provide no answers—all the way from how best to initiate negotiations for settlement of an apparently hopeless case to how to handle the naturally testy judge who gives every sign of becoming as impatient with one's client in the witness box as one has long been with that same client out of it.

With experience, difficulties diminish but all experience is hard won, all too often at the expense of the unfortunate client, whose consequent disillusionment adds to the volume of public cynicism about lawyers and the law.

Now no longer need bitter experience and the ad hoc advice of others be the only sources of practical guidance through the minefields of the law. Judge Lewis and Emilios Kyrou first came to the rescue eight years ago with their first edition of *Handy Hints*. This second edition retains all the wisdom, and wit, of its predecessor while adding much that is new: discussion of such esoteric topics as Chinese walls and alternative dispute resolution, of such familiar afflictions as the "I can't say no" syndrome and the "time to quit" condition; these and other topics timely for the '90s feature in this new edition.

The theme throughout is that common sense will solve many problems of practice in the law. But what is common sense in any given situation may only emerge in discussion and with wise counsel and, as the authors say, legal practice can on occasion be a very lonely affair if there is no one with whom to talk over troubles or discuss solutions. *Handy Hints* furnishes much common, and some uncommon, sense and for the lonely and troubled practitioner it provides welcome company and wise advice. Its authors have given us not only an invaluable guide to good practice in the law but also a delightful description of its many tribulations and how best to survive them in good shape.

Foreword to the First Edition

JOHN MORTIMER

My father, when he was busy persuading me to become a barrister, used to say that all you needed for success in the law was a certain amount of common sense and relatively clean finger nails. I believe I managed the common sense, although I don't know if the finger nails have always been impeccable.

He was exaggerating, of course. It's necessary to know a little law, and to know where to look up the rest. But the daily practice of a barrister or a solicitor is something utterly removed from the theoretical legal studies which go on in the safe atmosphere of schools and universities. The qualities the practising lawyer needs, courage, persistence, a refusal to abandon the most unlovable client or to be overawed by the highest tribunal, are no part of an academic training. Nor is the true art of cross-examination, the even more nerve-racking business of examination-in-chief, the skill needed to woo a judge and the knowledge of when to abandon him and woo the jury instead, taught in any university. Such lessons are only learnt in the hardest way in the hardest courts in which the lawyer begins his real life, for it seems to be the rule that the humblest courts are the most difficult and the least sympathetic. The truth is that the law is not an academic subject. It only comes to life when it's applied in real situations, to people in real trouble.

Gordon Lewis and Emilios Kyrou have written a most valuable book which gently and expertly bridges the gap between legal training and legal experience. A lawyer's duty to his client (you must do everything for him except deceive the court), his duty to his opponent and his duty to the tribunal before which he practises are discussed with admirable common sense. A great part of the civil lawyer's life is concerned with negotiation and the authors deal with such delicate manoeuvres with considerable expertise. If all their advice were taken the legal world might be a better place: it is no part of a lawyer's duty to encourage his client to behave more greedily or more ruthlessly than his better nature might suggest.

Lawyers are notoriously, together with income tax collectors, politicians and traffic wardens, the most disliked members of the community. They are thought to be dishonest, money-grubbing and insincere. And yet all our great freedoms, the presumption of innocence, the right not to be imprisoned without a trial, the right to silence and the requirement that police officers should be restrained from inventing too many verbal admissions, depend on the vigilance, courage and skill of lawyers. If they all follow the wise advice contained in this book we should not have much to fear.

Preface to the Second Edition

When the first edition of the book was written eight years ago, we sought to emphasise the "common sense" aspects of the practice of law rather than produce a scholarly work on areas of substantive law. By doing so, we hoped to capture those features of legal practice which have been accepted by generations of lawyers and which are impervious to change. For one thing, we did not wish to produce a second edition in a hurry!

We have been only partially successful in achieving our aims. While many parts of the book have stood the test of time, there have been significant changes in some areas of practice in the last eight years which have necessitated a second edition.

All chapters of the book have been updated. The main differences between the first and second editions are as follows:

- Chapter 5 (Confidentiality and Legal Professional Privilege) contains a discussion of privileged documents supplied to an opponent in error and search warrants executed on lawyers' premises;
- Chapter 6 (Conflict of Interest) contains a discussion on "Chinese walls";
- Chapter 14 is a new chapter dealing with Alternative Dispute Resolution;
- Chapter 19 is a new chapter headed Assisting the Disadvantaged (Pro Bono);
- Chapter 21 (Precautions Against Negligence) contains a new section on commercial transactions;
- Chapter 22 (Unprofessional Conduct) contains new sections on witnessing affidavits, defrauding partners, supervision of staff, conflict of interest, conducting another business, not honouring obligations, tax advice and defrauding the revenue, breach of undertaking, ignorance is no excuse and dishonesty not required;
- Chapter 25 (Contempt of Court) contains new sections on Lord Erskine's noble stand for the independence of the Bar,

abuse of process, obstruction, destroying documents, breach of orders or undertakings, failure to appear in court, scandalising and sub judice;

- Chapter 27 (Conducting a Case) contains a new section on starting out;
- Chapter 28 is a new chapter headed Instructing in Court;
- Chapter 29 is a new chapter headed From the Bench;
- Chapter 31 (General Mistakes and Misapprehensions) contains a new section on irrevocable authorities;
- Chapter 37 (Telephone) contains a new section on speaker phones;
- Chapter 38 is a new chapter dealing with faxes;
- Chapter 39 (Without Prejudice) contains a new section on "off the record";
- Part 7 is a new part headed Practice Management and contains new chapters on prioritising, file management and technology;
- Part 8 is a new part headed Working in the Law and contains new chapters on Back to Basics—Lessons from the 1980s, A Survival Kit For New Lawyers and Women in the Law;
- Part 9 is a new part headed Leaving the Law—Common Legal Diseases and contains new chapters on the "I Can't Say No" syndrome and the "Time to Quit" condition.

The second edition, unlike the first edition, uses gender neutral terms.

We hope that the second edition does justice to the trends that have emerged in the practice of law since the first edition was published and that *Handy Hints on Legal Practice* continues to be relevant and useful to legal practitioners in all common law jurisdictions.

G. D. LEWIS
E. J. KYROU

Melbourne
February 1993

Preface to the First Edition

This is a simple book. Its main purpose is to bridge, in a modest sort of way, the gap between what law students learn at university and what they need to know to practise law. Another important purpose is to provide a readily accessible guide to the basic features of legal practice which can be used by all practitioners.

The authors have felt for some time that there is a real need for a book of this kind which addresses matters that are of relevance and importance to law students and practitioners, and which seeks to provide a practical foundation for the practice of law.

It is not the purpose of the book to provide in-depth discussion of statute and case law in particular areas. Rather, the book seeks to provide a general overview of the legal and practical considerations that affect the practice of law. The book gives considerable emphasis to "common sense", which is an essential prerequisite to the practice of law.

The book is intended to have general application. It is relevant to both branches of the profession—barristers as well as solicitors—and to all common law jurisdictions. The book deliberately does not cover matters which are specific to a particular jurisdiction.

The book does not pretend to be exhaustive. The authors have concentrated on areas that they believe most commonly arise for consideration. It is hoped that the subject matter of the book will expand with subsequent editions.

Some parts of the book are based on articles written by G. D. Lewis in the Victorian *Law Institute Journal* during 1983, 1984 and 1985.

In view of the growing popularity of "gender neutral terms", the authors wish to emphasise at the outset that in using the word "he" throughout the book, they do not wish to be sexist.

The word is used merely for convenience and it is intended to refer to both males and females.

G. D. LEWIS
E. J. KYROU

Melbourne
January 1985

Acknowledgments for the Second Edition

We wish to thank Susan Woodford for her valuable research assistance and preparation of drafts of Chapters 14 and 49.

We also wish to thank the following people and organisations for their kind assistance in the preparation of the second edition of this book: Mick Batskos, who assisted with research; Joanne Cameron who prepared drafts of Chapters 41, 42, 43 and 46; Matt Edmonds who prepared drafts of Chapters 19 and 45, Fiona Blackmore who assisted with research; several partners and solicitors of Mallesons Stephen Jaques (including John Waters, Jim Higgins, Joy Geary, Robert Peters, John Bushby, Melissa Donoghue and Philip Martin) who made some suggestions to the authors in relation to the book; the staff of the Mallesons Stephen Jaques library who provided assistance to the researchers; and Michelle Davidson and Kelly Basset for their enthusiastic and professional typing of the manuscript.

Acknowledgments for the First Edition

The authors are indebted to several people and organisations for their kind assistance in the preparation of this book. They are the Law Institute of Victoria which gave permission for reproduction of material appearing in the *Law Institute Journal*; Mr Graham Fuller who gave permission for reproduction of parts of his articles entitled "En Garde" appearing monthly in the *Law Institute Journal* since 1978; Mr John Ahern who made some suggestions to the authors in relation to agreements on costs (discussed in Chapter 7); staff at the Leo Cussen Institute of Victoria who made some suggestions to the authors in relation to Chapter 27; several partners and solicitors of Messrs Corrs Pavey Whiting & Byrne, Melbourne, who made some suggestions to the authors in relation to Chapters 27, 28 and 29; Mr Robert Hatch, Director of Research and Information at the Law Institute of Victoria, who made some suggestions to the authors in relation to Chapter 28; Mr John Finemore, retired Chief Parliamentary Counsel for Victoria, who made some suggestions to the authors in relation to Chapter 35; the Auckland District Law Society which gave permission for reproduction of parts of a pamphlet entitled "A Guide to Legal Partnerships" in Chapter 37 of the book, and Mrs Merrilyn Thomas for typing the manuscript so efficiently and expertly.

Table of Contents

Part 3

RELATIONSHIP WITH THE PROFESSION AND THE COMMUNITY

Part 4

RELATIONSHIP WITH THE COURTS

Part 5

MISTAKES AND MISAPPREHENSIONS

Part 6

COMMUNICATION AND DRAFTING

Part 7

PRACTICE MANAGEMENT

Part 8

WORKING IN THE LAW

Part 9

LEAVING THE LAW—COMMON LEGAL DISEASES

Part 10

MISCELLANEOUS

Part 1

Relationship with Client

Chapter 1

Introduction

> "The White Rabbit put on his spectacles. 'Where shall I begin, please your Majesty?' he asked. 'Begin at the beginning' the King said, very gravely, 'and go on till you come to the end: then stop'."
>
> Lewis Carroll, *Alice's Adventures in Wonderland*, Ch. 12.

Legal practice was never meant to be easy. You may have a sound grasp of basic legal principles after completing your law course, but that is no guarantee that you will become a good practitioner. The skills required of a good law student are not identical with those required of a good practitioner.

A fundamental reason for this is the existence of a real-life client with a real-life problem seeking a real-life solution to his or her problem. Your client is not interested in the intricacies of the cases and statutes that you spent years mastering. Your client wants you to solve his or her problem quickly and with a minimum of fuss.

The practitioner-client relationship imposes many obligations on you. You have a duty to look after the interests of your client to the best of your ability. You must not only act honestly in the way you handle your client's affairs but you must also exercise a standard of care that is acceptable to the profession. Your duties to your client are fiduciary as well as contractual and therefore you must always place your client's interests before your own.

Your feelings towards your client and your views about the social utility or otherwise of your instructions—in the absence of fraud or criminality or similar exceptional circumstances—

should play no part in the manner in which you carry out those instructions.

The chapters in Part 1 of this book discuss some of the important elements of your professional relationship with your client.

Chapter 2

First Interview with Client

> "So often common sense, a knowledge of humanity and a flair for the business-like way of doing things matter far more than any knowledge of law."
>
> R. E. Megarry, *Lawyer and Litigant in England* (Stevens & Sons Ltd, London, 1962), p. 13.

You will always remember the first time you are called upon to interview a client.[1] You will never be more aware of a lack of grey hairs or a respectable number of birthdays than the moment the receptionist informs you that the client has arrived. How will you handle the interview? How will you convince the client that you know what you are talking about and that the client should be at ease in entrusting you with his or her affairs?

Interviewing a client is not an easy task. Considerable skill is involved. That skill cannot be acquired merely by reading this or any other book; it is built up through experience. All that this book can do is to point out some practical guidelines that may assist you in interviewing clients.

Accepting the client

The first decision you should make is whether you are able to accept the client's matter. As a practising solicitor, you are not obliged to act for a client in a particular matter unless you want to. Some of the considerations that you should take into account before accepting the matter include whether there are any potential conflicts of interest, whether the client's instructions

1. For a theoretical and empirical discussion of a first interview with a client, see A. Sherr, "Lawyers and Clients: The First Meeting" (1986) 49 *Modern Law Review* 323.

involve potential fraud, illegality or other impropriety and whether you are competent to handle the matter. If there is serious doubt on any of these matters it would be prudent to refuse to act for the client.

Take time to explain

Once you decide to accept a matter on behalf of a client, you must decide how you will conduct your first interview with the client. This will depend on the type of person the client is and the nature of the legal problem involved.

It is important to make an accurate assessment of your client at the earliest possible opportunity. If you are dealing with an experienced recovery clerk of a major finance company, it is obvious that you do not have to explain routine court procedures. On the other hand, most clients do not know much about the law or the legal system. This is why they have come to see you. Therefore, you must take some time to explain matters to them as fully as possible and as simply as possible at the earliest opportunity.

Few practitioners are so busy that they cannot afford a few minutes during interviews to tell clients what will be involved in resolving their legal problems. At the outset you should give your clients some indication of the likely costs. In litigious matters, it is vital that your clients know at the earliest stage whether or not they can afford to lose.

Simple language

The complexity of the language you use during interviews with clients once again will depend on the type of client you are dealing with. For most clients, it is essential to avoid legal jargon and to use only expressions that they will understand. In the case of a client who is not very familiar with the English language, you should be very careful in your choice of words.

Do not make the mistake of shouting at clients who are not fluent in English when you sense that they do not understand you. Speaking louder will not help them to understand; rather, you should try to use the simplest language you can in order to enable them to understand you. If the language barrier prevents communication, either arrange an interpreter, or refer the client to a practitioner who speaks the client's language.

Instructions to be complete

At the first interview with your client, ensure that your instructions are complete. Take comprehensive notes of the material facts. If the client is reluctant to disclose the full facts, assure the client that you are obliged to respect the confidentiality of all information provided to you and that in order for you to give appropriate advice, it is essential for you to be told the whole story. Ask pertinent questions—your client is not as skilled as you in appreciating what is relevant and what is irrelevant. Inexperienced clients have a tendency to emphasise matters which they consider are important, but which are in fact completely irrelevant. A client will not be offended if you courteously inform him or her that the matter is irrelevant.

Proper guidance by you during an interview will shorten the duration of the interview and this will reduce the cost to the client. It will also enable you to promptly initiate the appropriate steps to resolve your client's problem. If instructions are not complete, the consequences may be that the steps you take on behalf of your client will be inappropriate and a waste of money, or that you will need to arrange further interviews, which creates delay and further costs for the client. In short, get it right the first time.

In order to ensure that you obtain complete instructions from your client, you should arrange the interview time yourself rather than instructing your secretary to do so. After agreeing on an interview time with your client, you should tell your client to bring all relevant documents to the interview. If your client is not sure which documents are relevant then help him or her.

It is also advisable to ask your client to write down the important things that he or she wants to raise with you before attending the interview. This procedure will make it less likely that the client will forget to tell you something important. It is also likely to shorten the duration of the interview.

It would be helpful for you to inform your client of the probable length of the interview. This will give both of you a time frame to work within, and may assist the client to focus on important issues. If there is a maximum amount of time you can spend with the client for any reason, for example, because you have another client coming to see you at a particular time, then let the first client know in advance so that every effort is made to finish on time. Your client will be very unhappy if you have to cut short an interview because of other commitments of which your client was not aware. The client is likely to believe that you are not only rude but that you are giving other clients priority.

Instructions direct from client

It is vital that you receive instructions direct from your client. If you accept instructions from friends or relatives or persons who purport to act on a client's behalf, you may be inviting unnecessary complications. A classic trap—reflecting values of a past era—is to accept instructions from a client's husband on the assumption that the husband has authority to represent his wife.[2]

Be wary of accepting a new matter over the telephone from someone you have never met—unless of course you work for a firm and the person is an established client of the firm. You should ask for confirmation of your instructions in writing and arrange an interview with the person who telephoned you.

Evidence to support instructions

Ask for evidence to support instructions as soon as the client tells you the facts. Since most clients have an emotional involvement with their matter, their instructions may not be the best possible means of acquiring an objective statement of the facts.

Too often in litigious matters young practitioners wait until they are at the door of the court to seek substantiation of what their client told them initially. This is a dangerous practice, especially for information such as the date of an accident in personal injuries matters. If the client gives you a wrong date and you rely on this, you may later find that the cause of action is statute barred. You should try to verify the date and other material facts from police reports and from doctor, hospital or ambulance records.

If your client's instructions appear to be inconsistent with the objective facts then it is your duty to probe and query in order to determine what the real position is, and thus protect your client's interests. On the other hand, you should not be unduly suspicious of what your client tells you. It is not your role to pass judgment on your client; that is the role of the court.

2. *Mercantile Mutual Insurance Co. Ltd v. Gosper* (1991) 25 N.S.W.L.R. 32.

Do not give hurried advice

When a client first consults you, do not be afraid to tell the client that you do not know the answer to his or her questions, but that you will provide your advice after researching the matter. Do not volunteer advice which you hope you can verify by subsequent research.

If your client insists on obtaining a tentative indication from you as to what you think the advice will be, make sure you are as general as possible. Make it clear that although you think that may be the answer, the client should wait until you advise him or her properly before acting on your advice. Remember that it is not an admission of failure to confess that you do not have all the answers at your fingertips. Sometimes knowing the right questions to ask at an interview may be just as important as knowing the right answers.

At all times, try to ensure that your advice is correct and balanced rather than an unconscious attempt to please your client by giving the advice your client wants to hear.

It is not sufficient for you to tell your client only what the theoretical position is; you must, in addition, draw attention to practical considerations. For example, it is not sufficient to advise that your client has a good cause of action; you must also emphasise that much time and expense will be involved in obtaining judgment and that the judgment will only be worthwhile if the defendant has sufficient funds to meet the judgment or is insured.

Matters of principle

Beware of matters of principle. Some practitioners are persuaded to take proceedings when win, lose or draw, they will have a dissatisfied client on their hands. We all know the client who outlines to you a splendid cause of action which, if successful, will result in an order for $25 against an impecunious defendant. If you tell the client that litigation will be uneconomical and will result in the client being out of pocket, the response will probably be, "It is a matter of principle."

When a client insists upon litigating a matter of principle, it is vital that there be good communication between you and your client. If you decide to stand your ground and refuse to act, ensure that a letter is sent to the client confirming why.

Alternatively, if you decide to follow your client's instructions, then obtain them in writing and obtain an acknowledgment that the client has been advised that the proposed action is likely to be uneconomical, but despite that advice you are instructed to proceed.

Matters of principle often lose their appeal when the time comes for the client to pay the account. To guard against this, you should obtain costs in advance or regular progress payments, as the high principles proclaimed at the start of the proceedings so often disappear after an adverse result of which the client has been forewarned.

Limited instructions

Where a client limits your instructions to a particular aspect of any matter or transaction, you should confirm this in writing so that there can be no misunderstanding at a later date. This problem may arise, for example, in situations where the client has the opportunity to pursue several remedies but limits your instructions to one of the remedies. Again, there can be difficulties where a commercial matter has drafting and conveyancing aspects and your client instructs you that he or she will attend to the conveyancing personally.

Criminal matters

In criminal matters it is desirable for you to obtain instructions from your client while you are alone. In the case of a younger client, this is certainly preferable to having friends or relatives present because the client has probably already tried to justify himself or herself to them. To have others present at the initial instructions is to taint the purity of the version of the facts you are obtaining from your client. Any accused is reluctant to contradict an earlier version given to friends or relatives.

You should also bear in mind that on the question of prior criminal record, clients frequently fail to reveal their previous convictions in the presence of a spouse, child, or a friend who has never heard of the trouble. Once again this is a reason why you should see the client alone. Even if your client insists that there are no "priors", always check this fact with the police before putting your client's character in issue at the trial by challenging the character of any of the prosecution witnesses.

Do not be satisfied always with the details of the charge set out on the information that your client produces. If necessary, you can write to the informant and request further and better particulars of the charge. Press your client as to whether he or she has made a written statement to the police. If your client does not have a copy, or seems vague, write to the police and request a copy.

Remember that not only should you obtain a statement in relation to the alleged offence, but there is a second aspect, the plea for leniency, to be enquired into. Personal details, including family, education, outside influences and a medical history, are vital. Find out about the client's private life, including sporting interests, hobbies and involvement in community and other organisations. Obtain details of your client's employment. If necessary, obtain references from employers, teachers, church officials and other such sources.

The necessity of obtaining the fullest possible information from your client is obvious in criminal cases. However, this is often difficult because some clients are afraid or suspicious of practitioners who they see as persons in authority and part of the "system".

Such suspicions are perhaps more common with non-English speaking clients. The result is a reluctance on the part of the client to tell you the whole story for fear that you will pass on everything you are told to the police. It is a real test of your powers of persuasion and professionalism for you to gain the confidence of such a client.

Sometimes you will know that your client is sought by the police for interview. It is best to tell your client not to answer any questions at all or to refuse to answer questions unless his or her legal adviser is allowed to be present. If, before declining to answer questions, your client says, "I have done nothing wrong," so much the better.

Going to a police station and interfering with the conduct of an interview by the police has, on more than one occasion, led to real difficulties for practitioners. To put yourself in a position where you can be called as a witness to your client's interview can be a two-edged sword. In some situations, it would be unethical for you to act for a client if it is likely that you will be called as a witness at the hearing of your client's case.[3]

In most cases, the interrogation of your client by the police is the strongest evidence against your client and it is always desirable to take full instructions about the manner in which the interrogation was conducted. Obtain your client's version of the whole interrogation. Detailed and precise instructions as to the

3. See Ch. 6, p. 37.

manner in which the interrogation was conducted lay the foundation for challenging admission evidence.

At the local court level there are traffic offenders, the first offenders who come before the court on comparatively serious charges, and also the hardened petty criminals. You will find almost invariably that the first time offender will turn up with the informations issued against him or her neatly folded and still in their envelopes, whilst the person who is a constant offender will probably have had them washed in the pocket of his or her jeans on three or four occasions or else used them to jack up the leg of a chair in the kitchen.

Dealing with the third category we have mentioned, the seasoned petty criminals, you will find that they know the ropes and will invariably give you a version of the facts which will suit them and you. The real problems arise when you are acting for youngsters who do not appreciate that the defence of a prosecution is not a conspiracy between the two of you to defeat justice. You must explain the limits of what you can do for your client immediately after you have been given his or her name and address and been shown the information.

How to handle a client charged with a comparatively serious offence comes with experience. For one thing, you should never ask "Did you do it?". If your client tells you he or she is innocent, you must accept that unless the objective facts available to you unequivocally show that what you have been told is a lie.

For example, if your client tells you he or she was sober at the time of being "booked" for driving whilst under the influence of alcohol but the blood alcohol reading at that time was .250, you can assume that your client's recollection of what happened is hopeless. In such a case, you should proceed on the assumption that you will hear what *really* happened for the first time at court, unless the police informant is prepared to discuss the matter beforehand.

Courtesy

It is important to be courteous to your client at all interviews and at the first interview in particular. Attempt to make clients more comfortable by offering them a cup of tea or coffee before obtaining instructions from them. Throughout the remainder of the interview show that you are interested in your client's problem, even if you have heard the same story a hundred times before. Never be patronising or aggressive. It always makes a bad impression on clients if you cut them off in mid-sentence.

You should give your client your undivided attention during interviews. Instruct your secretary not to come into your office to talk to you or to give you something whilst your client is there unless it concerns that client. No telephone calls should be put through to your office until your client leaves. Apart from being rude and annoying, interruptions to an interview are unfair to your client because you are being paid to listen and give advice, not to speak to someone else.

When you are unable to start the interview on time, ask your secretary or receptionist to apologise to the client for the delay. If you expect to be detained for a considerable period due to circumstances beyond your control, take the time to explain the situation to the client and provide a realistic estimate of the likely delay. This will enable the client to decide whether to wait or make another appointment.

When you are ready for your client, make sure you look ready. An untidy desk, papers everywhere, and messages all over the place do not inspire confidence. Contrary to the popular myth that clients like to see how busy their solicitor is and a crammed desk reinforces that, clients want to feel that the matter they are discussing with you is your only worry in the world. It is very hard to feel that in an environment where you seem to be surrounded by files that relate to someone else's problems and do not seem to be able to lay your hands on anything that is vaguely relevant to the client sitting in front of you.[4]

If you follow the simple guidelines outlined above, it is more likely that you will enjoy a satisfactory relationship with your client and that the first interview will not be the last time you see the client.

4. This paragraph is quoted from J. Fenton, "Concentrate on Service" (1987) 61 *Law Institute Journal* 359.

Chapter 3

Maintaining Contact with Client and Termination of Retainer

> "I needed a lawyer; I couldn't get in touch with you; I got another lawyer; I don't need you any more . . ."
>
> J. G. Foonberg, *How to Start and Build a Law Practice* (American Bar Association, Chicago, 1976), p. 40.

Maintaining contact with client

It is always prudent for you to write to your client as soon as possible after receipt of instructions to confirm the matters discussed at the interview. Some Law Societies in fact have rules of professional practice which require solicitors to write to their clients to set out relevant matters, such as costs.[1]

You should ask your client to keep in touch with you, to advise you of any change of address, employment or telephone number and to pass on any additional information that he or she may obtain. It is very embarrassing if, at some stage of a transaction or proceeding, a critical decision must be made promptly but you find yourself unable to obtain instructions because your client has changed address or is on holiday.

You must keep your client informed of progress in relation to his or her matter. This is especially so for matters where several months must elapse before the next step can be taken. You will

1. For example, r. 12(2)(a) of the *Solicitors' (Professional Conduct and Practice) Rules* 1984 (Vic.) requires a solicitor after first taking instructions from a client who is a natural person to provide a written estimate of costs or the method of calculation of those costs.

save your client unnecessary confusion and frustration by sending a brief letter or making a short telephone call to explain the situation. Unavoidable delay will be tolerated by your client if the reasons for the apparent inactivity are explained and the client is given regular progress reports.

You should not resent your client taking the initiative in trying to find out what is going on. You should not regard your client as an encumbrance and his or her enquiries as a nuisance which slows down the progress of the case.

If, on the other hand, your client is irrational and telephones you every day for a progress report when you have already told him or her that it will be months before the case will come on for hearing, then tell the client what every telephone call is costing. You will be amazed by the sudden reduction in the frequency of the telephone calls.

Too often practitioners are criticised for being slow when the fault is not theirs but rather that of delays in the court lists. Immediately an action is set down in a list, invite your client in, show him or her the list and explain why there will be a delay prior to the hearing. An explanation such as, "Your action is in a queue of cases awaiting hearing and it is unlikely that your action will be heard for another 12 months" is all that is required. After the interview, perhaps letters could be sent from time to time, indicating how the queue is moving and making some estimate of when the case is likely to be heard.

You should inform your client of all offers of settlement in any proceeding, even if, in your professional opinion, the amount of the offer is inadequate. If you reject an offer without consulting your client, you would be acting without instructions and you could be sued by your client. It is wise always to obtain your client's written confirmation of the acceptance or rejection of any offers.

In order to maintain a satisfactory relationship with your clients, you should avoid delay. You should respond promptly to any correspondence and telephone calls and you should not pass on the client's matter to another practitioner in your office without first consulting the client. Clients often feel frustrated and neglected when they have to deal with different practitioners every few months. Invariably, the practitioner who inherits the file will not be fully acquainted with it and the client will form the impression that his or her affairs are not being attended to properly.

If you fail to maintain appropriate contact with your client throughout the duration of the legal problem you may find that next time that client has a legal problem you may not be contacted about it and the client may go elsewhere.

Termination of retainer

A retainer is the contract by which you are engaged to act for a client. Whilst a client may terminate the retainer at any time, there are limitations on your ability to terminate it.

A retainer is normally an "entire contract" whereby you promise to act for the client in a particular matter until its completion and the client promises to pay you for your services upon completion of the matter. If the client exercises the right to terminate the retainer prior to the completion of the matter, then normally you have a right to retain that client's documents or other personal property until your proper costs are paid. This right is called a "solicitor's lien" and is further discussed in Chapter 9.

If you purport to terminate the retainer prior to the completion of the matter then normally you will be committing a breach of contract. This means that you will have to return the client's documents and will not be entitled to payment for the work you have done pursuant to the retainer prior to its termination.

Sometimes you may be able to terminate the retainer without committing a breach of contract if you have good cause and give reasonable notice to the client. "Good cause" includes a failure by the client to provide funds for payment of disbursements, a request by the client for you to do something illegal or dishonourable or a refusal by the client to provide you with instructions so that your ability to act is hindered. It may not be "good cause" where having commenced proceedings on behalf of a legally aided client you decide to cease to act for that client because the legal aid is terminated shortly before the hearing.[2]

Upon termination of the retainer for "good cause", the client will be liable to pay for the work you have done.[3]

Because of the loss of legal fees that will result from your refusal to complete a matter for a client, you may not be able to afford to cease acting for a client before completion of the matter. It is therefore in your interest to try to make the relationship as cordial as possible.

2. *Chisholm v. State Transport Authority* (1986) 41 S.A.S.R. 317.
3. See *Halsbury's Laws of England* (4th edn), Vol. 44, paras 97, 99, 100.

Chapter 4

Adhering to Instructions

> "For I am a man under authority, having soldiers under me: and I say to this man, Go, and he goeth; and to another, Come, and he cometh; and to my servant, Do this, and he doeth it."
>
> *The Holy Bible*, Matthew, Ch. 8, v. 9.

Obey instructions

In general, you are under a duty to obey your client's instructions. You are the agent of your client in relation to the matters falling within your retainer. Like all agents, you can be liable to your client if you act contrary to your client's instructions and thereby cause harm to your client.

If you act without authority, you are not necessarily guilty of misconduct. However, you will be guilty of misconduct if you knowingly act without authority.[1] You must not substitute your own judgment for the specific instructions of your client,[2] even if you believe your own judgment is more likely to operate in your client's best interest.

Failing to comply with this duty, apart from possibly rendering you liable for damages to your client, might result in disciplinary action being taken against you by your Law Society.

Where you have "apparent" or "implied" authority, it may be permissible for you in some situations to act without consulting your client,[3] but this principle has limitations and in order to

1. *Wheatley v. Bastow* (1855) 7 De G. M. & G. 558; 44 E.R. 218.
2. M. M. Orkin, *Legal Ethics* (Cartwright & Sons Ltd, Toronto, 1957), p. 95.
3. J. Disney and others, *Lawyers* (2nd edn, Law Book Co. Ltd, Sydney, 1986), p. 638.

safeguard yourself you should always obtain express authority. For example, even if you have ostensible authority to compromise a proceeding on behalf of your client, a court asked to enforce the compromise may exercise its discretion and refuse to do so.[4]

Lord Denning has said that where there is a dispute over the precise scope of a solicitor's instructions:

> "The word of the client is to be preferred to the word of the solicitor, or, at any rate, more weight is to be given to it . . . The reason is plain. It is because the client is ignorant and the solicitor is, or should be, learned. If the solicitor does not take the precaution of getting a written retainer, he has only himself to thank for being at variance with his client over it and must take the consequences."[5]

Although Lord Denning's proposition that the word of the client should be preferred to the word of the solicitor has not met with universal judicial acceptance, a prudent practitioner should always avoid a situation developing in which it is a case of the practitioner's word against that of the client.

Always confirm in writing instructions from the client to follow a course of action which is contrary to the advice you have given. Remember that if the nature of your advice or lack of it is ever an issue in court, there is no certainty as to who will be believed.

Settlements

Where you accept an offer of settlement for a particular amount on behalf of a client, it is not uncommon for the client to complain that you had no instructions to accept that amount in settlement. You will probably claim that in fact you had verbal instructions to accept the amount in settlement, but that the client is reneging on the settlement because the client now thinks more money could be obtained. It is difficult to resolve disputes such as these where accusation and counter-accusation are made. The simple answer is that if you had taken the trouble to obtain instructions in writing and have those instructions signed by the client, the dispute would not have arisen at all.

The desirability of written instructions in a settlement situation is common sense. All of us have second thoughts about bargains we strike. All of us wonder whether we could have obtained

4. *Insbury Pty Ltd v. Craig* [1990] 1 Qd R. 309.
5. *Griffiths v. Evans* [1953] 1 W.L.R. 1424; 2 All E.R. 1364.

more for our car as a trade-in on a new vehicle or whether we could have purchased the new house a little more cheaply if we had haggled a little longer with the estate agent.

Similarly, it is reasonable to expect a litigant who has settled to wonder what may have been in Pandora's box, what massive amount the court may have given as compensation for injuries. Perhaps clients are sometimes dishonest, but, far more often, they can convince themselves that their version of a settlement is true, in the hope that they will be able to re-open the matter.

Plaintiffs whose cases have been settled talk to relatives, neighbours, work colleagues and other litigants. It is not new for them to hear that their compensation is trivial compared with the huge amounts received by other people for comparatively minor injuries. Neither is it new for clients, after hearing often quite ill-informed comment, to wonder whether they have been duped by you.

The area of settlements is a minefield of potential professional problems. It is certainly worth the time to have your client sign a statement such as:

> "I hereby authorise and instruct [practitioner] to effect settlement of my claim against Y (Supreme Court Action No. 12345 of 1993) for the sum of $. . . plus costs. In giving these instructions I acknowledge that I will be required to pay the amount of $. . . in respect of certain unpaid expenses and that I will be obliged to contribute a maximum amount of $. . . towards the total legal costs of the action. I also acknowledge that I have been advised by [practitioner] that it is anticipated that I will receive approximately $. . . in my own pocket after the payment in full of all outstanding legal costs and expenses."[6]

With this sort of objective evidence, the "my word against yours" confrontation is avoided and you are spared a great deal of embarrassment in furnishing explanations to your Law Society.

If the client's knowledge of English is poor, then special care in explaining the terms of settlement is necessary, particularly to ensure that the client is not under a misapprehension as to the net amount to be received.

6. Some Law Societies require this type of statement to be provided to a client who is a natural person prior to settlement of a litigious matter. See, for example, *Solicitors' (Professional Conduct and Practice) Rules* 1984 (Vic.), r. 12(2)(b).

Doing good by stealth

At all times you must avoid getting yourself into trouble by trying to do good by stealth. It is extremely unrewarding to take on the decision-making process with a view to acting in the client's best interests without the client's knowledge.

Some practitioners take this course because they want to intermingle their egos with the client's cause of action. Somehow the practitioner measures his or her own abilities by the results achieved on behalf of the client. With surprising frequency, practitioners are prepared to either ignore the client's instructions or to assume that their actions will be ratified by the client later.

Do not take it upon yourself to conduct a matter on behalf of a client without the client's full knowledge and instructions. That is like a real estate agent putting up a board outside your house and selling it for a magnificent price without first asking you whether you want to sell. You should do no more than put all the options and alternatives to your client, advise him or her of your views and then carry out the client's instructions.

Instructions direct from client

Make sure you act only on your client's instructions. If you receive instructions to act or prepare documents through the agency of a third party, such as an accountant, a real estate agent, a spouse[7] or a relative of the client, it is essential that the instructions are confirmed by the client before you take any steps in the matter.

7. See *Mercantile Mutual Insurance Co. Ltd v. Gosper* (1991) 25 N.S.W.L.R. 32 and above, p. 8.

Chapter 5

Confidentiality and Legal Professional Privilege

> "There are two kinds of people who blow through life like a breeze.
> And one kind is gossipers, and the other kind is gossipees."
>
> Ogden Nash, 1938.

Confidentiality

There is an implied term of the contract between you and your client that you will preserve the confidentiality of all communications between you and your client. This means that a client can sue you for damages if you fail to keep his or her affairs confidential. Alternatively, the client can apply to the court for an injunction to restrain you from committing a breach of confidence.

Few practitioners disclose their clients' affairs with the deliberate aim of causing their clients embarrassment or harm. However, the absence of an intention to cause harm would not absolve you from liability. Most young practitioners get very excited about their work and naturally enough talk about it with their friends and colleagues. Although there is nothing wrong with discussing your work in a general way with friends and colleagues, be careful that your discussion does not become too specific. You may find that your friend or colleague acts for a person who is in dispute with your client!

Similarly, never discuss your cases in a crowded lift on the way to your office or a barrister's chambers—you never know who the other people in the lift are.

The contractual duty of confidence can never override any statutory or common law duty to disclose a communication between you and your client. Accordingly, the fact that a document is subject to your contractual duty of confidence to your client would not excuse you from producing the document to the police if it comes within the scope of a valid search warrant.[1]

Legal professional privilege

In addition to the contractual obligation of confidence, there is a rule of law that confidential communications between you and your client are "privileged" from disclosure. This applies not only to disclosure in judicial and quasi-judicial proceedings, but also to all forms of compulsory disclosure—such as search warrants and statutory notices to produce documents or provide information to some authority[2]—except where a statute excludes the privilege.[3]

The privilege is generally referred to as "legal professional privilege", which is an inappropriate name because the privilege belongs to the client and not to you. Accordingly, you are not at liberty to waive the privilege and disclose confidential information you obtain from your client unless your client expressly authorises you to do so.

The privilege continues indefinitely, even after the transaction in question has been completed and even after the client terminates your retainer and employs another practitioner.[4] Not even the death of the client destroys the privilege.[5]

1. *Parry-Jones v. Law Society* [1969] 1 Ch. 1.
2. *Baker v. Campbell* (1983) 153 C.L.R. 52; *Commissioner of Taxation v. Citibank Ltd* (1989) 20 F.C.R. 403. See also *Rosenberg v. Jaine* [1983] N.Z.L.R. 1; *Descoteaux v. Mierzwinski* (1982) 141 D.L.R. (3d) 590. The position in England is different. In *Parry-Jones v. Law Society* [1969] 1 Ch. 1 the Court of Appeal decided that legal professional privilege was a rule of evidence which could be relied on only in judicial and quasi-judicial proceedings; in relation to search warrants and other forms of administrative action involving a power to require compulsory disclosure, only the contractual duty of confidence was relevant and in each case this was subject to and overridden by any inconsistent duty imposed by statute or the common law. However, the effect of the *Police and Criminal Evidence Act* 1984 (U.K.) is to give privilege a much broader application as "items subject to legal privilege" are excepted from material which can be seized with or without a warrant.
3. *Corporate Affairs Commission (N.S.W.) v. Yuill* (1991) 172 C.L.R. 319.
4. *Attorney-General (N.T.) v. Maurice* (1986) 10 F.C.R. 134 at 140.
5. *Bullivant v. A.-G. (Vic.)* [1901] A.C. 196 at 206.

The privilege subsists even if the client will not suffer any detriment if the information in question is disclosed.[6]

Legal professional privilege is founded on public policy. The courts have over a long period determined that it is a principle of public policy that the preservation of the confidentiality attaching to practitioner-client communications is essential to the administration of justice.[7] The rationale is that without an absolute assurance of confidentiality, citizens will be reluctant to consult practitioners to enforce their rights or might be reluctant to disclose all the details when they do see a practitioner, with the consequence, in each situation, that justice might not be done.

The following is a brief summary of the law:

1. The privilege applies to a communication between you and your client where the communication is referable to your professional relationship and where the communication is intended to be confidential. A communication between two persons, one of whom happens to be a practitioner, is not privileged unless a practitioner-client relationship is contemplated or exists between them in respect of the subject matter of the communication.
2. The communication must be made for the sole purpose of seeking or giving legal advice or for use in existing or anticipated legal proceedings. A communication between you or your client and a third party (such as a witness) is privileged only if it was made for the sole purpose of use in existing or anticipated legal proceedings.[8]
3. The communication may be oral or written. If the communication is written, the relevant document must have come into existence for the sole purpose of seeking or giving legal advice or for use in existing or anticipated legal proceedings.[9] Accordingly documents which constitute or evidence transactions such as wills or written contracts prepared by you are not subject to legal professional

6. *Dunesky v. Elder* (1992) 35 F.C.R. 429.
7. *Greenough v. Gaskell* (1833) 1 M.Y. & K. 98 at 103; 39 E.R. 618 at 621.
8. *Wheeler v. Le Merchant* (1881) 17 Ch. D. 675; *Nickmar Pty Ltd v. Preservatrice Skandia Insurance Ltd* (1985) 3 N.S.W.L.R. 44.
9. *Grant v. Downs* (1976) 135 C.L.R. 674. In England and New Zealand, the "sole purpose" test has been rejected in favour of the "dominant purpose" test: *Waugh v. British Railways Board* [1980] A.C. 521; *Guardian Royal Exchange Assurance of N.Z. Ltd v. Stuart* [1985] 1 N.Z.L.R. 596.

privilege. Neither are entries in your trust account ledger.[10] Similarly, a memorandum prepared by you for the dual purposes of notifying your managing partner that the firm may be sued and of referring that memorandum to the lawyers acting for your firm's insurers for their information is not privileged.[11] However, a bill of costs may be privileged if it discloses the nature of the advice sought or given.[12]

4. Documents which are not otherwise privileged cannot become privileged merely by your client giving them to you for safekeeping or by passing them through your hands.[13] The question is not whether the documents are received by you for the purpose of tendering legal advice but whether they are brought into existence solely for that purpose.
5. A copy of a privileged document is usually privileged unless it was made for purposes entirely unrelated to advice or litigation.[14]
6. A copy of an unprivileged document, even if made for the sole purpose of use in litigation, is usually not privileged. The position is otherwise where a document (such as a summary) is created from source material which is not privileged for the sole purpose of use in litigation and where legal skill was applied in the creation of the document.[15] Such a document is sometimes referred to as a "lawyer's work product".
7. It is not clear whether parts only of a document may be protected by legal professional privilege.[16]
8. If a third party overhears an oral communication between you and your client or obtains a copy of a written communication between you and your client, it used to be thought that the privilege would not prevent the third party

10. *Allen, Allen & Hemsley v. Deputy Commissioner of Taxation* (1989) 20 F.C.R. 576 at 583.
11. *Occidental Life Insurance Company of Australia Ltd v. Bank of Melbourne Ltd* (unreported, Vic. Sup. Ct, O'Bryan J., 2 August 1991).
12. *Packer v. Deputy Commissioner of Taxation (Qld)* (1984) 73 F.C.R. 205.
13. *Choo Cheng Kui v. Quinn* (1984) 11 F.C.R. 217 at 219.
14. S. B. McNicol, *Law of Privilege* (Law Book Co. Ltd, Sydney, 1992), pp. 94-95.
15. S. B. McNicol, *Law of Privilege* (Law Book Co. Ltd, Sydney, 1992), pp. 95-97.
16. *Waterford v. Commonwealth* (1987) 163 C.L.R. 54 at 66-67 per Mason and Wilson JJ., 85-86 per Deane J. and 103 per Dawson J. Compare *HongKong Bank of Australia Ltd v. Murphy* (unreported, Vic. Sup. Ct, Smith J., 24 December 1992).

from giving evidence of what he or she heard or from tendering the copy document in evidence.[17] However, recent English cases[18] have established that there is an equitable right to restrain a person from using or relying on a document obtained in error. In *Westpac Banking Corp. v. Australian Broadcasting Corp.*[19] the Supreme Court of New South Wales restrained the publication of news items which quoted parts of letters of advice from Westpac Banking Corporation's solicitors.

9. The privilege does not apply to communications which are made for the purpose of facilitating a crime or fraud, even if you are not aware of the purpose.[20] However this exception does not apply to a confession of a prior crime or fraud by a client to you.[21]
10. Because the privilege is founded on public interest considerations, it may not apply where preservation of the confidentiality of a particular practitioner-client communication would be contrary to a higher public interest which requires the communication to be disclosed.[22] For example, if a privileged communication would tend to establish the innocence of a person charged with a crime, the requirements of natural justice override the privilege.[23] Similarly, you cannot rely on legal professional privilege to refuse to divulge information supplied by your client concerning the whereabouts of a ward of court.[24]
11. The name of your client is normally not privileged and accordingly you can be compelled to disclose it.[25]
12. The privilege is confined to communications and does not apply to facts learned by you with your own senses.

17. *Calcraft v. Guest* [1898] 1 Q.B. 759.
18. *Goddard v. Nationwide Building Society* [1986] 3 All E.R. 264; *English & American Insurance Co. Ltd v. Herbert Smith & Co.* (1987) 137 N.L.J. 148; *Guinness Peat Properties Ltd v. Fitzroy Robinson Partnership* [1987] 2 All E.R. 716. See also *R. v. Uljee* [1982] 1 N.Z.L.R. 561.
19. (1991) A.I.P.C. 90-804. See also *R v. Lewis* [1987] 2 Qd R. 710.
20. *R. v. Cox and Railton* (1884) 14 Q.B.D. 153; *Attorney-General (N.T.) v. Kearney* (1985) 158 C.L.R. 500 (abuse of statutory power); S. B. McNicol, *Law of Privilege* (Law Book Co. Ltd, 1992), pp. 104-113.
21. *Tuckiar v. R.* (1934) 52 C.L.R. 335 at 346.
22. *R. v. Bell; Ex parte Lees* (1980) 146 C.L.R. 141; 54 A.L.J.R. 412.
23. *R. v. Barton* [1973] 1 W.L.R. 115; S. B. McNicol, *Law of Privilege* (Law Book Co. Ltd, 1992), pp. 101-104.
24. *Burton v. Earl of Darnley* (1896) 8 L.R. Eq. 576n.
25. *Bursill v. Tanner* (1885) 16 Q.B.D. 1; *Southern Cross Commodities Pty Ltd (in liq.) v. Crinis* [1984] V.R. 697.

Accordingly, if you observe that your client walks with a limp, you would not be precluded from disclosing this fact on the grounds of legal professional privilege.

13. Privilege may be waived either expressly or impliedly.[26] A common question which arises in practice is whether privileged documents which are inadvertently provided to an opponent (especially during discovery) cease to be privileged. The position appears to be as follows:[27]

(a) There are two relevant issues. The first is whether it is unethical for you to use privileged documents which have been supplied to you by an opponent in error. The second is whether your opponent can apply successfully for an injunction to restrain you from using such documents.

(b) In some jurisdictions, such as Victoria, the Law Society takes the view that a solicitor who obtains access to privileged documents without any improper conduct on his or her part or on the part of the client, has an obligation to look at the documents and use the information for the benefit of the client.

(c) Courts in England and Australia have said that they do not agree with the view that it is ethical for a solicitor to use privileged documents supplied by an opponent in error and have urged Law Societies which take a contrary approach to review their position.

(d) Privilege can only be said to be waived by unintended disclosure if the circumstances are such that the waiver should be implied. Whether that waiver should be implied will usually turn on the issue of fairness. Thus if the party who acquired knowledge of the privileged documents would have difficulty conducting its case while trying to ignore the content of the documents, there would be an argument that fairness required that the party that inadvertently disclosed the privileged documents should bear the consequences of its mistake. Similarly, if a party discloses part of a

26. *Attorney-General (N.T.) v. Maurice* (1986) 161 C.L.R. 475.

27. See generally on this issue *Hooker Corp. Ltd v. Darling Harbour Authority* (1987) 9 N.S.W.L.R. 538; *Key International Drilling Co. Ltd v. TNT Bulkships Operations Pty Ltd* [1989] W.A.R. 280; *Guinness Peat Properties Ltd v. Fitzroy Robinson Partnership* [1987] 2 All E.R. 716; *Derby & Co. Ltd v. Weldon (No. 8)* [1991] 1 W.L.R. 73; *English and American Insurance Co. Ltd v. Herbert Smith & Co.* [1988] F.S.R. 232.

privileged document and seeks to claim privilege for the balance but the balance is relevant to that which was disclosed, it may be unfair to allow that party to insist on maintaining the privilege.[28]

(e) Where privilege has not been waived intentionally or by implication, the party entitled to the privilege can seek equitable relief including orders for the return of copies of the privileged documents. In determining whether such relief should be granted, a number of matters are relevant, including:

(i) how the recipient obtained the documents;

(ii) whether the person seeking to protect the confidentiality of the documents has acted expeditiously;

(iii) whether the documents have been obtained by fraud or mistake;

(iv) whether it would be futile to make the orders;

(v) whether the recipient of the documents was aware that the mistake had been made.[29]

(f) In many cases, if there is no dispute about the privileged nature of the documents, the opposing solicitors and their respective clients resolve the matter by agreement whereby the documents are returned and undertakings are provided that the information in the documents will not be used for the purposes of the proceeding.

(g) Having regard to the friction and bad feeling that usually arises when one solicitor attempts to use privileged documents supplied by an opponent in error, unless agreement can be reached on what should be done, the better course may be to retain the documents in question in a sealed envelope and refer the matter to the court for determination.

14. Where a client directly or indirectly puts in issue the substance of a privileged communication, the privilege may be lost insofar as is necessary to do justice between the parties.[30]

28. *HongKong Bank of Australia Ltd v. Murphy* (unreported, Vic. Sup. Ct, Smith J., 24 December 1992).

29. *HongKong Bank* case.

30. *HongKong Bank* case.

15. The privilege does not apply in situations where a statute expressly or by necessary implication provides that the privilege is inapplicable.[31]
16. The onus of establishing that a particular communication is privileged is on the person claiming the privilege.[32]

Because legal professional privilege belongs to your client and not to you, you have a duty to invoke it in all circumstances where it is applicable unless your client instructs you to the contrary. The privilege should be invoked not only in relation to discovery, interrogatories and testimony in court but also whenever any person purporting to act pursuant to statutory authority requests information or documents falling within the scope of the privilege.

Search warrants

There have been a number of cases concerning the effect of search warrants and other statutory requests for information on legal professional privilege.[33]

The Law Council of Australia has reached agreement with the Australian Federal Police on the guidelines to be followed when a search warrant is executed on a lawyer's premises.[34] A similar agreement was reached with the Australian Taxation Office in relation to statutory requests for information under taxation legislation.[35] The effect of the guidelines is to restrict the inspection of any document by the officer executing the warrant or making a statutory request where legal professional privilege is asserted.

The officer must permit the practitioner a reasonable time to seek instructions from his or her client. The practitioner must also be permitted sufficient time to examine the documents and may also seek advice on them.

If the practitioner claims that particular documents are privileged, the officer will refrain from inspecting the

31. *Corporate Affairs Commission (N.S.W.) v. Yuill* (1991) 172 C.L.R. 319; S. B. McNicol, *Law of Privilege* (Law Book Co. Ltd, 1992), pp. 113-135.
32. *National Crime Authority v. S* (1991) 29 F.C.R. 203.
33. *Allen, Allen & Hemsley v. Deputy Commissioner of Taxation* (1989) 20 F.C.R. 576; *Commissioner of Taxation v. Citibank Ltd* (1989) 20 F.C.R. 403; *Arno v. Forsyth* (1986) 9 F.C.R. 576 (search warrants under *Crimes Act* 1914 (Cth), s. 10; *Allitt v. Sullivan* [1988] V.R. 621 (search warrants under *Crimes Act* 1958 (Vic.), s. 465).
34. The guidelines are published in (1990) (Oct.) *Australian Law News* 58.
35. The relevant guidelines are published in (1991) (Sep.) *Australian Law News* 23.

documents. Instead the documents will be placed in a sealed envelope. The practitioner is then permitted three days to consult with his or her client and advise the officer whether the claim for privilege will be waived or abandoned. If the claim for privilege is maintained, proceedings must be instituted so that the issue can be decided by a court.

What should you do if you are confronted with a search warrant? First, you should look closely at the terms of the warrant and take a copy of it. The warrant must describe the documents to be seized with sufficient particularity; if it is excessively wide, it will be invalid.[36] If the warrant appears to be valid on its face, ask the officer executing the warrant for identification and record the details for future reference.

Ask the officer to explain the purpose of the warrant and what documents he or she is looking for. Also ask whether you are suspected of involvement in the commission of the alleged offence.

Then work out precisely which documents are covered by the warrant. If any documents are to be seized pursuant to the warrant, make a list of them and retain copies. Ask for a detailed receipt. It is important that there should be no doubt about what documents were seized.

If you believe that some of the documents are protected by legal professional privilege but no agreement can be reached to exclude these from the scope of the warrant, you should photocopy the documents and place the originals in a sealed envelope to be delivered to the registry of the appropriate court.[37] The court should be informed of your claim for legal professional privilege. Formal arrangements (such as the commencement of proceedings) should then be made to enable the court to determine the question of privilege.

In appropriate cases you may need to obtain urgent advice from counsel or even apply for an ex parte injunction if you believe there is some irregularity with the warrant or the way it is being executed.

Most search warrants relate to the affairs of a client rather than the practitioner at whose premises the warrant is being executed. In such a situation you should immediately inform your client of

36. *Arno v. Forsyth* (1986) 9 F.C.R. 576.
37. In Victoria, if the warrant is issued under the *Crimes Act* 1958, s. 465, the sealed envelope is to be delivered to the justice or magistrate who issued the warrant. See *Allitt v. Sullivan* [1988] V.R. 621.

what is happening and obtain instructions. In the absence of instructions to the contrary, you cannot make any concessions or waive any rights, including the right to claim legal professional privilege.

If there is a doubt about whether a particular document is privileged, claim the privilege and let the court decide the issue. Do not decide the matter yourself because you may be liable to your client if you make an error in deciding that a document is not privileged.

If you are an inexperienced practitioner and are faced with a search warrant, do not panic. Be methodical in your approach and seek assistance from more experienced colleagues.

Chapter 6

Conflict of Interest

> "No man can serve two masters: for either he will hate the one, and love the other; or else he will hold to the one, and despise the other. Ye cannot serve God and mammon."
>
> *The Holy Bible*, Matthew, Ch. 6, v. 24.

As a practitioner, your primary duty is to use your utmost skill and experience and all relevant information available to you to further the interests of your client. Accordingly, you should avoid doing anything which may potentially conflict with that duty. Failure to avoid a conflict of interest may constitute unprofessional conduct.

Acting for both parties to a transaction

A distinction is sometimes drawn between litigious and non-litigious matters. Whilst it is clear that you cannot act for two opposing parties in actual or contemplated litigation, in most jurisdictions there is no absolute rule precluding you from acting for both parties in non-litigious matters.[1] However it is generally unwise to do so and in certain circumstances it might be misconduct to do so.

The question of conflict of interest in non-litigious matters often arises in situations where you act in one transaction for

1. A number of Law Societies have rules of professional practice which restrict the circumstances in which a solicitor may act for both parties, and impose safeguards, such as the requirement that written consent be obtained from both parties. See, for example, *Solicitors' (Professional Conduct and Practice) Rules* 1984 (Vic.), rr. 10 and 11. In addition, some professional indemnity insurance policies have special provisions for liability arising from a conflict of interest.

both vendor and purchaser or mortgagee and mortgagor or lessor and lessee. The practice of some practitioners, in jurisdictions where there is no prohibition against acting for both parties, is to act for both parties unless it can be demonstrated that there are special circumstances which give rise to a conflict between the parties or indicate potential for such a conflict.

If, despite the undesirability of so doing, you decide to act for both parties to a transaction, it is incumbent upon you to ensure that every possible step is taken to safeguard the interests of each client. You must ensure that you give the same care and attention to the interests of each client as you would be bound to give if you were acting for only one. This is a difficult task because acting for both parties in a transaction may inhibit the professional judgment normally exercised by you when acting only for one of the parties. If you acted for both parties and favoured the interests of one to the detriment of the other, you would be guilty of unprofessional conduct.[2]

The case of *Spector v. Ageda*[3] has provoked debate on the question of conflict of interest in non-litigious matters. In that case Ageda and Gravesande had borrowed money under an agreement with Maxwell. Spector, who was Maxwell's sister and a lawyer, was later asked by the borrowers to act for them in the discharge of their obligations under the agreement. Spector knew the agreement was probably unenforceable against them but did not tell them. To make matters worse, Spector had altered the agreement after it had been signed by the borrowers and apparently without their knowledge. The alteration was to their detriment. Megarry J. said:

> "A solicitor must put at his client's disposal not only his skill, but also his knowledge, so far as is relevant; and if he is unwilling to reveal his knowledge to his client, he should not act for him. What he cannot do is to act for the client and at the same time withhold from him any relevant knowledge that he has."[4]

Gifford[5] submits that a practitioner is precluded from acting for either party if the practitioner would probably find that he

2. *Re A. B. (a solicitor)* [1939] A.L.R. 208; *Wan v. McDonald* (1992) 33 F.C.R. 491.
3. [1973] 1 Ch. 30.
4. *Spector* at 48.
5. K. H. Gifford, *Legal Profession Law and Practice in Victoria* (Law Book Co. Ltd, Sydney, 1980), p. 355.

or she is under a duty to make use of confidential information for the benefit of one client which has been acquired in the course of acting for the other. There is also a conflict of interest if the practitioner should warn one party to make inquiries which would be inimical to the interest of the other.

In *Goody v. Baring*[6] Danckwerts J. stated that it was improper for a solicitor to act for two or more parties in a conveyancing transaction. He said: "It seems to me practically impossible for a solicitor to do his duty to each client properly when he tries to act for both a vendor and a purchaser." In *Gavaghan v. Edwards*[7] the same judge remarked: "In many cases it may work perfectly all right, but if anything whatsoever goes wrong with regard to the sale, a solicitor who is acting for both parties is almost certainly placed in a position where the interests conflict and a difficult situation is likely to arise."

It has also been judicially stated that "The man who undertakes to serve two masters may easily find himself in a position where he must be false to one and possibly to both"[8] and that "It may be that a solicitor who tries to act for both parties puts himself in such a position that he must be liable to one or the other, whatever he does."[9]

Do not be under the misapprehension that it is proper for you to act for both parties to a transaction because they consent or even insist that you act for both of them. A client can never be the arbiter of what professional propriety requires. The decision is yours alone. Knowing the problems involved, you should decline to act for both parties.

The problem is acute in country areas where refusal to act for both parties may mean that one of the parties will be greatly inconvenienced by having to go to another town to find another practitioner. However much you may desire to avoid this inconvenience to someone who may be a well-established client, you should bear in mind that the risks associated with finding yourself in a conflict of interest situation are just too great.

Even if it were originally proper for you to act for both parties to a transaction, once a dispute arises between the parties you must cease acting for one of them. In most cases, you will need to cease acting for both of them.

6. [1956] 1 W.L.R. 448 at 450; 2 All E.R. 11 at 12.
7. [1961] 2 Q.B. 220 at 225.
8. *Jennings v. Zilahi-Kiss* (1972) 2 S.A.S.R. 493 at 511-512.
9. *Moody v. Cox* [1917] 2 Ch. 71 at 91.

Prior clients

You should not act contrary to the interests of a prior client. For example, if you acted for X and then you are retained by X's previous opponent Y, you may find yourself in a conflict of interest situation. You have a duty not to disclose confidential information you obtained while acting for X but you also have a duty to do your best for your new client Y which includes reliance on any relevant information in your possession, irrespective of its source. In such a situation, if you rely on the information obtained from X, you may be liable to X for breaching client confidence; if you do not rely on the information, you may be liable to Y in negligence for failing to use your utmost skill, experience and knowledge.[10] An injunction can be obtained by X to restrain you from breaching confidence.

In the case of a firm, the knowledge of one partner is imputed to all partners and accordingly one partner cannot act for Y if another partner previously acted for X and thereby obtained confidential information which is relevant to Y's matter.

Chinese walls

The conflict of interest rules create a problem for many modern law firms with multiple clients because the rules, in effect, prevent them from acting in many transactions. In an attempt to resolve these difficulties, firms have relied on so-called "Chinese walls".[11] This involves establishing procedures to prevent information in the possession of one solicitor from being communicated to other solicitors in the same office—that is, "quarantining" legal practitioners who had dealt with client X from those practitioners now dealing with client Y. This seeks to attract the principle that because no confidential information from X will be used in acting for Y, it is unlikely that either X or Y will be prejudiced if the firm acts for Y and therefore it would not be improper for the firm to accept a retainer from Y.[12] Both X and Y would need to give their informed consent to the arrangement in order for it to be acceptable.

The use of "Chinese walls" has been questioned by recent decisions in Australia, the United Kingdom and Canada, and it

10. *Mills v. Day Dawn Block Gold Mining Co. Ltd* (1882) 1 Q.L.J.R. 62.
11. See R. Tomasic, "Chinese Walls, Legal Principle and Commercial Reality in Multi-Service Professional Firms" (1991) 14 *University of New South Wales Law Journal* 46.
12. *Rakusen v. Ellis, Munday & Clarke* [1912] 1 Ch. 831.

now seems that in many cases "Chinese walls" will not be accepted by the courts as legitimate means of overcoming conflict of interest problems, especially in criminal cases.

In *Mallesons Stephen Jaques v. KPMG Peat Marwick*,[13] the court granted an injunction restraining a law firm from representing the Commissioner for Corporate Affairs who had retained the firm to assist in the prosecution of a person who had previously obtained advice from the firm. Although no confidential information about the previous client was conveyed to those lawyers engaged by the current client, and the lawyers working for the Commissioner were located in a separate building, it was held that there was "a real and sensible possibility" that the firm had placed itself in the position of conflict of interest.

Similarly in the United Kingdom[14] and Canada,[15] the courts have restrained practitioners from acting against previous clients.

It is possible that in civil cases the use of "Chinese walls" may be restricted to cases where information about a former client is unrelated to the new matter.[16]

In family law matters, the courts are often reluctant to permit a firm of solicitors to act for one party if that firm had previous dealings with both parties.[17]

Chinese walls have also been questioned by some Law Societies.[18]

Personal interest

You should not act for a person in a transaction to which you are yourself a party with an adverse interest.[19] It is certainly improper for you to take advantage of your client's inexperience, age or any infirmity. You cannot advise an ignorant client to act to his or her detriment and your own

13. (1991) 4 W.A.R. 357. See also *D. & J. Constructions Pty Ltd v. Head* (1987) 9 N.S.W.L.R. 118.
14. *David Lee & Co. (Lincoln) Ltd v. Coward Chance* [1991] Ch. 259; *Re A Firm of Solicitors* [1992] 1 All E.R. 353.
15. *MacDonald Estate v. Martin* (1991) 77 D.L.R. (4th) 249.
16. *Fruehauf Finance Co. Pty Ltd v. Feez Ruthning* [1991] 1 Qd R. 558.
17. *Thevenaz and Thevenaz* [1986] F.L.C. 91-748; *Magro and Magro* (1989) F.L.C. 92-005; *Griffis and Griffis* [1991] F.L.C. 92-233.
18. The Law Institute of Victoria has adopted conflict of interest guidelines which appear to reject Chinese walls. See (1991) 65 *Law Institute Journal* 351.
19. *Spector v. Ageda* [1973] 1 Ch. 30 at 47.

benefit, or conceal from the client that you are personally interested.[20] Nor is it proper for you to receive a secret profit in the course of acting for your client.

In order to completely preclude a conflict between a client's interest and your own interest, you should not mix a business relationship with your professional responsibilities to your client. For example, you should not borrow from a client, or arrange a loan from a client to a person or company with which you are associated, unless the client obtains independent advice or is in the business of lending.[21] The reason is obvious. There is a conflict between your client's interest in securing favourable terms as lender and the interest of yourself or the associated person or company in securing favourable terms as borrower.[22] In such a situation the conflict of interest is so great that it is preferable that you should not act for the client.

If you do act for the client, at the very least you should act in good faith, make full disclosure of all relevant circumstances and strongly advise your client to obtain independent legal advice. In *O'Reilly v. Law Society of New South Wales*[23] Kirby P. observed that a solicitor who intermingled his or her affairs with those of a client should disclose the interest fully and candidly to the client, preferably in writing, advise and facilitate the provision of independent advice where that is appropriate and do so in more than a perfunctory way.

The position is succinctly expressed by Street C.J. in *Law Society of New South Wales v. Harvey*[24] as follows:

> "The price of being a member of an honourable profession, whose duty to his client ought not to be prejudiced in any degree, is that a solicitor is denied the freedom to take the benefit of any opportunity to deal with persons whom he has accepted as clients . . . A solicitor ought not to intermingle his personal affairs, in a sense including the affairs of companies, ventures or others with whose financial position he has a personal connection, with the affairs of his client."

20. *Southern Law Society v. Westbrook* (1910) 10 C.L.R. 609.
21. Professional conduct and practice rules in some jurisdictions prohibit a solicitor from borrowing a client's money, or arranging for the client to lend money to the practitioner's immediate family or associates. See, for example, *Solicitors' (Professional Conduct and Practice) Rules* 1984 (Vic.), r. 8.
22. *Law Society of New South Wales v. Harvey* [1976] 2 N.S.W.L.R. 154.
23. (1988) 24 N.S.W.L.R. 204 at 209.
24. [1976] 2 N.S.W.L.R. 154 at 171, 172.

Gifts

You should always think carefully before accepting a substantial gift from a client because this could lead to unwelcome litigation. The court, in dealing with such a gift, starts with the presumption that undue influence exists on your part and throws upon you the burden of satisfying the court that the gift was uninfluenced by your position.[25]

Where you may be a witness

Rules of Bar Associations often preclude a barrister from taking instructions in a case in which the barrister is likely to be a witness. Such an absolute prohibition usually does not apply to a solicitor, although it may be inappropriate for a solicitor to act in certain situations. One example is where it is anticipated that allegations of personal dishonesty or misconduct are likely to be made against the solicitor when giving evidence.

In the case of *Chapman v. Rogers*[26] Campbell C.J. stated:

> "For the reason that it is desirable to avoid any suggestion of real or apparent conflict between the duty to the court and the obligation to the client, I consider that it is generally unwise for a solicitor, who is not himself appearing as advocate or as instructing solicitor in court but who is aware that it is likely that he will be called as a material witness (other than in relation to formal or non-contentious issues), to continue, either personally or through his firm, to represent the client if this can be reasonably avoided."

Where you may be sued

Where in the course of acting for a client in relation to a matter you become aware that your client may have a cause of action against you in respect of your handling of that matter, you should advise your client to obtain separate legal advice about your conduct and whether you should continue to act in the matter. While, for this purpose, it will be necessary for you to state in general terms the aspects of your advice or conduct which should be investigated, you must be careful not to make any admissions which may prejudice your professional indemnity insurance.[27]

25. *Wright v. Carter* [1903] 1 Ch. 27 at 57.
26. [1984] 1 Qd R. 542 at 545.
27. See *Keppie v. Law Society of the Australian Capital Territory* (1983) 65 F.L.R. 147 at 159-160 for a discussion of the conflicts of interest that may arise in this context.

Associated bodies

You should not act for a client who has a dispute against an organisation with which you are substantially associated, such as a local council of which you are a councillor or a company of which you are a director. On the other hand, it is not necessarily improper for you to act for a potential competitor of a company of which you were once a director.[28]

Be quick to detect a conflict of interest

You should always ask yourself at the time of obtaining initial instructions whether a conflict of interest could possibly arise. A conflict of interest could arise in a situation where you least expect it. For example, assume a motor accident occurs which is caused by the negligence of X and which injures a husband and wife (A and B) who were in another vehicle driven by the husband (A). If A and B instruct you to institute proceedings against X, then you must verify that the accident was caused solely by the negligence of X. If there is a possibility that A's conduct either caused or contributed to the accident, then you should not act for both A and B in case B may need to sue A if it is found that the accident was caused wholly or partially by the negligence of A.

Similarly, where a creditor sues a primary debtor and a guarantor, it may not be appropriate for you to act for both the primary debtor and the guarantor because the guarantor would have a right of indemnity against the primary debtor for such amounts as the guarantor is found liable and pays to the creditor.[29]

When acting for an insurance company seeking recovery of amounts paid under a policy pursuant to its right of subrogation, there are often two distinct interests involved. This will arise, for example, where a person's goods are damaged by a carrier's negligence but not all the goods are insured. You should not issue proceedings in respect of only one of those interests without ascertaining from the other whether or not there is any objection to that course. You should point out that the proceedings you propose issuing would debar the other interest from recovering at a later date.

28. See the discussions of the case of *TVW Enterprises Ltd v. Miller* in (1985) 59 *Australian Law Journal* 567.
29. *Halsbury's Laws of England* (4th edn), Vol. 20, para. 211.

An insurance company may not wish to take any action where a "knock for knock" agreement is involved but may request that its interest be included in the proposed proceedings or, if proceedings have already been commenced by the insurer's solicitors, then the client's personal interest can be included in those proceedings.

It is important that some agreement is reached as to who is to conduct the proceedings, as to consultation from time to time (especially if settlement is contemplated) and as to the sharing of damages and costs, in order to avoid any misunderstandings or disputes on these matters at a later date.

When you are instructed by an insurance company to defend an action on behalf of an insured, you should be wary of the possibility of a conflict of interest between the insurer and the insured. You should not, for example, make a damaging admission on the instructions of the insurer without first consulting the insured, otherwise you could be held liable to the insured.[30] You should bear in mind that both the insured and the insurer are your clients.

Non-clients

Apart from the wisdom of acting for one party only, it is also necessary at the outset to define clearly to all concerned, when dealing with more than one party, who your client is and for whom you are not acting. This is necessary to avoid "non-clients" incorrectly assuming you are protecting their interests. The non-clients acting on their own account should also be advised that in order to protect their interests, it is necessary for them to consult a practitioner of their own. If you fail to adopt these precautions, you may find yourself liable to the non-clients. Avoid being manipulated into a situation in which you believe you are not acting for the non-clients but the non-clients believe you are protecting their interests. That risk can be eliminated by a simple letter clarifying the situation.

30. *Groom v. Crocker* [1939] 1 K.B. 194 at 203.

Chapter 7

Costs

> "In New Jersey the black-necked stilt is sometimes called 'lawyer' on account of its 'long bill'."
>
> E. Kahn, "The Seven Lamps of Legal Humour" (1984) *De Rebus* 251.

Disputes between practitioners and clients over legal fees are common and generally represent a large proportion of complaints received by Law Societies. The reason for this is not so much that a lot of practitioners overcharge their clients but that many of them fail to give adequate explanations to their clients at the outset regarding the legal fees that will be involved in handling a matter.

The best way to avoid misunderstandings and arguments with your client when the time comes to render a bill is to explain very carefully to your client, upon acceptance of instructions, matters such as how much you think the legal fees will be, the types of disbursements (such as barristers' fees) that will be incurred and whether there is any prospect of someone other than the client paying the legal costs.[1]

Party/party and solicitor/own client costs

Most clients who consult you in relation to a litigious matter will be vaguely familiar with the general rule that a successful party is entitled to costs. This is the rule that costs follow the event. However, not many clients appreciate that very rarely does an order for costs against an unsuccessful party cover all the

1. Some Law Societies require solicitors to provide this type of information at the outset to a client who is a natural person. See, for example, *Solicitors' (Professional Conduct and Practice) Rules* 1984 (Vic.), r. 12.

costs that will be charged by the practitioner acting for the successful party and that the successful party normally has to pay part of those costs out of his or her own pocket.

In other words, few clients appreciate the distinction between party/party costs and solicitor/own client costs. Party/party costs embrace all such costs as are necessary and proper for enforcing or defending a client's rights.[2] Solicitor/own client costs on the other hand embrace all costs that are incurred except those which are of an unreasonable amount or are unreasonably incurred.[3] It follows that solicitor/own client costs will normally be higher than party/party costs.

Unfortunately when the court orders an unsuccessful party to pay the successful party's costs, it usually does so on the party/party basis and not on the solicitor/own client basis.[4] The difference must be borne by the successful party.

Unless your client is forewarned of this possibility, he or she may become very confused and angry because he or she will not be able to understand why, if he or she is awarded the costs of a proceeding, he or she should be required to pay anything at all. Having personally heard the judge order that the defendant pay his or her costs, your client will no doubt conclude that you are cheating him or her!

The best way to illustrate the distinction between party/party and solicitor/own client costs is through an example. Suppose that you accept instructions from a client named Jo Bloggs to sue a newspaper proprietor in defamation. Bloggs appeared normal enough at the beginning but you soon suspect that Bloggs is neurotic and schizophrenic as well as paranoiac. Your suspicions are confirmed when for a whole month prior to the trial Bloggs telephones you at home at midnight, 2 a.m., 4 a.m. and 6 a.m.!

The trial is successful and Bloggs is awarded $20,000 damages plus costs. You inform the defendant's practitioner that Bloggs'

2. *Smith v. Buller* (1875) 19 L.R. Eq. 473 at 475. Most rules of court define party/party costs.
3. *EMI Records Ltd v. Ian Cameron Wallace Ltd* [1983] Ch. 59. Most rules of court define solicitor/own client costs. There has traditionally been an intermediate position between party/party costs and solicitor/own client costs, namely solicitor/client costs. Solicitor/client costs are similar to party/party costs except that a more generous allowance is made for costs actually incurred by the successful party: *Frankenburg v. Famous Lasky Film Service Ltd* [1931] 1 Ch. 428 at 436.
4. *Broughton v. Rodd* (1867) 6 S.C.R. (N.S.W.) Eq. 102 at 109. Most rules of court provide for payment of costs to a successful litigant on the party/party basis.

costs amount to $6,200, $1,200 of which is represented by the 120 nocturnal attendances for the previous month. The defendant's practitioner refuses to pay a cent over $5,000 on the ground that the nocturnal attendances were neither necessary nor proper for enforcing Bloggs' action.

You readily concede the point and accept a cheque for $25,000 from the defendant. Because $5,000 does not cover all your professional costs, you will have to deduct $1,200 from the damages awarded to Bloggs so that Bloggs will ultimately receive a cheque for $18,800 from you. Of course the cheque will be accompanied by a covering letter which fully explains what your costs are and why $1,200 had to be deducted from the award of damages.

In the above simplified example, it is clear that $5,000 represents party/party costs, $6,200 represents solicitor/own client costs and $1,200 represents the difference between them. As between Bloggs and the defendant, it was not necessary for Bloggs to telephone you four times per night for a whole month and accordingly it would be unreasonable for the cost of those attendances to be borne by the defendant. On the other hand you provided a service to Bloggs every time Bloggs telephoned and accordingly it is fair that Bloggs should be obliged to pay for the costs of such service personally. You are entitled to charge Bloggs for persecuting you!

The notion that there is a distinction between party/party costs and solicitor/own client costs causes a great deal of confusion and ill feeling in clients and it will be a constant thorn in your side for as long as you practise as a solicitor. The only way to deal with it is by adequate explanation to clients.

At the time that you receive instructions to commence proceedings on behalf of a client, you should explain the nature of solicitor/own client costs vis-á-vis party/party costs and alert the client to the prospect that he or she may have to contribute something towards the costs of the action. You should confirm that advice in writing and, before any settlement is ultimately achieved, you should attempt to estimate the amount of solicitor/own client costs that your client will be responsible for and have your client sign a written acknowledgment, firstly instructing you to effect settlement for a specified amount and then acknowledging the likely amount that will be received when the case is completed.[5]

5. See above, pp. 18-19.

You should always alert your client to the rule that, generally speaking, costs incurred before the issue of proceedings are not allowable as party/party costs and therefore will have to be borne by your client.

Taxed costs

Another concept that sometimes causes confusion with clients is taxation of costs.[6] When a client is in court and hears that he or she is awarded $X in damages plus "taxed costs" the client is likely to think that he will have to share his or her good fortune with the tax department. You should carefully explain what is involved in the concept of taxed costs, namely that the costs of the action will be comprehensively itemised in a bill of costs and that the bill will then be scrutinised by a court official called the "Taxing Master". If the Taxing Master considers that any item on the bill is unjustified or excessive, the Taxing Master will "tax off" or delete an appropriate amount from the bill and your client will only be entitled to claim the balance, as certified by the Taxing Master, from the unsuccessful opponent.

If there is a prospect that any disbursement that you incur on behalf of a client will not be allowed on taxation, you must forewarn the client that he or she may have to pay for the disbursement even if successful in the action. If you fail to forewarn the client, you will be personally liable for the disbursement.[7]

Taxation of costs is not confined to litigious matters. Whenever a client is unhappy with a bill from you, the client can demand that you supply a bill in taxable form, that is, a bill which lists comprehensively all items of work that you completed on behalf of the client. The client can then make an appointment with the Taxing Master to have the bill taxed. Once again, if the Taxing Master considers that any item on the bill is unjustified or excessive, it will be taxed off and the client will only be obliged to pay the balance of the bill as certified by the Taxing Master.

For example, if you need to go overseas to interview witnesses and you travel first class without your client's prior approval, it is very likely that the difference in cost between first class and economy class will be disallowed on taxation.

6. The procedures and principles of taxation of costs are usually specified in statutes, such as the *Supreme Court Act* 1986 (Vic.), or rules of court.
7. *Re Blyth & Fanshawe* (1882) 10 Q.B.D. 207.

The parties in the first situation and the solicitor and client in the second situation could agree on a figure for costs in lieu of having the bill taxed. This commonly occurs because the procedure for having a bill taxed can be costly as well as time-consuming and inconvenient.

In some jurisdictions, barristers' fees may be taxed in much the same way as solicitors' bills.[8]

Costs in advance

There is nothing objectionable in your refusing to take on a matter unless your client pays to you an amount which you estimate will cover your costs and disbursements. This amount, however, belongs to the client and must be kept in your trust account until the matter is completed and a proper bill of costs is rendered.[9] Asking for costs in advance is wise where you have doubts about your client's ability to pay and this is especially so for clients consulting you for the first time.

However, if it is obvious that a client is impecunious, it would be insensitive to ask for funds in advance. In such a case you should either apply for legal aid on behalf of the client or refer him or her to a free legal service. Alternatively, if you have a gambling streak and think that the client has a valid claim, you can take on the matter and hope to be paid ultimately.

If the client is a disadvantaged member of the community, you should consider undertaking the work on a non-paying basis.[10]

If you do not request costs in advance but will be requiring your client to keep you in funds from time to time to cover disbursements, then inform your client of this at the outset and give the client an outline of the types of disbursements that will be incurred and their likely magnitude. If your practice is to cease acting for a client who cannot put you in funds to cover disbursements, then once again your client should be informed of this at the outset.

Lump sum bills of costs

Another concept which will cause you great trouble in practice is the lump sum bill of costs. Contrary to the myth, you cannot determine the amount of legal fees by the weight of a file or by thinking of a figure and then preparing a bill to justify it.

8. See, for example, *Supreme Court Act* 1986 (Vic.), s. 67.
9. *Johns v. Law Society of New South Wales* [1982] 2 N.S.W.L.R. 1.
10. See below, Ch. 19.

In some jurisdictions, you cannot enforce a "lump sum" bill to your client which baldly states "To professional costs rendered, $20,000". In these jurisdictions, you are obliged to set out in itemised form the services rendered and the charge for each individual item. And we stress "each item".

In your early days in practice, you will probably see principals laboriously preparing four and five page bills which list each telephone and personal attendance upon a client and everything else that was done on the client's behalf and which finish up with one lump sum at the end. Do not be misled. This is still a lump sum bill which (subject to any statutory provisions to the contrary)[11] cannot be sued upon: *Malleson, Stewart, Stawell and Nankivell v. Williams.*[12] The rationale is that a bill must contain sufficient details to enable the client to decide whether or not to seek to have the bill taxed by the Taxing Master.

A client can, of course, waive the right to receive a bill in taxable form and the right to have a bill taxed.

Many practitioners do in fact send out lump sum bills and their clients do not query them. The lump sum bill, if rejected by the client, is normally not enforceable against that client and must be replaced by a bill in taxable form.

A problem that sometimes arises is whether you are bound by the amount claimed in a lump sum bill of costs if your client does not accept the bill and insists on receiving a bill in taxable form. In other words, if you charge your client $500 in a lump sum bill but the bill in taxable form adds up to $700, can you ask the Taxing Master to ignore the first bill when taxing the second bill?

The courts have taken different approaches to this question. You should find out what approach the courts in your jurisdiction take before sending your client a lump sum bill which intentionally or unintentionally understates your costs. In some jurisdictions, it is permissible to reserve a right to withdraw a lump sum bill and render a bill in taxable form for a larger amount if your client objects to the initial bill.[13]

Most jurisdictions also impose certain prerequisites to a valid bill of costs. Two prerequisites that are prescribed in Victoria are that a bill must be signed by a partner of the firm concerned and that one month must expire from the delivery of a proper bill to a client before a practitioner can sue upon it.[14]

11. See, for example, *Supreme Court Act* 1986 (Vic.), s. 61.
12. [1930] V.L.R. 410.
13. See, for example, *Supreme Court Act* 1986 (Vic.), ss 61(5) and 74(7).
14. *Supreme Court Act* 1986, s. 61.

Interim bills

Another general rule is that a bill cannot be rendered for a matter until the matter is completed.[15] This is because most of the matters handled by a practitioner involve an "entire contract" between the practitioner and the client so that the practitioner is not entitled to any remuneration until the matter is completely finalised.

This means that, subject to statutory provisions to the contrary,[16] interim bills are generally not enforceable. Therefore, in the absence of a valid costing agreement between you and your client, a client would be acting within his or her rights in refusing to pay an interim bill. However, many practitioners follow the practice of submitting interim bills and in most cases clients pay them without complaint. Some clients in fact prefer to pay for legal services gradually in small sums rather than paying a large amount upon completion of the matter.

Contingency fees

Contingency fees, whereby you are paid a percentage of any damages awarded to your client if his or her action succeeds, are generally not permitted in common law jurisdictions. They are permitted in the United States and Canada.

Contingency fees have been the subject of considerable debate in Australia and the United Kingdom and in some jurisdictions, such as Victoria, proposals to legalise some contingency fee arrangements have been put forward.[17]

Overcharging

You must be careful not to overcharge a client because this could amount to unprofessional conduct. If a scale exists for the work that you have done, then you must not charge above scale. If a scale or other binding rule does not exist, then in general you should charge a sum which is fair and reasonable having regard to all the circumstances of the case, including:

(a) the complexity of the matter or the difficulty or novelty of the questions raised;

15. *Underwood, Son & Piper v. Lewis* [1894] 2 Q.B. 306. See above, p. 16.
16. See, for example, *Supreme Court Act* 1986 (Vic.), s. 61.
17. See Australian Senate Standing Committee on Legal and Constitutional Affairs, *Cost of Legal Services and Litigation Discussion Paper No. 3: Contingency Fees* (1991).

(b) the skill, labour, specialised knowledge and responsibility involved;

(c) the time spent on the matter;

(d) the number, length and importance of the documents prepared or perused;

(e) the amount or value of any money or property involved; and

(f) the importance of the matter to the client.[18]

Some firms use time costing, whereby each practitioner is assigned a charge rate per hour. When a matter is completed, the time spent on it is worked out (often this is provided by a computer printout) and this is multiplied by the charge rate. Many commercial clients accept being charged on a time-costing basis. However, for the ordinary client in a litigious matter, you must adhere to scale unless a costing agreement has been entered into between you and your client.

Even if time costing is applicable, do not use it mechanically. Take into account matters such as those listed above before determining the fee. Sometimes it may be appropriate to charge above the time-costing figure (especially if the work was urgent and was completed largely outside normal office hours); at other times you may need to charge below it.

Discounts

Contrary to the belief of some young practitioners, there is nothing improper in charging a client less than the fee specified by an applicable scale. The scales set the maximum charges only; they do not prohibit charging less than scale where you consider this is appropriate.

Practitioners sometimes render accounts to their clients in which they set out an amount that would normally apply, add the magic words, "but in the circumstances, say . . ." and then insert a reduced amount. Some practitioners fondly believe that this practice impresses clients and makes them think more of them so that they will bring more business to them. This is not always the case. The practice may in fact make the client suspicious about whether or not you have mucked up the whole thing, and, as a result of a pricked conscience, felt obliged to give the client a break.

18. See *Cordery on Solicitors*, (8th edn, Butterworths & Co. (Publishers) Ltd, London, 1988), p. 168.

There is a story about a practitioner who felt so sorry for a client who had lost an action that he wrote to the client stating that he would not charge the client anything. The next thing the practitioner heard was that the client had visited the Law Institute of Victoria and complained that the solicitor had been so negligent that he felt ashamed to render a bill.

Agreement on costs

Apart from a bill of costs which has been calculated in accordance with statutory scale allowances (if any are applicable) and which at the client's option is subject to taxation to determine whether the amount claimed is proper, you may claim costs pursuant to an agreement.

Agreements on costs between practitioners and clients are generally governed by statutes such as the *Supreme Court Act* 1986 (Vic.) or subordinate legislation such as rules of court.

The courts, from time to time, have emphasised that an agreement about costs must be fair and reasonable having regard to all the circumstances of the case. The courts have not hesitated in setting aside any agreement where they have considered that the costs claimed are excessive and far beyond what the practitioner would have been entitled to claim in the absence of the agreement.

Similarly, courts have set aside agreements where the client has not fully understood the agreement or was induced to enter into it by the fraud, misrepresentation or other improper conduct of the practitioner concerned. In some jurisdictions, a court may set aside an agreement where the solicitor has been guilty of default, negligence, delay or other improper conduct in the performance of his or her duties under the agreement.

An agreement as to costs should state precisely what services you propose to provide for the agreed fee. Accordingly, in a litigious matter it is necessary to state the name of the court, whether the agreed amount includes barristers' fees or other disbursements, whether the fee will apply if liability is admitted and whether the fee includes the cost of interrogatories and various other interlocutory applications in the course of the proceeding. It is also necessary to indicate whether the fee will apply only if the matter is settled at the door of the court or whether it will extend to cover the costs of the trial. Sometimes it is desirable to build into an agreement an additional agreed daily fee for the trial of an action.

Where you make an agreement with a client to charge fees on a time basis, your client does not waive his or her right to request a detailed bill. You would accordingly be expected to deliver a detailed bill indicating precisely the time spent on each service rendered. It is possible that such a bill will be in far greater detail than a bill of costs prepared in accordance with the statutory scales. For example, you would be expected to set out the time spent in drafting or dictating a letter and in checking, signing and posting it. Of course, the agreement should state whether the time charge includes or excludes the time of administrative staff such as the typist.

Acting for yourself

When, contrary to our advice in Chapter 10, you act for yourself and are successful in litigation, you may recover costs in the ordinary way except that you will not be allowed costs for instructing yourself or for attendances on yourself or for similar items which would involve a duplication of yourself as client and as lawyer.[19]

Organisation of files

The way you organise your files should be orientated towards the proper costing of the matter upon its completion. Proper keeping of records of activities such as telephone conversations, conferences and attendances in court will make it easier to accurately calculate and prepare a bill of costs. Otherwise you will have to play the guessing game of who telephoned who and who did what.

The guessing game is wasteful and not much fun, especially for matters that commenced five years ago. In the absence of adequate proof that you performed an item of work that is listed in your bill of costs, it is likely that you will have arguments over it with your client or with the practitioner acting for your client's opponent and if the bill comes before the Taxing Master, you may find that the item is "taxed off".[20]

19. *Ogier v. Norton* (1904) 29 V.L.R. 536 at 538; *London Scottish Benefit Society v. Chorley Crawford and Chester* (1884) 13 Q.B.D. 872.
20. *Morris v. Bonnie Dundee Coal Co. Pty Ltd* [1969] Q.W.N. 31.

Chapter 8

Entitlement to Documents

> "The proprietor of a hotel . . . may detain . . . any property . . . brought by a guest into the hospitium of the inn . . . He is not, however, entitled to detain the guest himself, nor take clothes from his person."
>
> *Halsbury's Laws of England* (4th edn reissue), Vol. 24, para. 1144.

Question of ownership

If a client pays your bill and demands his or her file, to what documents is the client entitled? Though this problem arises frequently in practice, not many practitioners know the precise answer.

Most practitioners have a fair idea of what a solicitor's lien is—a matter that we discuss in Chapter 9—but the solicitor's lien is not relevant once the client pays your bill.

The position is determined largely by ownership; the client can ask for documents belonging to him or her but not documents belonging to you. The notion of ownership in this context is not easy to apply.

In *Wentworth v. De Montfort*[1] the following principles were set out:

1. Where a solicitor acts only as an agent for a client in doing some act, the ordinary rules of agency apply so that a document brought into existence or received by the solicitor when so acting belongs to the client.

1. (1988) 15 N.S.W.L.R. 348.

2. Where a solicitor acts in a capacity other than as agent for the client, property in documents brought into existence or received by the solicitor depends on principles referable to the relationship of a professional person and client. Relevant factors to be considered include:
   (a) whether or not the client was charged for the creation of the document; and
   (b) whether the solicitor created the document primarily for the client's benefit and protection or for the solicitor's own benefit and protection.

The following types of documents were held in the *Wentworth* case to generally belong to the client:

(a) documents involving counsel created or received for the benefit of the client (even though it may also be for the solicitor's benefit) including original or copy documents and counsel's brief;
(b) correspondence and notes of conversations between a solicitor and court official (although a solicitor is entitled to copy these).

The following types of documents were held to generally belong to the solicitor:

(a) cheque requisition forms;
(b) financial records (whether computerised or otherwise) kept in relation to transactions concerning moneys of a client held in trust and disbursements of those moneys (although the client is entitled to information about his or her financial affairs on the records and to inspect and copy where appropriate);
(c) notes of telephone or personal attendances on persons other than the client or at court and correspondence with persons other than the client may belong to either depending on the nature and content of the notes and whether made for the primary purpose of the solicitor or client;
(d) internal records and memoranda of a solicitor as to work done or to be done;
(e) internal photocopying requisitions.

In Cordery[2] the following guidelines are laid down:

1. Documents in existence before the retainer commences and sent to you by the client or by a third party during the

2. *Cordery on Solicitors* (8th edn, Butterworths & Co. (Publishers) Ltd, London, 1988), pp. 89-90.

retainer are held by you as agent for and on behalf of the client or third party. On the termination of the retainer you must dispose of them as the client or third party may direct.

2. Documents which come into existence during the retainer and for the purpose of business transacted by you pursuant to the retainer fall into four categories:

   (a) Documents prepared by you for the benefit of the client and which are paid for by the client, belong to the client.[3] These documents include draft, original and copy deeds prepared in non-contentious matters, briefs to counsel, and file copies of letters written by you on behalf of the client.

   (b) Documents prepared by you for your own benefit or protection, the preparation of which is not regarded as an item chargeable against the client, belong to you.[4] These documents include copies of letters written to the client, entries of attendances, inter-office memoranda, entries in diaries, timesheets, computerised records, office journals and books of account.

   (c) Documents forwarded by the client to you during the retainer, the property in which was intended at the date of despatch to pass from the client to you, belong to you.[5] These documents include letters, authorities, and written instructions given by the client to you.

   (d) Documents prepared by a third party during the retainer and forwarded to you (other than at your expense) belong to the client. These documents include letters from an opposing party's practitioner, receipts for disbursements incurred by you on behalf of your client and expert opinions (including medical reports).

Cordery[6] concludes that a solicitor seeking to retain documents must show that:

(a) there was no duty to prepare them;

(b) they were not prepared for the benefit of the client; and

(c) the client was not liable to pay for them specifically or under any general item in the bill of costs.

3. *Re Ellis and Ellis* [1908] W.N. 215.
4. *Re Thomson* (1855) 20 Beav. 545; 52 E.R. 714.
5. *Re Wheatcroft* (1877) 6 Ch. D. 97.
6. *Cordery on Solicitors* (8th edn, Butterworths & Co. (Publishers) Ltd, London, 1988), p. 90.

On the other hand, Cordery states that a client wishing to take possession of documents must show that:

(a) they were a necessary part of the business transacted; and

(b) the client has paid in one form or another for their preparation.

Halsbury sums it up in this way:

> "Documents coming into existence in the course of business transacted under a retainer, and either prepared for the benefit of the client or received by the solicitor as agent for the client, belong to the client. However, documents prepared by the solicitor for his own protection or benefit, and letters written by the client to the solicitor, belong to the solicitor."[7]

In the absence of a solicitor's lien, it is your duty, when called upon by your client, to deliver to the client in a reasonable condition such documents of the client as you possess.[8]

Medical reports

A continuing problem is that of the embarrassing medical report. At times the situation is encountered where, as part of the conduct of a civil action, you arrange for the client to undergo a medical examination on the basis that the examining doctor will furnish a report to you. The ultimate cost of the report is the responsibility of the client.

Sometimes medical reports contain references to malingering by the client or some psychiatric disorder suffered by the client. Medical reports prepared for the purposes of a plea for leniency in criminal proceedings, in particular, frequently contain assessments of morbid psychiatric conditions and make gloomy predictions of anti-social behaviour on the part of the client.

Many doctors believe that it can be detrimental for a patient to become aware of a frank assessment of his or her condition, prospect of recovery and future treatment. However, accepting that Cordery's proposition 2(d) above is correct, you would be required to hand over the medical report to the client upon request because it is a document prepared by the doctor during the currency of the retainer and sent to you at the client's expense.

7. *Halsbury's Laws of England* (4th edn), Vol. 44, para. 103.
8. *Re Long* [1929] V.L.R. 318.

Because of the perceived dangers of a patient having access to medical reports, there is a growing tendency for doctors to be more and more guarded in subjective assessments of clients in medical reports. Some doctors who are concerned that there is a prospect of the client becoming aware of material in a medical report which would be disturbing, place a condition upon the provision of the medical report. The report contains words to the effect: "I give this medical report to you on the condition that the contents of paragraphs X and Y are not made available to your client."

Whilst it may be argued that it is unfair for the client to be required to pay for a medical report if he or she is not going to have full access to it, the condition may be justified because the client's benefit is the use of the information contained in the report for the purpose of litigation rather than physical possession of the document or the publication of its contents. Nevertheless, if a client insists on having access to the whole of a report, it is doubtful whether a condition imposed by the doctor which seeks to restrict access to parts of it would be binding on the client.

Chapter 9

Solicitor's Lien

"Yond' Cassius has a lien [sic] and hungry look; He thinks too much: such men are dangerous."

Shakespeare, *Julius Caesar.*

Nature of solicitor's lien

As a solicitor, you have a right to retain possession of documents or other personal property of a client or former client until payment of the amount of your costs. This right to retain possession is called a "lien".

A solicitor's lien extends to all deeds, papers or other personal property which belong to the client and which come into your possession with the client's consent in the course of your employment and in your capacity as solicitor.[1] If you hold money in your trust account on behalf of a client, the lien attaches only to the amount of your bill of costs and not to the whole of the trust funds.[2] No lien attaches to a client's will.[3]

The lien is a general lien and attaches to a client's property in respect of all professional costs owed by the client to you whether or not such costs have any connection with any of the property in question. However, the lien applies only to professional costs which are properly due to you. If a client exercises the right to have a bill of costs taxed then the lien subsists only in respect of the amount certified by the Taxing

1. *Cordery on Solicitors* (8th edn, Butterworths & Co. (Publishers) Ltd, London, 1988), p. 237.
2. *Miller v. Atlee* (1849) 3 Exch. 799; 154 E.R. 1068; *Re Jalmoon Pty Ltd* [1986] 2 Qd R. 264.
3. *Balch v. Symes* (1823) Turn. & R. 87; 37 E.R. 1028.

Master as being due to you. The lien does not apply to moneys owing by the client to you in a capacity other than as solicitor. For example, if you personally lend money to a client on the security of a mortgage, a solicitor's lien would not attach to the mortgage documents.[4]

Your right to retain possession of documents or other property pursuant to a solicitor's lien is enforceable against your client and his or her representatives (such as a personal representative or a trustee in bankruptcy) but the right is qualified against third parties. This is because you cannot have any better right to retain a document than your client would have if the client had possession of it.

Accordingly, just as a third party could have compelled your client to produce documents in court pursuant to a subpoena you can also be compelled to do so.[5] However, you would retain the right to have the documents returned to you at the conclusion of the proceeding.

A solicitor's lien is discharged if your client pays you the amount of your costs or gives you security for such amount, if you hand over the documents or other property to your client, or if you waive the lien.[6]

In addition to the general solicitor's lien over a client's documents or other property in your possession, you may also have a particular lien over property recovered or preserved, or the proceeds of any judgment obtained, by you through your work on your client's behalf.[7]

Such a lien differs from the general lien because it only extends to costs properly incurred by you in obtaining the property or the judgment on your client's behalf. Another difference is that the particular lien cannot be enforced without seeking the assistance of the court.

4. *Pelly v. Wathen* (1849) 7 Hare 351 at 364; 68 E.R. 144 at 150.
5. *Hope v. Liddell* (1855) 7 De G.M. & G. 331; 44 E.R. 129. See also *Re Hawkes, Ackerman v. Lockhard* (1898) 2 Ch. 1.
6. *Cordery on Solicitors* (8th edn, Butterworths & Co. (Publishers) Ltd, London, 1988), pp. 248-250. Some Law Societies have rules of professional conduct which oblige solicitors to return to a client funds and documents held by the solicitor pursuant to a lien if the solicitor fails to deliver to the client a bill in taxable form within a prescribed time. See, for example, *Solicitors' (Professional Conduct and Practice) Rules* 1984 (Vic.), r. 5.
7. *Cordery on Solicitors* (8th edn, Butterworths & Co. (Publishers) Ltd, London, 1988), p. 250.

Practical problems

Although it is relatively easy to summarise the nature of a solicitor's lien, it is much more difficult to work out the answers to the many problems that arise in practice in relation to such liens.

Three situations commonly arise in practice:

1. A dissatisfied client changes his or her solicitor and comes to see you in relation to an incomplete matter handled by the former solicitor. You request the client's papers from the former solicitor but that solicitor refuses to hand them over until his or her costs are paid. The client cannot pay such costs until the matter is completed.
2. A client comes to see you in relation to a matter that has been completed by a former solicitor. The client needs some papers from the file relating to the matter but cannot obtain them without paying the former solicitor's costs. The client refuses to pay because he or she considers the former solicitor's costs exorbitant.
3. A client who wants to sue a former solicitor for negligence comes to see you. The client is antagonistic to any costs which the former solicitor wishes to render for work which the client considers second rate. The former solicitor is reluctant to hand over the documents which may be the basis of a negligence action against him or her and therefore insists on payment of his or her costs.

The extent to which the former solicitor can claim a lien over the client's documents depends upon the circumstances in which the professional relationship between them was terminated. The legal position is as follows:

1. If the former solicitor was discharged by the client in the course of an action, otherwise than for misconduct, the former solicitor cannot, so long as the costs are unpaid, be compelled to produce or hand over to you the client's documents which are in that solicitor's possession. This is so even if you are prepared to give an undertaking that the solicitor's taxed costs will be paid.[8]

   Moreover, a mere allegation on the part of the client that the former solicitor was negligent or is seeking to overcharge the client will not affect the former solicitor's

8. *Re Rapid Road Transit Co.* [1909] 2 Ch. 96; *Re Castle* (1867) 6 S.C.R. (N.S.W.) 195; *Hughes v. Hughes* [1958] 3 All E.R. 175.

lien.[9] If the client feels the former solicitor's bill is excessive, the remedy is to have it taxed.

2. If the former solicitor discharged himself or herself, the general principle is that the solicitor must hand over the client's documents to you upon receiving an undertaking from you that you will preserve the solicitor's lien over the documents and will return the documents at the end of the litigation.[10]
3. If the former solicitor was discharged by the client for misconduct, then the situation is the same as in example 2.
4. If the former solicitor discharged himself or herself or was discharged by the client for misconduct and you gave him or her an undertaking to pay his or her taxed costs, rather than an undertaking to preserve the lien and to return the documents, it is submitted that the former solicitor would be obliged to hand over the documents to you. If you secure payment of the former solicitor's costs—such as through payment into court—then the former solicitor can be compelled to hand over the documents to you.[11]
5. If the former solicitor discharged himself or herself from a matter and then refused to hand over to you the client's documents in his or her possession in exchange for an undertaking to retain the papers and return them upon completion of the matter, the former solicitor will be liable to pay the costs of any proceeding commenced to have the papers delivered to you.

It can be seen from the above propositions that the former solicitor's lien is not lost by handing the documents over to you if it is made clear that the lien is to be preserved.

Although, in the absence of misconduct, a solicitor who is discharged by a client is entitled to retain the client's papers until his or her costs are paid and is not obliged to accept any undertakings in respect of the payment of costs from a new solicitor, some commonsense and give and take is desirable if our legal system is to work.

Where proceedings, especially criminal proceedings, are imminent but the client is unable to raise enough money to pay

9. *Lewis v. Powell* [1897] 1 Ch. 678.
10. *Robins v. Goldingham* (1872) 13 L.R. Eq. 440; *Conquest v. Maffey* (1897) 22 V.L.R. 616; *Re Stuart Robertson* (1926) 43 W.N. (N.S.W.) 107; *Gamlen Chemical Co. (U.K.) Ltd v. Rochem Ltd* [1980] 1 All E.R. 1049.
11. *Beneficial Finance Corp. Ltd v. Conway (No. 2)* [1971] V.R. 594 at 607.

the costs of a former solicitor, that solicitor should take such steps as would avoid prejudice to the client's cause of action or the successful defence of criminal charges whilst at the same time protecting his or her own position. The solicitor may have a legal right to insist on retention of the documents until his or her costs are paid but an uncompromising assertion of such a right may give rise to criticism from the Bench.[12]

Undermining of lien by opposing solicitor

Assume that your client is the plaintiff and is keen to resolve the litigation as quickly as possible. There is a change in the defendant's solicitors and the new solicitor advises you that the previous solicitor is claiming a lien over the documents. Your opponent requests you to provide him or her with copies of all relevant documents from your file to enable the matter to proceed. Since your client's interests would be advanced by providing the documents so that delay is avoided, should you accede to the request? By doing so, would you be undermining the lien of the original solicitor?

In our view, your duty to your client to advance his or her interests means that it would be appropriate for you to co-operate with the new solicitor by providing relevant documents from your file, such as pleadings and copy discovered documents.

12. *Re Castle* (1867) 6 S.C.R. (N.S.W.) 195 at 199.

Chapter 10

Acting for Friends or Relatives

> "There is always something about your success that displeases even your best friends."
>
> Oscar Wilde.

It has often been said that your worst clients will be your friends and relatives. This is not because there is anything improper or unethical in acting for friends or relatives or because your friends or relatives are mean and seek to take advantage of you. Rather, it is the extra familiarity between you, over and above the practitioner-client relationship, that causes problems.

From your point of view, you may relax some of your discipline because you may think that nothing will go wrong in the transaction or, even if it did, your friends or relatives would not sue you, especially if you have agreed to take on the matter gratuitously. Taking on a matter gratuitously may lead to the further problem of you giving the matter less priority than the files of your paying clients.

Obtaining instructions

There may also be difficulty in obtaining instructions. For paying clients, you normally receive instructions at personal interviews, by letter or by telephone and you take detailed notes of all conversations. In the case of friends or relatives, instructions may be given at the dinner table, mingled with general social conversation. In such a situation there is the danger either that instructions are vague and general, or that they are not precisely understood or recorded by you.

There is even the risk that you may be tempted to dispense with instructions altogether and instead act upon what you think your instructions would be if you asked your client. Assumed or implied instructions are very dangerous indeed.

From the clients' point of view, it is often the case where a friend or relative acts for them, that they give instructions as general as "Do what you think is best without bothering me about the details." In effect, they consider that they are giving you a power of attorney to do everything you think fit on their behalf. If you do what you think best for them, but the result is an unsatisfactory one, they generally feel aggrieved and think that you have not done all that you could for them. They may feel that you have adopted a different standard of care in relation to their matter vis-á-vis your other clients. They might be right!

On the other hand, some friends and relatives might be reluctant to demand from you the service to which they would be entitled if a "normal" solicitor-client relationship existed. It is very difficult to make demands upon someone who is doing you a favour or handling a matter for a reduced fee. It takes courage indeed to demand that your next door neighbour rise at 6 a.m. to keep a promise to help you fix your roof.

Cutting corners

Another problem is that friends and relatives often have the confidence to tell you to finalise a matter quickly and to cut as many corners as possible. Accordingly, you may be tempted to cut a corner which you think will not in any way prejudice your client, but our experience has been that cutting legal corners invariably leads to litigious collisions.

Out of your depth

If you have recently started a practice of your own, you may find that friends and relatives will retain you as their solicitor so that they can help you establish yourself. Any newcomer to private practice needs this sort of support but you should take care to ensure that you are not enticed into handling matters outside the scope of your competence. It is preferable for you to point out to your friends and relatives that you are not competent to handle the matter and to refer them to another practitioner who you know is competent in the area. The alternative may be to take on the matter and make a mess of it to the detriment of yourself, your clients and your relationship with them.

Friends and relatives can certainly become dissatisfied ex-clients and ex-friends if, through your incompetence, you have increased their costs or have mishandled their legal affairs. They may even sue you!

Discounts

Friends and relatives have the familiarity to ask for huge discounts whenever you act for them. They are sometimes the first to complain about the size of the bill after their matter is completed. Even after you have established yourself in practice, they may not be able to get out of their heads the notion that they are doing you a favour by referring their legal work to you.

Conflict of interest

Acting for friends and relatives may also pose conflict of interest problems. For example, it may be wise to refuse to draw up your parents' wills if you are to be a principal beneficiary under those wills. The same principle could apply in a situation where you are buying a property from friends or relatives, or where you are borrowing money for the purposes of your practice and ask your friends or relatives to guarantee your obligations.

Confidentiality

There is a risk that your obligation to maintain the confidentiality of communications between you and your clients may be neglected when your clients are friends or relatives. Communications from clients often provide items of juicy gossip. Where the client is a friend or relative, you must resist the temptation to discuss their affairs with other friends or relatives. If you succumb to the temptation, you may not only lose a friend and a client, but might also face a complaint of unprofessional conduct.

Loss of objectivity

Another difficulty that arises is that when acting for someone who is close to you, you may so identify yourself with that person's problems and interests that you lose your professional objectivity. This would be detrimental to both yourself and your client.

Do not second guess another practitioner's advice

It is often in the best interests of your friends and relatives, as well as yourself, that they be represented by someone else. If they are so represented then, although there would be no objection to you talking to them generally about their legal problem, you should avoid giving them advice. There is nothing more annoying than meddling professional relatives.

Where you refer a friend or relative to another practitioner you should never act in a way which might interfere with the ability of that practitioner to fulfil his or her obligations to the client.

Acting for yourself

Apart from the dangers of acting for friends and relatives, it is also inadvisable ever to act for yourself except in very minor matters. Remember the old proverb, "One who is his [or her] own lawyer has a fool for a client"!

Chapter 11

Sex in the Office

> "Parties to a cause of divorce may not litigate by day and copulate by night."
>
> *Holt v. Holt*, 77 Fed. (2nd) 538 at 540 (1935).

The professions which seem most vulnerable to accusations of sexual impropriety or harassment are the medical and teaching professions. However, the legal profession has had its share of accusations and complaints—not many, but enough to indicate that from time to time in the practitioner-client relationship there is either mutual physical attraction between practitioner and client or unwanted advances made by a practitioner towards a client.

Different situations

There are two separate situations. The first is an act of sexual intercourse between two consenting adults, one a practitioner, the other a client. The second is one of sexual harassment of the client by the practitioner.

In the first instance, the relevant Law Society should mind its own business, unless it can be demonstrated that the personal relationship between the practitioner and the client has resulted in a conflict of interest situation or an impairment of the practitioner's competence to discharge his or her professional obligations to the client. That observation is equally applicable whether the relationship is heterosexual or homosexual.

The position is totally different in the case of sexual harassment. Over the years Law Societies have received a number of complaints from female clients about male solicitors. Such behaviour is intolerable in any context, whether professional relationships are involved or not. The conduct presents a very difficult situation from the point of view of investigation. Unfortunately, in some cases, the best that a Law Society can do, in the absence of independent evidence, is to counsel the practitioner and hope that this will prevent repetition of the conduct.[1]

Lamb's case

The decision of the High Court of Australia in *Bar Association of Queensland v. Lamb*[2] involved sexual relations between a solicitor and a client.

Mr Lamb, who was a Queensland solicitor, applied for admission to the Queensland Bar. In his application for admission to the Bar, Mr Lamb had admitted that, while a solicitor, he had had extra-marital intercourse with his client in a matrimonial matter after the decree absolute but before questions of custody and maintenance had been determined. It was held that although the conduct complained of warranted the criticism that it was "unprofessional" and "reprehensible", it nevertheless fell short of amounting to such unprofessional conduct as would render Mr Lamb unfit to remain a solicitor or to become a barrister.

The matter had come before the High Court by way of an application by the Bar Association of Queensland for special leave to appeal against the decision of the Supreme Court of Queensland to admit Mr Lamb as a barrister. In the Supreme Court the Acting Chief Justice of Queensland had said, "The critical question is whether the adulterous and unprofessional conduct, in the circumstance in which it occurred, should disqualify the applicant from admission to the Bar." His Honour then gave reasons why he answered the question in the negative.

In the High Court, Windeyer J. said that although he considered the conduct complained of "reprehensible", it was not sufficient to justify the disqualification of Lamb from membership of the legal profession. Thus, although the members of the High Court were clearly unimpressed by Mr Lamb's behaviour, they were not prepared to put him out of business.

The reason why the Bar Association of Queensland took the matter to the High Court was probably that, in involving himself

1. Equal Opportunity legislation in some jurisdictions makes sexual harassment unlawful in relation to the performance or provision of services in some circumstances.
2. [1972] A.L.R. 285.

in a sexual relationship with his client whilst the questions of custody and maintenance remained outstanding, Mr Lamb created a situation of potential detriment to his client. The High Court added that the application of the Bar Association of Queensland was "understandably and properly made".

Apart from *Lamb's* case, it is difficult to find any real authority on the propriety or otherwise of a sexual relationship between a practitioner and a client. It is really a question of degree.

It would be unprofessional conduct for a practitioner acting for a distressed and confused client in a matrimonial matter to take advantage of the client's state of mind and seduce him or her.

Similarly, if a client offers sex as part payment for legal services rendered, it would be improper for the practitioner to accept.

On the other hand, if a practitioner is acting for a client in a commercial matter and they become friends and eventually have sexual intercourse, it is unlikely that the practitioner would be held to have acted improperly.

Although there is no blanket commandment "Thou shall not have sexual intercourse with clients," you should always be careful when a professional relationship with a client starts to become more intimate.[3]

The experience of the Law Institute of Victoria

Some of the practical situations the Law Institute of Victoria has had to deal with have been almost bizarre.

In 1976 a solicitor, who refused to give his name, telephoned and asked, "Is it OK to have sexual intercourse with my client?" The caller was obviously in a state of barely contained ardour and because of the sense of urgency in his voice, one could form a mental picture of two trembling would-be participants eagerly awaiting the outcome of the call to the Law Institute. Clearly it was a situation which could not await a ruling in writing from the Ethics Committee. One had to do the best one could. He was told that it all depended on the nature of the professional relationship. Before the Institute had a chance to finish telling him that he was not entitled to take advantage of the emotional dependence of his client upon him, particularly in a matrimonial case, there came an agitated interjection, "But I'm a conveyancer!"

3. The U.S. position is discussed in J. Pitulla, "Unfair Advantage" (1992) (November) *American Bar Association Journal* 76.

The Law Institute hardly ever receives complaints of sexual molestation from the clients of conveyancers or probate solicitors. Perhaps in the case of probate matters the files on the desk are so large that there may not be an opportunity to gain physical access to the client.

Doctors

Whatever the confusion which may exist about a lawyer's responsibilities in this area, it is clear that the safest course for doctors is to abstain from having sexual relations with patients. In *Bhattacharya v. General Medical Council*[4] the Privy Council was faced with allegations of sexual misconduct by a doctor towards his female patient during a period of almost six years. The relationship was regular and, at times, almost overt, but neither factor caused the Privy Council to alter the decision of the General Medical Council to strike the doctor's name off the roll.

Even the fact that the improper relationship had existed prior to the commencement of the professional relationship was not considered to be an excuse by the Privy Council. Their Lordships held that the tendency of conduct to debase or degrade the standing and reputation of the profession varied from case to case; while the maintenance of a long standing pre-existing association with one who becomes a patient may in general be less serious than the deterioration of a professional relationship into an improper association, the former was still capable of amounting to infamous conduct in a professional respect.

This case is to be contrasted with that of *Medical Board of Victoria v. Cato*[5] where the Medical Board of Victoria was refused leave to appeal to the High Court against a Supreme Court ruling that a doctor who had "passionately embraced and kissed" a young woman patient when she was ill and at home alone in bed was not guilty of infamous conduct in a professional respect. She had called the doctor and was in bed in a low cut black negligee when he arrived. After the "improper" kissing incident the doctor had a sexual relationship with her but it was held that at that time the doctor-patient relationship had ended and had been replaced by a purely social relationship.

4. [1967] 2 A.C. 259.
5. Unreported, High Court of Australia, 23 August 1985.

Although the High Court was clearly more lenient to Dr Cato than the Privy Council was to Dr Bhattacharya, it still appears that a doctor will get into trouble more readily by having sexual relations with a patient than a solicitor who has such relations with a client.

A cynic might ask, does that mean that in general terms lawyers are entitled to be over-sexed but not dishonest with their trust accounts, while doctors can be neither? Perhaps the distinction is valid because only doctors are able to abuse their clients under the guise of necessary physical examination. As undressing and climbing onto the consulting couch have never been prerequisites to legal services, clients are far less likely to unwittingly subject themselves to their lawyer's advances.

Part 2

Relationship with Other Practitioners

Chapter 12

Introduction

> "He is . . . not worthy of his robes if he allows his law to override his common sense."
>
> R. E. Megarry, *Lawyer and Litigant in England* (Stevens & Sons Ltd, London, 1962), p. 15.

Apart from your duty to act in the best interests of a client, you also owe a duty to other practitioners. That duty is to conduct yourself in an honest, reasonable and reliable manner towards your colleagues because it is of the essence of the legal profession that its members must be able to rely on each other's word, whether that word is given by way of an oral promise, a letter or by way of a formal undertaking.[1]

In all your dealings with other practitioners, try to maintain the tradition of co-operation and courtesy between members of the profession so far as is possible without prejudicing the interests of your client. The maintenance of co-operation and mutual assistance within the profession not only makes the practice of law more enjoyable but also strengthens the profession and the administration of justice generally.

Assisting an inexperienced colleague with a problem in an area in which you are experienced will in all probability be reciprocated one day when you have a problem in which the colleague may be an expert.

Helping a colleague may also be to your financial advantage in the form of referral of work to you if the colleague cannot act for any reason, such as the existence of a conflict of interest.

If you disregard the tradition of co-operation and make life difficult for your colleagues, you will probably find that they will

1. K. H. Gifford, *Legal Profession Law and Practice in Victoria* (Law Book Co. Ltd, Sydney, 1980), p. 375.

respond in a similar fashion. The result will be not only unpleasantness within the profession but also a decline in its public standing.

The chapters in Part 2 of this book look at some practical aspects of your professional relationship with other practitioners.

Chapter 13

Conducting Negotiations

"Why, may not that be the skull of a lawyer?
Where be his quiddities now, his quillets, his
cases, his tenures and his tricks?"

Shakespeare, *Hamlet*, V, i, 104.

Much of your professional time will be taken up in discussing your clients' matters with practitioners acting for other parties. The nature of these discussions will be determined largely by the type of matter being discussed. For example, discussions relating to a conveyancing matter are normally routine. Discussions relating to litigious matters, on the other hand, may range from friendly chats on the progress of an action to lively arguments on points of law or fact.

As most actions are settled out of court, discussions with other practitioners in a litigious matter will commonly involve negotiations to settle the matter. Your client will expect, and you have a duty to ensure, that any settlement that is reached is in the best interests of the client.

Negotiations with other practitioners require skill and vigilance. One slip and you could prejudice the interests of your client. Unfortunately, good negotiation skills are often not taught in law school and need to be developed through practical experience. However, there are some simple points that are worth making.

Conceal your ignorance or inexperience

When conducting negotiations with a practitioner acting for your client's opponent, never be intimidated if that practitioner is more experienced than you. If you have just started to practise law, do not volunteer this information to the practitioner on the other side because that practitioner might try to take advantage of your inexperience.[1]

Even if the other practitioner knows that you are inexperienced, try to give the impression that you know what you are about. Some practitioners think that if you are not a principal or otherwise feature on your firm's letterhead, you must be stupid.

If you are in doubt as to how to respond to a question or proposition put to you by an opponent, say that you will have to consider the matter or obtain instructions. Then seek assistance from a more experienced colleague. Never admit that you do not know much about the file because it is not yours, or that you are unfamiliar with the area of law involved in the matter. Such statements can only be detrimental to your client.

Above all else, during negotiations never be stampeded into actions or statements which exceed your instructions or which involve disclosure of information to which your opponent is not entitled.

Don't say too much

When negotiating, do not say more than you have to. You must be careful not to provide a voluntary set of answers to interrogatories! Remember, the purpose of the communication is normally to threaten action, to seek a concession or to discuss a solution. The communication is made on behalf of your client with a view to advancing the client's case and protecting his or her interests. Do not say anything that would have the opposite effect of prejudicing your client's case.

If your opponent is being nosey, for example, by asking what witnesses you will be calling, politely tell your opponent to mind his or her own business.

If you are negotiating a settlement with an opponent over the telephone and you tell your opponent that your client is prepared to offer $10,000 all in, how should you respond if your opponent asks you whether that is the maximum that you have to offer, if you have instructions to go to $15,000 if necessary?

We are of the view that in such a situation your opponent deserves exactly what he or she gets. Your instructions are no business of your opponent and therefore you should refuse to

1. See, for example, *Lewis v. Combell Constructions Pty Ltd* (1989) 18 N.S.W.L.R. 528; *Insbury Pty Ltd v. Craig* [1990] 1 Qd R. 309.

answer the question. Arguably, an answer such as "Yes, that is the limit of my instructions" would also be proper.

Some purists may say that such an answer is a lie and therefore unethical. However, your overriding duty in such a situation is to protect your client's interests. When a client gives you a maximum settlement figure, it can be inferred that it is part of your instructions to settle for less if this is possible. Apart from possibly breaching your obligation to maintain professional confidentiality, you may prejudice a favourable settlement by disclosing all your cards.

Sometimes, if you have had numerous dealings with a particular practitioner over a long period and you both know when the other is or is not telling the truth, then it may be advantageous to come clean straight away.

These questions of "tactics" should be canvassed with your client before launching into negotiations.

Off the record

Beware of invitations from your opponent to speak "off the record" without first clarifying precisely what is meant by this expression.[2]

Bluff

Through experience you will come to know when someone is bluffing. You will also learn of the reputations that particular practitioners have. Some practitioners have a reputation for always telling the truth when they say anything positive. If Jo Bloggs tells you that there is an independent witness who is prepared to say that your driver was travelling at 150 kilometres per hour in a built-up area, then pay heed if Bloggs has such a reputation. If, on the other hand, Bloggs has a reputation for dishonesty, then pay no heed at all. Let Bloggs produce the witness and let the witness be tested by cross-examination.

Know the facts

Before embarking on negotiations with your opponent, refresh your memory regarding the facts of the case. This will put you at a great advantage against an opponent who is fuzzy about the facts and it will enable you to cope with unexpected problems which may arise.

2. See below, p. 238.

Concessions

Your first responsibility is to your client. While it is sometimes in order for you to grant concessions or indulgences to an opponent, you must always ensure that your client's interests will not be prejudiced in any way. You should never grant a concession if this will give an unwarranted advantage to your client's opponent. For example, do not agree to an adjournment if this might result in one of your major witnesses becoming unavailable. You must always be wary of opponents who continually ask for concessions and indulgences as a delaying tactic.

Your instructions to act generally involve a discretion to assume responsibility for the day-to-day running of the case. However, from time to time significant decisions may have to be made which should be discussed with your client. Some requests from your opponent for concessions or indulgences can be regarded as so significant that they are outside the scope of your general discretion to act. In these circumstances, it is highly desirable that you seek your client's instructions.

Remember that if your client gives specific instructions not to grant a particular concession then you have a duty to comply with those instructions. No matter how reasonable your opponent's request for a concession may seem, you cannot accede to it; instructions are simply not negotiable.

If you are acting for a plaintiff, be wary of practitioners who protract unduly the period of negotiations, without any genuine intention to settle the matter. Their purpose may be to delay the matter coming to court for as long as possible.

Too frequently, young practitioners are led like lambs outside the relevant limitation period without proceedings being commenced. Some practitioners preach the gospel of "issue now and talk later".

You should insist on prompt compliance with the time limits applicable to interlocutory steps. If the defendant's practitioner is not adhering to the time limits, take out a summons. Rather than prejudicing negotiations, such action may encourage genuine discussions, especially if the defendant has no defence.

Don't boast

To talk about your negotiating triumphs is tactically unwise. The less your opponents know about how you operate, how you gauge your first offer, whether your first offer has any fixed relationship to your final offer and how you approach payments into court or equivalent procedures such as offers of compromise, the better.

Don't get emotional

Never take negotiations so seriously and personally that you become emotional. The practitioner you are negotiating with is simply doing his or her job and you should not complain if your opponent puts arguments or adopts tactics that make your task a little more difficult.

If you become emotional, you may lose your professional detachment and objectivity and this is not in the best interests of your client.

There is no room for threatening or abusive behaviour towards other practitioners or for rudeness, such as leaving correspondence and telephone messages unanswered, or for sexist or patronising labels such as "love", "pet", "girlie", "sweetie", "boy", "son" or "young man".

Avoid point scoring

You should not fall into the trap of focusing on narrow issues during negotiations and losing sight of your overall objective of reaching an optimal result for your client. The tactics you adopt should be calculated to achieve this objective; they should not be seen as ends in themselves.

Avoid the temptation of engaging in point scoring, particularly if your opponent is being difficult. Scoring a point may make you feel good temporarily but it is unlikely to contribute to the achievement of your client's objectives in the long term.

Confirm in writing

Always confirm in writing what is said over the telephone. Unfortunately, not all practitioners are honest and trustworthy. A simple and easy way to avoid disputes as to what was said or agreed to over the telephone is to put it in writing. If it is you who has put a proposal, then it is easy for you to confirm in writing. If your opponent puts a proposal and, despite requests, fails to put it in writing, then you can write as follows:

> "I refer to our telephone conversation on . . . and confirm your suggestion that . . . If this does not accord with your

recollection of what was said, please advise me immediately."

Skilful negotiating abilities are certainly an invaluable asset. Sometimes they are just as important as a thorough understanding of the law. If you are able to negotiate a favourable settlement for a client, you will be absolving the client from the delay, expense and inconvenience generally associated with court proceedings.

Chapter 14

Alternative Dispute Resolution Procedures

> "Every human benefit and enjoyment, every virtue, and every prudent act, is founded on compromise and barter. We balance inconveniences, we give and take, we remit some rights, that we may enjoy others; and we choose to be happy citizens rather than subtle disputants."
>
> Edmund Burke, Speech on Conciliation with America, 22 March 1775, quoted in W. Pengilley, "Alternative Dispute Resolution: The Philosophy and the Need" (1990) 1 *Australian Dispute Resolution Journal* 81 at 93.

Although concern about the costs of litigation is not new, it has received widespread publicity and unprecedented attention by public authorities in recent years. The spiralling costs of legal services, considerable delays in court lists and the recognition of the high human cost of litigation—stress, anxiety, attention diverted from personal and business pursuits—have contributed to a growing interest in ADR techniques as real alternatives to litigation.

ADR refers to Alternative Dispute Resolution, although it is also known as Additional Dispute Resolution,[1] and Assisted Dispute Resolution. It applies to those strategies and techniques used to resolve disputes outside the formal adjudicative system of the courts. Types of ADR processes include mediation,

1. The Hon. Sir Laurence Street, "Foreword" (1990) 1 *Australian Dispute Resolution Journal* 3.

conciliation, arbitration, expert appraisal, negotiation and counselling.[2] These are often quicker, cheaper and less stressful forms of dispute resolution than court proceedings.

In this chapter, ADR will refer to those processes that involve an independent third party, thereby distinguishing ADR from direct negotiation which is discussed above in Chapter 13.

If you ignore ADR techniques because you believe that ADR is inferior to litigation as a means of resolving disputes then you are in for a rude awakening for two reasons.

The first is that court-directed mediation is increasing in both popularity and efficacy and is now a feature of many courts and tribunals.

The second is that clients are becoming increasingly aware of the benefits of ADR. Some clients in fact insist that their lawyers have expertise in ADR. Some insurers, for example, have stated publicly that lawyers on their panels must not only be aware of ADR but have a real commitment to it.

It has been suggested in the United States that the failure of a lawyer to advise his or her client on the full range of dispute resolution processes available may constitute professional negligence, leaving the lawyer liable to pay damages.[3]

To advise a client properly, you need to have a good knowledge and understanding of ADR processes to be able to identify when those processes may be appropriate.

Where neither party is willing to compromise, or where one party insists on having his or her day in court to publicly air his or her grievances, then ADR techniques may not be helpful.

On the other hand, certain types of disputes are recognised as being suitable for ADR—notably disputes over money with no emotional overlay. ADR strategies are also appropriate where the parties must, or wish to, maintain a continuing business association, and where a speedy, non-acrimonious resolution is required.

What role can you, as a lawyer, play in ADR? Apart from advising on ADR options, you have a critical role in preparing your client's case for presentation at mediation, drafting submissions, making oral submissions at mediation, controlling, directing and assisting the client at mediation, protecting the

2. K. Spencer, "ADR—An Introduction" (1991) 65 *Law Institute Journal* 40.
3. J. David, "Lawyers—Engage in ADR!" (1991) 65 *Law Institute Journal* 51; H. Astor and C. M. Chinkin, *Dispute Resolution in Australia* (Butterworths, Sydney, 1992), p. 186.

client's interests during negotiation, drafting settlement agreements and drafting ADR clauses in documents.[4]

To meet the requirements of the courts, and the needs of your clients, you should become acquainted with ADR strategies and techniques. You can do this through courses, workshops and seminars, as well as reading about ADR in textbooks and journal articles.

4. H. Astor and C. M. Chinkin, *Dispute Resolution in Australia* (Butterworths, Sydney, 1992), p. 187; A. Batterby, "Lessons to be Learned from ADR Procedures" (1991) 65 *Law Institute Journal* 53, 54.

Chapter 15

Use of Counsel[1]

> "Advice is seldom welcome; and those who want it the most always like it the least."
>
> Chesterfield, 1784.

For young solicitors, briefing experienced counsel can be an intimidating experience, and too often they find themselves in the role of book-carrying sycophants, silent witnesses to settlement discussions and faceless dummies sitting in court to observe what happens. The same young solicitors are also often putty in the hands of an aggressive and experienced barrister's clerk.

Let us look at some of the basic rules that you should adopt for your own protection whenever you brief counsel:

Marking a fee

1. It is your obligation to mark an appropriate fee for counsel on every brief. It is a very dangerous practice to deliver an unmarked brief. Too often this is taken by counsel as an invitation to mark whatever fee counsel considers the client would be willing to pay. Indeed, the New South Wales Court of Appeal has stated that a barrister has a right, if delivered an unmarked brief, to charge whatever fee he or she thinks proper.[2]

1. This chapter is more apt for jurisdictions which have a separate Bar. For an excellent discussion of the relevant principles and practical issues, see *Working with Barristers—A Guide for Solicitors* (Law Institute of Victoria, 1991); *Working with Barristers—A Solicitor's Guide to Relations with the Bar* (Law Society of New South Wales, 1992).
2. *Re Evatt; Ex parte New South Wales Bar Association* (1967) 86 W.N. (Pt 2) (N.S.W.) 17 at 32.

2. If counsel requests a fee to be marked on the brief in excess of that fixed by scale, you must advise your client that the fee is above scale and that even if the client wins the case, the excess fee will not be allowed on taxation as between party and party and therefore will have to be borne by the client.[3]

   In such circumstances, it is desirable to confirm your advice in writing and obtain written authority from your client to agree to the above-scale fee, because the onus is on you to prove that the excess fee was authorised and that your client was properly advised. If you cannot discharge the onus and your client refuses to pay the excess, you will be liable to pay it yourself.[4]

3. Similar considerations apply to unusual fees such as "cancellation fees" which have received judicial criticism[5] and are unpopular with many solicitors.

4. Counsel is not required to accept a marked brief for either an opinion or advice in conference. However, an agreement can be reached with the barrister's clerk on the time rate or other basis upon which counsel's charges will be made.

Queen's Counsel[6]

1. On taxation of costs, the fees of Queen's Counsel may be regarded as an unusual expense and accordingly you should advise your client that such fees may not be recoverable from an opponent. You should always obtain your client's express authority before briefing silk.

2. Briefing Queen's Counsel is a touchy business. First, you must decide if it is an appropriate case for silk and, secondly, you must determine what is an appropriate fee in the particular case. Too often young solicitors turn to junior counsel for advice as to whether there should be a leader. This is an undesirable practice from both points of view. The relevant principle has been stated by the High Court of Australia as follows:

   > "Would a prudent person not compelled by poverty come into court in such a case without two counsel? In

3. *Re Blyth & Fanshawe* (1882) 10 Q.B.D. 207.
4. *Re Blyth*. See also above, p. 43.
5. See *Commissioner of the Australian Federal Police v. Razzi* (1991) 30 F.C.R. 64.
6. Some jurisdictions have abolished the title of Queen's Counsel.

answering that question regard must be had, inter alia, to the importance of the case, the probable duration of the trial, the probability of conflict of evidence entailing the necessity of careful cross-examination and the general practice as to employing two counsel."[7]

In deciding if it is appropriate to allow the fees of senior counsel on a taxation of costs, the question is whether the retention of senior counsel was reasonably necessary for the attainment of justice or the enforcement of the party's rights.[8]

Cost considerations

1. On taxation of costs, in normal circumstances, no fee will be allowed to counsel or a solicitor for a conference in addition to a fee for drawing or settling a document.
2. The normal brief fee is considered to comprise both a fee for preparation and a fee for appearance. Whatever the barrister's clerk may argue, preparation and reading fees are normally not allowable as a separate fee over and above the brief fee. For counsel to be entitled to a separate preparation or reading fee, there would have to be prior agreement between you and counsel. However, on a party/party taxation, preparation and reading fees are usually not allowable as separate fees except in matters of great complexity or voluminous documentation.[9]
3. You should be aware that in some jurisdictions such as England, South Australia and Victoria, the "two thirds" rule, whereby junior counsel's fees are fixed at two thirds the fees charged by Queen's Counsel, has been abolished and accordingly junior counsel are not entitled on taxation to any higher fee than they would have been entitled to receive if they had appeared alone.
4. For your own protection, any variations from the basic costing principles applicable to briefing counsel should always be referred to your client for instructions.
5. Counsel will look to you for payment of his or her fees and not to your client. Therefore, to enable you to pay counsel's

7. *Kroehn v. Kroehn* (1912) 15 C.L.R. 137 at 141.
8. *Oldaker v. Currington* [1987] V.R. 712.
9. *Magna Alloys & Research Pty Ltd v. Kevin Lindsay Coffee (No. 2)* [1982] V.R. 97 at 109, 112.

fees promptly, it is preferable to obtain money in advance from your client for this purpose.

6. Before a solicitor's bill of costs can be taxed, it is necessary to pay counsel's fees. In any event, from the point of view of efficient office management, it is highly desirable to pay counsel's fees as quickly as possible from moneys received from your client for that purpose.
7. Failure to pay counsel's fees may, in some circumstances, amount to unprofessional conduct.[10]
8. In some jurisdictions, barristers' fees may be taxed in much the same way as solicitors' bills.[11]

Negotiations and settlements

1. Do not allow yourself to become a doormat. If you are unhappy about a settlement which is being urged upon you by counsel, or if you see that your client is being bullied into a settlement, call "Enough!". You are the instructing solicitor. You will see the client again. Counsel probably will not.
2. There is no difference between the intellect of barristers and solicitors. What barristers have is familiarity with appearing in court and knowledge of the basic rules of procedure and evidence. Accordingly, from the point of view of dealing with your client in an out-of-court settlement situation, you are as good as the next man or woman. It will be to you that your client will turn for reassurance and for help. Your client is familiar with you whereas the barrister, irrespective of how eminent or able, is a recently introduced stranger.
3. You should have your own views about your client's legal rights and entitlements. If you practise in a country area, you will probably have a much greater knowledge of community standards and previous verdicts than a barrister on circuit.
4. Remember that on circuit, if counsel has the fifth case in the list and cases 1, 2, 3 and 4 are proceeding, counsel would be less than human if the payment into court or offer of settlement, which was ridiculously low at the start of the week, did not become more attractive as the days of inactivity pass.

10. *Carver v. Legal Profession Disciplinary Tribunal* (unreported, N.S.W. C.A., 27 September 1991).
11. See, for example, *Supreme Court Act* 1986 (Vic.), s. 67. See also above, pp. 43-44.

5. There are different kinds of settlements. There are outstanding settlements, good settlements, average settlements, poor settlements, cowardly settlements and abject surrender settlements. Your client's morale is at its lowest immediately before the case comes on, and you have an enormous responsibility to protect your client against himself or herself.
6. Except where it is unavoidable, you should not allow counsel to speak with your client in your absence. It is unfair to the barrister and equally unfair to your client and yourself. If counsel has a right to sue you for fees, then, consistent with that obligation, it is your responsibility to instruct counsel. If your instructions are unacceptable, counsel will return the brief.

Dealing with other side's counsel

1. Where you have not briefed counsel but the opposing solicitor has briefed counsel you should normally deal with the opposing solicitor except where you are representing your client at a pre-trial conference or at a hearing and the other side is represented by counsel appearing alone.[12]
2. Where both sides are represented by counsel, you should communicate with the other side's counsel through your counsel rather than directly. Barristers are, generally speaking, prohibited from communicating directly with the solicitor for the other party other than in circumstances of necessity.

General

1. When counsel appears at the hearing of a matter, then subject to counsel's duties to the court and the right to advise another course of action, counsel must adopt and adhere to such instructions as you give him or her on behalf of your client. Counsel is not entitled to go on a frolic of his or her own while appearing. However, counsel is entitled to insist on, and as a general rule, ought to have, complete control over how instructions are carried out and over the actual conduct of the matter in court. If such control is not given, counsel would be entitled to return the brief.[13]

12. *Working with Barristers—A Guide for Solicitors* (Law Institute of Victoria, 1991), pp. 11, 14.
13. *Halsbury's Laws of England* (4th edn reissue), Vol. 3(1), paras 518-519.

2. Do not get into a rut. For the sake of some free advice over the telephone and an occasional invitation to dinner, you should not get into the habit of briefing the same barrister. Brief the counsel best qualified to handle the particular case. Have a "stable" of barristers from which to choose if your first choice is unavailable.
3. Never send a brief to counsel without first checking whether he or she is available to accept it. Cases where briefs have sat on counsel's desk collecting dust well past the hearing date because counsel was on holidays are not rare. A short telephone call prior to sending the brief is all that is required.
4. It is your obligation to prompt counsel if he or she is taking too long to complete a matter. If a brief requires urgent attention by counsel, do not say so in the body of your memorandum to counsel. Counsel will not realise it is urgent until he or she reads the memorandum. Instead, use an appropriate eye-catching notation on the back sheet and couple this with a follow-up telephone call.
5. It is advisable to record the date a brief is delivered to counsel and to select a date in your diary by which you expect the brief to be returned. If the brief is not returned by that date, then you should contact counsel and urge him or her to complete the matter. If further delay occurs, request counsel to return the brief and then brief another barrister. You should not wait until your client or an opponent presses you before contacting counsel. You cannot excuse delay by shifting the blame to counsel.
6. If you find that a particular barrister is always tardy, then, irrespective of how much you may like that barrister and wish not to offend, you should not use that barrister again. Your first priority is to protect your client and yourself.
7. Do not get into the habit of over-using counsel or treating him or her as an extension of your office. Before briefing counsel, ask yourself whether the time, effort and cost needed to brief counsel justify the task at hand, or whether it would be simpler and easier for you to perform the task yourself.
8. Exercise some care in preparing a brief. Do not just instruct your secretary to tie a red ribbon around the file and send it off to counsel with a request to draw pleadings or give an opinion on a particular matter. Solicitors who engage in this "file dumping" abdicate their responsibilities as instructing

solicitors and are very unpopular with barristers.[14] Carefully prepared briefs will enhance your professional reputation among barristers and they are likely to give you preference over other solicitors.

9. Be selective in what documents you include in counsel's brief, thereby saving counsel's valuable time. Where possible, your brief should include a summary of the facts and statements of witnesses. If you have done preliminary research on the matter on which you seek counsel's opinion, then inform counsel of your views, together with any relevant authorities you have looked at. Counsel may be assisted by your research and preliminary conclusions. It also makes you feel you are slightly better than a post office or clearing house for documents passing between your client and counsel.
10. If you are seeking counsel's advice, make sure that you carefully formulate the questions upon which you seek counsel's opinion.
11. The date fixed for a hearing, if known at the time of delivery of a brief, should always be included in the brief. If it is not then known, you should advise counsel of the date as soon as it comes to your attention.

14. See *Federal Commissioner of Land Tax v. Jowett* (1930) 45 C.L.R. 115 at 117.

Chapter 16

Communication with Another Practitioner's Client or Witness

> "Why are lawyers loathed? Possibly because it is our job to make the worst appear the better course: perhaps it is that there are more opportunities for cheating in the law than in other professions. It is rather like golf—it is very easy to cheat."
>
> Lord Chief Justice Lane, Address to the Law Institute of Victoria, July 1981.

General rule

It is accepted by the legal profession that it is improper for one practitioner, whether directly or through an employee or agent, to contact the client of another practitioner in a particular matter without the latter's consent. Logically, the principle is defensible because, if it were open to a practitioner to go behind the back of the opposing practitioner to gain admissions from the other party, then litigation would become even more hazardous and commercial negotiation unworkable.

Gifford states the principle as follows:

> "A practitioner should never interview or communicate with the client of another practitioner except with the approval of that practitioner. This is so even if the client himself approaches the practitioner."[1]

1. K. H. Gifford, *Legal Profession Law and Practice in Victoria* (Law Book Co. Ltd, Sydney, 1980), p. 376.

A related principle is that a solicitor should not attempt to prevent a colleague from communicating with or obtaining instructions from that colleague's client.[2]

Where delay is prejudicing your client

In some cases you may be faced with the situation in which the opposing practitioner is not taking any steps in a matter and even refuses to answer correspondence. When faced with that situation you will certainly be pressed by your client as to what is happening and why the matter is being delayed.

Gifford[3] suggests that in those circumstances you would be justified in informing the practitioner in default that you will communicate with his or her client direct, unless the practitioner completes his or her part of the transaction within a specified period. Such communication should be in writing. If nothing happens at the expiration of the specified period, you could then write directly to the defaulting practitioner's client. A copy of the letter should be sent to the defaulting practitioner.

The form of letter is important and certainly its terms should be neutral. In a delayed conveyancing transaction, for example, the following form of letter might be appropriate:

> "I act for the purchasers in respect of the sale of your house at . . . The contract provides that settlement should take place on the . . . It is vital for my clients that settlement is not delayed as they have sold their own home and have arranged to vacate on the. . . Although Messrs B & C act for you, I have written to them on . . . occasions without response, and many telephone calls remain unanswered. There are many procedural steps which must be completed to ensure that settlement will take place on the due date. Would you please contact your solicitors immediately and instruct them to take appropriate action to protect your interests. If they are no longer acting for you, would you contact me immediately so that we can discuss the future of this transaction. A copy of this letter has been sent to Messrs B & C."

The above suggested procedure should be resorted to only in an extreme situation where further delay will prejudice the

2. See *Horak v. Secretary of the Law Institute of Victoria* (unreported, Vic. Sup. Ct, Phillips J., 18 October 1991).
3. K. H. Gifford, *Legal Profession Law and Practice in Victoria* (Law Book Co. Ltd, Sydney, 1980), p. 376.

interests of your client. It should not be used simply to overcome your annoyance or frustration.

Where the client is a company

Sometimes it is difficult to apply the rule forbidding communication with the client of another practitioner because you cannot be sure who the client actually is.

This is especially so where the other practitioner's client is a company. In those circumstances, can you go past the practitioner on the other side and speak to the managing director or other persons in positions of authority within the company in order to obtain information that is not readily available other than through direct inquiry? Is the test to be applied a question of the responsibility and seniority of the person you desire to contact?

Take for example the case of an industrial accident where an employee is severely injured and has no recollection of the circumstances surrounding the accident. If the accident was witnessed by a supervisor of the company employing the injured plaintiff, would you, if you were acting for the plaintiff, be justified in making contact with the supervisor to ascertain what he or she saw and perhaps to obtain a statement about any safety measures which might have prevented the accident? Strictly speaking you probably could contact the supervisor but you would no doubt be buying into a dispute with the opposing practitioner if you did.

The question arose at the Law Institute of Victoria in another context. A firm of solicitors was acting on behalf of the receivers and managers of a company which was in liquidation. The solicitors took proceedings on behalf of the company through the receivers against another company which was alleged to be indebted to the company in liquidation.

The solicitors acting for the defendant company made application to the Supreme Court of Victoria for an order for security for costs. In support of that application, an affidavit was filed which made reference to a telephone call by the solicitors for the defendant to a managing clerk employed by the receivers to handle most of the day-to-day work in connection with the receivership of the plaintiff company. The solicitors acting for the defendant had identified themselves before questioning the managing clerk regarding the financial circumstances of the plaintiff company. The managing clerk apparently gave full and detailed answers to the questions put to him.

The solicitors for the receivers of the plaintiff company took objection to the approach that had been made by the defendant's solicitors and sought a general ruling from the Ethics Committee of the Law Institute of Victoria as to the propriety of that approach.

The Ethics Committee ruled as follows:

1. The clients in this case were the receivers and managers of the plaintiff company.
2. The employees of the plaintiff company were not identical with the client, but were separate individuals and would be available to be called as witnesses in any action by either side.
3. There is no rule of law or practice precluding inquiries being made of witnesses as distinct from clients.
4. The proper practice for a solicitor making such an approach would be to identify himself or herself, to declare that he or she is a solicitor and to advise the witness which party he or she represented.

In the course of its deliberations, the Ethics Committee referred to the Rules of Professional Ethics of the New York County Lawyers' Association. The stance of that body is interesting. It has a rule that a lawyer shall not communicate on the subject of the representation with a party known to be represented by another lawyer in the matter, unless the other lawyer consents or the communication is authorised by law.

In its comment on that rule, the Lawyers' Association said that the rule prohibited communication concerning the matter in representation by a lawyer for one party with managing agents of a party that is a corporation or organisation, because such persons speak for the organisation. It does not prohibit communication with "lower echelon employees" who are not representatives of the organisation.

The Lawyers' Association considered that whether a specific employee is a representative of a client would depend on the circumstances, and in particular whether the employee had significant managerial responsibility in the matter in question.

This might sound all right but it seems to beg the question "Where is the line of demarcation?". For example, in litigation involving alleged fraud by a company which is claiming an insurance cover in respect of the destruction of its building by fire, is it proper for the practitioner acting for the plaintiff company to have discussions with the claims supervisor of the defendant insurer to determine the grounds on which fraud is suspected? Alternatively, after proper identification, would it be in order for the practitioner acting for the defendant insurer to contact a regional manager of the plaintiff company to obtain that manager's version of the sequence of events leading up to the fire being discovered?

Difficult questions of degree arise. Some practitioners argue that because of the artificial nature of a corporate body, the best rule to introduce would be to forbid a practitioner contacting any employee of a corporation which is on the other side in litigation and which has legal representation.

A suggested approach might be to avoid communicating with people within a company who normally have authority to make admissions on the company's behalf or to instruct in the conduct of the proceeding.[4] This will usually include at least the chief executive officer and the general manager.

Another situation that came before the Law Institute of Victoria involved a third party insurance claim brought by a wife passenger against her husband driver after the vehicle driven by the husband had been involved in a collision. Proceedings were commenced on behalf of the wife claiming damages for personal injuries arising out of the collision. Liability was admitted. The solicitors acting for the plaintiff had alleged that, as a result of severe head injuries suffered by the wife passenger, her interest in sexual activity with her husband had waned.

The solicitors for the plaintiff invited the defendant husband to attend a conference, prior to the hearing, for the purpose of obtaining a proof of evidence from him about the deterioration in the matrimonial relationship. The solicitors acting for the third party insurer of the defendant husband's vehicle heard of the conference and took strong exception to what had taken place.

The matter was referred to the Ethics Committee of the Law Institute of Victoria, which took the view that, irrespective of the fact that the case was an assessment, and that the parties were related, the plaintiff's solicitors had acted improperly in holding such a conference without first obtaining the consent of the solicitor for the third party insurer.

4. Litigation Lawyers' Section of Law Institute of Victoria, "Ethical Restraints on Interviewing Witnesses" (1990) 64 *Law Institute Journal* 910.

Witnesses[5]

Neither a client nor a practitioner has any property in a witness. Therefore, you can interview a witness even though you know that person will be called by the other side and indeed even if that person has already commenced to give evidence for the other side. However, in the latter situation you should observe the "salutary rule" that "a solicitor for the adverse interest should be circumspect and delicate in approaching a person whose evidence has been opened by the other party."[6] If approaching the witness, it is prudent to inform that person on whose behalf you are acting and ensure that no attempt is made to influence the evidence to be given.

In criminal matters, it is advisable to seek the permission of the prosecutor, or the Crown solicitor, before approaching a Crown witness. An unauthorised approach could leave you open to an accusation that you have attempted to interfere with the witness.

Although you cannot suggest to a witness what evidence should be given or to change any evidence already given,[7] it is not improper for you to tell a witness whom you propose to call that he or she is not obliged to speak to the other side and that you would prefer for him or her not to do so.

Unrepresented prospective defendants

Although no special ethical restrictions apply when interviewing unrepresented prospective defendants, it would be prudent to:

(a) inform the person of the subject matter in question and on whose behalf you act;

(b) make it clear to the person that you are not acting for or advising him or her; and

(c) inform the person that he or she may choose not to discuss the matter with you.

Where there is a possibility that a witness may be later joined as a defendant, it would be prudent to advise him or her to seek legal advice or representation by another practitioner before you obtain a written statement from that witness.

5. See also below, Ch. 26.
6. *Bar Association of Queensland v. Lamb* [1972] A.L.R. 285 at 286.
7. *Kennedy v. Council of the Incorporated Law Institute of New South Wales* (1939) 13 A.L.J. 563.

The above precautions will assist you in overcoming any allegations later that you obtained admissions through trickery or that your conduct was misleading or even dishonest.[8]

8. Litigation Lawyers' Section of Law Institute of Victoria, "Ethical Restraints on Interviewing Witnesses" (1990) 64 *Law Institute Journal* 910.

Chapter 17

Client Threats Against Another Practitioner

> "The first thing we do, let's kill all the lawyers."
>
> Shakespeare, *Henry VI (Pt 2)*, IV, ii, 86.

What do you do when your client threatens to kill the practitioner on the other side? The academics will quickly reply that you must telephone the practitioner on the other side to warn of the threat and, at the same time, telephone the police. But is it so simple? How do you know your client is serious about what is threatened? And if he or she is not serious, what are the ramifications of your telephone call to the police and to the other side?

Assume you act for the husband in a divorce action in which custody of the children is in issue. Not only does the wife seek custody but she asserts that the husband should not have access either. The husband is a cane-cutter in Queensland and, rightly or wrongly, he believes that his wife's attitude has been largely influenced by the solicitor representing her.

Recently, in a telephone conversation with you, he said that he was going to come to Victoria to "straighten out my wife and to kill that bastard who is advising her". What should you do in the circumstances?

You "think" that your client is serious in his stated intention of violence and would feel much easier if you telephoned the solicitor on the other side with whom you have had many dealings in the Family Court of Australia over the years. The sort of telephone conversation you have in mind would probably go like this: "Is that you there, Charlie? You know that custody matter of X we've got on, well, I thought I'd just give you a call to tell you that my client's going to kill you. Now, how have things been going generally? Charlie? Charlie, are you still there Charlie?"

That sort of conversation can be imagined but what are the likely consequences if the threats made by your client are nothing more than gorilla-like breast beating with no intention to implement them at all?

One can visualise the early part of the cross-examination of the husband at the hearing taking the following course:

Barrister for the wife:	"Mr X, you're a violent man?"
X:	"No."
Barrister for the wife:	"Mr X, I put it to you that as recently as two weeks ago you advised your solicitor you were going to 'straighten out' my client and you were going to kill my instructing solicitor."

Presumably at the end of his cross-examination, X will come up to you and say, "What the hell did you mean by passing on my conversation to the other side? You've just cost me the custody of my children".

The answer to this sort of dilemma, we suppose, is to know your client and to appreciate that the consequences of wrongly assessing the gravity of threats of violence can be drastic. You must also bear in mind that to disclose the threats made by your client may be a breach of confidence and legal professional privilege. Although no privilege attaches to communications which are in furtherance of a crime or fraud, you may have some difficulty excusing your actions if the threat was nothing more than bluff.

The problem of threats against other practitioners at first sight appears to be esoteric. However, acts of violence against members of the legal profession are not rare, particularly in the family law jurisdiction. Barristers, solicitors, parties, witnesses and even judges have been injured or killed, or their property damaged.

Some years ago parties to proceedings were fatally shot near the Melbourne Supreme Court building. As we understand it, there had been threats made by one of the litigants during the course of the proceedings that if he lost he would kill the successful parties and their witnesses. His solicitor took the threats seriously but despite advising the court and the police of the threats, the tragedy could not be averted.

It is unexpected problems like the one posed here which raise concern about the value of textbooks on professional conduct. Basically, you can lay down all the rules in the world but in the end when coping with this sort of problem, you must rely upon your own maturity, your own common sense, your own knowledge of your client and your own understanding of the obligations to your client, your colleagues, the court and the law as a whole.

In relation to the hypothetical case, all we can say is that if you are handling a custody dispute in the Family Court of Australia on behalf of a wife where the husband is a cane-cutter in Queensland then you had better look out!

Part 3

Relationship with the Profession and the Community

Chapter 18

Introduction

"He that goes to the law holds a wolf by the ears."

Robert Burton, *Anatomy of Melancholy* (1621). Quoted in E. Kahn, "The Seven Lamps of Legal Humour" (1984) *De Rebus* 251.

It has often been said that membership of a profession is different from membership of a trade. One of the hallmarks of a profession is a tradition of devoted and disinterested service quite apart from financial reward. Another is a tradition of co-operation between members of a profession.

For lawyers, there is another and more crucial aspect: because they are part of the administration of justice, there are unique duties imposed upon them, quite apart from their duties to their clients and their colleagues.

You will discover that your relationship with your profession and the community is a complex one which is dictated not so much by written canons of behaviour as by ethics and traditions passed on over many years.

It is a precondition of your entry into and continued membership of the legal profession that you are a fit and proper person to have your name on the roll of practitioners. You therefore have an overriding duty not to do anything that would render you a person who is not fit and proper to have your name remain on the roll.

This duty is essentially negative. It has often been expressed as a duty to refrain from conduct which would be reasonably regarded as disgraceful or dishonourable by your professional colleagues of good repute and competency.[1]

1. *Re a Solicitor* [1912] 1 K.B. 302 at 312.

We cannot hope to state exhaustively all the features of your relationship with the profession and the community. The chapters in Part 3 of this book focus only on the most common of those features.

Chapter 19

Assisting the Disadvantaged (Pro Bono)

> "All men have equal rights to liberty, to their property, and to the protection of the laws."
>
> Voltaire, *Essay on Manners*, 1756.

As the practice of law becomes increasingly commercial and business-focused, it is easy to forget that being a lawyer means being a member of an honourable profession which has a strong tradition of protecting the rights of disadvantaged members of the community.

In most jurisdictions, lawyers have been granted the privilege of a monopoly over the provision of legal services. This privilege imposes a corresponding responsibility on lawyers to contribute something back to the community. One way of doing this is by becoming actively involved in programmes to assist the disadvantaged.

"Pro bono"

Most programmes to assist the disadvantaged are labelled "pro bono" work. Consistent with our preference for simple English words rather than foreign expressions we will not use the expression "pro bono" in this chapter. We will use the expression "free work for the disadvantaged".

For the sake of completeness, however, it is useful to look briefly at the origins of the expression "pro bono". "Pro bono publico" translates from Latin into "for the public good" and, broadly defined, as it applies to the legal profession, means doing legal work for free. In practice, pro bono work is more strictly defined as the provision of free or discounted legal services to protect or enforce the rights of those who would otherwise be unable to obtain access to the legal system. More specifically, pro bono work tends to be concentrated on helping the disadvantaged in the community.

U.S. experience

The American legal profession has a long tradition of performing free work for the disadvantaged. In many major cities, local Bar Associations co-ordinate free work schemes, referring work to firms who have registered their desire to do such work.

In addition to this, private legal firms also have a strong commitment to the cause of free work for the disadvantaged. In 1992, almost every lawyer in the top 100 U.S. legal firms averaged over 20 hours per year of free work for the disadvantaged. Many firms averaged over 50 hours per lawyer; five even averaged more than 100 hours per lawyer.[1]

Areas of work in which free legal services are provided include work relating to refugees, landlord and tenant law, AIDS-related representation, battered women, civil rights, death penalty cases, homelessness, elderly and social security, representation of charitable organisations and advising in human rights cases.

Experience in other jurisdictions

Most other countries have a less extensive and distinguished history of free work for the disadvantaged; however, it is fair to say that most lawyers would provide at least some degree of free legal advice to family, friends and social clubs and charities with which they are associated.

There are many ways that young lawyers can become involved in the provision of free legal work to those less fortunate than themselves. Some local Law Societies or Bar Associations co-ordinate referral schemes that act as referral agencies for free work for the disadvantaged. These agencies are always keen to add firms' names to their lists of potential workers. Young lawyers should encourage their managing partners to register their firm's interest in undertaking free work for these agencies.

Some firms operate a system of seconding lawyers to public help agencies or charitable organisations. One U.S. firm rotates one associate every three months through a secondment at a

1. See (1992) *The American Lawyer*, Pro Bono Survey (July/August).

local tenants advice bureau. Such arrangements are not unique in the United States. Some Australian firms provide staff on secondment to community legal centres.

Lawyers interested in specific types of work for the disadvantaged should be encouraged to think of innovative ways that they can help relevant agencies with the support of their firms. If you can link the development of an area of your legal practice with any such agencies, then you might be able to convince your firm that it is in both their and the public agency's interest that you be seconded to the agency.

Many firms and Law Societies are developing policies for free work for the disadvantaged. Some Law Societies recommend that all practising lawyers contribute at least ten hours per year to a programme of free work for the disadvantaged. This equates to less than two full days' work. The Los Angeles County Bar Association recommends each lawyer should perform 35 hours of free work annually. Firms without clear policies should be encouraged by young lawyers to develop a programme of free work for the disadvantaged which sets targets or budgets for such work.

As a young lawyer keen to make a positive impression at your firm, you may be hesitant to put forward creative suggestions on free work schemes to the partners of your firm. "Won't they think I'm a radical—only out to cost the partners money?" While such thoughts are understandable, young lawyers should not be discouraged from promoting free work for the disadvantaged. You will more than likely be pleasantly surprised to find that even the toughest common lawyers or wealthiest senior partners all recognise their obligations as members of the legal profession to contribute to the community through free work for the disadvantaged.

Provided the cost of a free work programme is agreed upon and budgeted for in advance, most firms welcome the opportunity to show the community that the law is a worthy profession and that lawyers and their firms are prepared to put something back into society.

Chapter 20

Undertakings

> "Never let it be said of you that you have failed to honour such an obligation . . . It is far better to lose money than reputation."
>
> Lock, *Advice to a Young Solicitor* (1947), p. 3.

For the law to function, there must be mutual trust between members of the legal profession and the courts. To some extent this is dependent upon undertakings being given and honoured.

Nature of undertaking

An undertaking is a verbal or written promise either to do or refrain from doing something. It may be given to another practitioner or to the court. An undertaking is a very serious matter and should never be taken lightly.[1]

There is a distinction between a personal undertaking and an undertaking given on behalf of a client. A personal undertaking is one that is given by you on your own behalf, such as an undertaking not to disclose information without the court's consent. An undertaking on behalf of a client is one that is binding on your client and not on you. For example, you may undertake that your client will deliver answers to interrogatories within a specified time.

Personal undertaking

Personal undertakings are enforceable against you. The court can compel you to do or refrain from doing a certain act, or it can order you to compensate a person who has suffered loss

1. *Halsbury's Laws of England* (4th edn), Vol. 44, para. 255.

because you have failed to observe an undertaking.[2] Accordingly, if you undertake that the stamp duty on a document used in court will be paid, you will be liable to pay it yourself.[3]

Because you cannot be compelled by anyone to give a personal undertaking, you should normally not give one. You should certainly not give a personal undertaking unless you have complete control over the subject matter of the undertaking. Never give a personal undertaking to do something that is dependent on your client's cooperation because not all clients are honest and reasonable.

For example, you should not personally undertake that your client's affidavit of documents will be filed in court within a week unless the affidavit has been sworn and is in your office. Similarly, you should not give a personal undertaking to a third party as to how you will disburse trust funds because your client may alter instructions previously given about those trust funds and you would normally be bound to comply with the new instructions irrespective of your undertaking.[4]

Apart from any possible liability you may incur as a result of breaking an undertaking, your reputation as a practitioner of honesty and integrity will be impaired.

If you give a personal undertaking with your client's authority, you can seek reimbursement from your client for any amounts paid by you in compliance with your undertaking.[5]

Undertakings on behalf of client

Undertakings that are given on behalf of a client are enforceable against the client only if they are given with the client's express authority.[6] Accordingly, do not give an undertaking on behalf of a client unless you are authorised to do so, otherwise the undertaking may be held to be a personal undertaking. A client's instructions should never be anticipated.

2. *Cordery on Solicitors* (8th edn, Butterworths & Co. (Publishers) Ltd, London, 1988), p. 110. See also *John Fox v. Bannister, King & Rigbeys* [1987] 3 W.L.R. 480 at 483; *Udall v. Capri Lighting Ltd (in liq.)* [1987] 3 W.L.R. 465.
3. *Re Meyer* (1906) 23 W.N. (N.S.W.) 55.
4. Ethics Committee of Law Institute of Victoria, "Undertakings" (1989) 63 *Law Institute Journal* 1134.
5. *Halsbury's Laws of England* (4th edn), Vol. 44, para. 258.
6. *Marsden v. Marsden* [1972] Fam. 280 at 287.

It is preferable to obtain instructions in writing with an acknowledgment by the client that you have given advice on the enforceability and other consequences arising from the undertaking.

You must always make it clear whether or not you are giving a personal undertaking. If you are giving an undertaking on behalf of a client, it is not sufficient to say, "On behalf of my client I undertake . . ."; instead, you should say, "I have been instructed that my client undertakes . . . .". One way of safeguarding against any confusion is to obtain a written acknowledgment from the party to whom the undertaking is given that the undertaking is binding only as between that party and your client.[7]

Undertakings to be clear

You should also ensure that any undertaking you give is clearly and precisely expressed and is not capable of having more than one meaning.

Use of word "undertake" not necessary

You should take care not to inadvertently give an undertaking to your opponent. It is not necessary for the word "undertake" to be used for an undertaking to be provided. The court looks to the substance of what is said.

Enforcement of undertakings

The obligation to carry out an undertaking can be enforced by either party to litigation. Thus, if you act for the defendant and undertake to enter an appearance on behalf of the defendant, both the defendant and the plaintiff can seek an order compelling you to honour your undertaking.[8] However, it should not be thought that undertakings are enforceable only when given in litigious matters; they are enforceable in non-litigious matters as well. It is not relevant that no consideration was given for the undertaking.[9] On the other hand, undertakings are not enforceable unless given in your professional capacity as a practitioner.

7. F. Riley, "Undertaking on Behalf of Clients . . . Solicitors May Be Personally Liable" (1989) 27 (December) *Law Society Journal* 20 at 22.
8. *Squires v. Weeks* (1893) 9 W.N. (N.S.W.) 122.
9. *United Mining & Finance Corp. Ltd v. Becher* [1910] 2 K.B. 296.

An undertaking given by an employee solicitor on behalf of a firm is normally binding on the firm, even if the employee did not have actual authority to give it.

In some jurisdictions, professional conduct rules require solicitors to comply with any personal undertaking and provide that a breach of the undertaking will amount to unprofessional conduct.[10]

It usually amounts to a contempt of court if you breach a personal undertaking given to the court, or if you do not comply with an order compelling you to perform a personal undertaking given to another person. You can therefore be imprisoned for breaking a personal undertaking.[11] This underlines the need for care when, in a given situation, you are considering whether to give an undertaking.

10. See, for example, *Solicitors' (Professional Conduct and Practice) Rules* 1984 (Vic.), r. 9(1).

11. *D v. A & Co.* [1900] 1 Ch. 484; *Re a Solicitor* [1966] 1 W.L.R. 1604; *Udall v. Capri Lighting Ltd (In liq.)* [1987] 3 W.L.R. 465 at 471.

Chapter 21

Precautions Against Negligence

> "The rule that you are to love your neighbour becomes in law, you must not injure your neighbour . . . You must take reasonable care to avoid acts or omissions which you can reasonably foresee would be likely to injure your neighbour."
>
> *Donoghue v. Stevenson* [1932] A.C. 562.

In everything you do, you must protect yourself against the possibility of being sued for negligence.

If you are found to be negligent, you can be liable to your client in tort as well as in contract and you may even be liable to third parties.[1] In most cases you would not be able to charge your clients for negligent work that you have performed on their behalf.[2] In addition, your negligence could constitute unprofessional conduct and thus disciplinary proceedings may be instituted against you.[3]

A solicitor may be liable in contract to a client because it is an implied term of the contract for professional services between them that the solicitor will use his or her best skill and care in carrying out the client's instructions. A solicitor may be liable in tort to a client if he or she is negligent in carrying out the client's

1. *Ross v. Caunters* [1980] Ch. 297; *Macpherson & Kelley v. Kevin J. Prunty & Associates* [1983] V.R. 573; *Hawkins v. Clayton* (1988) 164 C.L.R. 539; *Johnson v. Perez* (1988) 166 C.L.R. 351.
2. *Heywood v. Wellers* [1976] Q.B. 446; *Cachia v. Isaacs* (1985) 3 N.S.W.L.R. 366.
3. *Re a Solicitor* [1972] 1 W.L.R. 869 at 873; *Wan v. McDonald* (1991) 33 F.C.R. 491.

instructions on the basis of the *Donoghue v. Stevenson*[4] duty of care and/or the *Hedley Byrne v. Heller*[5] duty of care.

There are suggestions in some cases that large law firms which offer specialist services in complex commercial transactions may owe a higher standard of care and therefore may be more readily liable in tort.[6]

The position of barristers, or solicitors acting as advocates, is slightly different; they enjoy an immunity from liability to a client in respect of their conduct of a trial and such pre-trial work as is intimately connected with the conduct of the trial.[7] The immunity is grounded on the advocate's overriding duty of candour to the court, the need for protecting persons participating in the curial process from the threat of litigation for words spoken in court, and the undesirability of permitting collateral attacks on decisions of criminal and civil courts.[8]

In addition to contractual and tortious liability, a solicitor may be liable as a fiduciary and under statutes which extend professional liability.[9]

Because the obligations and responsibilities of practitioners are many, you would be less than human if you did not make some mistakes during your career. But even a good track record over many years will not absolve you from liability in even a single isolated case where your standard of care fell below that which is expected of members of the profession.

Although, through professional indemnity insurance, you may not be personally responsible for payment of any damages to your client, the harm done to your professional reputation can be enormous. Furthermore, if your reputation is damaged, the standing of the profession may also suffer.

Even if it is not possible to eliminate all mistakes, you should aim to keep them to a minimum. This can only be done by

4. *Donoghue v. Stevenson* [1932] A.C. 562.
5. *Hedley Byrne & Co. Ltd v. Heller & Partners Ltd* [1964] A.C. 465. See also *L. Shaddock & Associates Pty Ltd v. Parramatta City Council* (1981) 55 A.L.J.R. 713.
6. *Kleinwort Benson Australia Ltd v. Armitage* (unreported, N.S.W. Sup. Ct, Cole J., 26 April 1989).
7. *Rondel v. Worsley* [1969] 1 A.C. 191; *Saif Ali v. Sydney Mitchell & Co.* [1980] A.C. 198; *Giannarelli v. Wraith* (1988) 165 C.L.R. 543.
8. *Donellan v. Watson* (1990) 21 N.S.W.L.R. 335 at 343.
9. D. Godsell, "Professional Liability under the TPA and FTAs" (1992) 66 *Law Institute Journal* 804; B. Akhurst, "Responsibilities of Solicitors under the Trade Practices Act 1974" (1987) 61 *Law Institute Journal* 909.

adopting suitable precautions against the occurrence or recurrence of errors by you and those who work with you.

The following list of precautions illustrates the types of measures that you should adopt with a view to eliminating errors.[10]

Litigious matters

1. Always verify the statute of limitations periods that are applicable to a particular matter.[11] Do not assume that you have six years in all cases. Specific time limits are prescribed by many statutes such as aviation, revenue and administrative law legislation.

2. Do not withhold or delay the issue or service of proceedings simply because you are in the midst of, or about to commence, negotiations with an insurance company or third party, unless in return for not issuing or serving process you can obtain:

   (a) an unequivocal undertaking in writing to waive and not to plead any defence under any statute of limitations;

   (b) a written admission of liability; and

   (c) an agreement in writing to the payment of interest from an agreed date.

   This is the real test of the bona fides of those with whom you are dealing. Do not place yourself in the situation of negotiations dragging on and the defendant relying on the statute of limitations immediately you are out of time.

3. It is always preferable to issue promptly and to effect service soon after. Issue first—talk later, as it were. Withholding or delaying service only creates situations beyond remedy if, at a later date:

   (a) you are unable to find the defendant for service;

   (b) the defendant is the wrong party sued; or

   (c) you have chosen the wrong jurisdiction, cause of action, or some other technical point is raised which you could have cured, but are now unable to.

10. Some of the examples are based upon articles written in the Victorian *Law Institute Journal* by Mr G. Fuller under the banner "En Garde—It Can Happen To You".

11. *Nikolaou v. Papasavas, Phillips & Co.* (1989) 166 C.L.R. 394; *Halsbury's Laws of England* (4th edn), Vol. 44, para. 135, n. 8.

Remember also that in some jurisdictions interest on any damages recovered will run only from the issue of proceedings. Therefore, the earlier proceedings are issued, the higher the amount of interest that will be awarded by the court.

4. If proceedings of any nature are to be instituted on behalf of a client "purely for tactical purposes" you should explain in writing:
   (a) why you advise the issue of process;
   (b) what are the prospects of success; and
   (c) the consequences which will flow from failure of the process;

   and obtain written instructions whether or not to proceed.[12] It is most difficult at a later date, in the absence of any such written advice and authority, to explain total failure of the tactic when the client is faced with liability for the whole of the costs.

5. It is common practice for solicitors to delay the issue of personal injury proceedings until the injuries have stabilised, and this is often encouraged by counsel on the basis that, until stabilisation, it is difficult to determine in what court the proceedings should be issued. This practice, however, may lead to problems which would not have arisen if proceedings had been issued promptly. Be positive. Make a judgment on the court to be selected on the material presently available, knowing that if it later becomes necessary, there are procedures which enable you to move either up or down the court hierarchy as may be required.

6. If you are consulted by a client on the eve of expiration of the statute of limitations period and there is no time to draw up a statement of claim, issue a generally endorsed writ (where the rules of court permit this) and deliver a statement of claim later.

7. If you are acting for a plaintiff and there are two possible defendants, each of whom is denying liability, sue them both in the same action by joining them as defendants. If the rules of court provide procedures (such as pretrial discovery) to enable you to decide who should be sued, then use such procedures.

12. *Halsbury's Laws of England* (4th edn), Vol. 44, para. 136, n. 2.

8. In litigation files, original process and other documents are required either to be issued, filed or served in compliance with various statutory requirements. It is essential that notations of compliance with those requirements are made on copies of the documentation on the file by the person actually carrying out the task. Such notations should be signed for later identification. Failure to observe this simple procedure as standard practice could prove embarrassing at a later date if an affidavit or other evidentiary material is required to establish compliance. Where the task was carried out by a secretary or clerk and an affidavit may be necessary, have it sworn straight away in case the secretary or clerk leaves your office and contact is lost.
9. When you are consulted by a defendant in a situation where insurance cover may exist, it is important to ask your client whether or not any insurance cover is held for the claim made or any part of it. Where cover may be available, the claim, particularly the issue of proceedings, should be reported immediately to the insurer involved and instructions should be sought as to who is to conduct the defence of the proceedings.
10. Learn the facts as soon as possible. If your client's instructions reveal the existence of witnesses, then obtain a signed statement from them as soon as possible and keep in touch with them until the case is settled or is heard.[13] Also formulate your views on whether the action is worth pursuing as soon as possible. Do not allow the action to drag on until the pretrial conference with counsel before you turn your mind to the question of whether the action is viable or not.
11. Immediately the question of a counterclaim arises during the course of instructions, check on the dates involved. Make the counterclaim promptly and observe the time limits required under the particular rules of court. If, despite all efforts on your part, the counterclaim is out of time, then apply immediately to the court for leave to counterclaim in the action. If leave is refused, then immediately issue a separate action on your client's behalf within the statute of limitations period. An application could be made later to consolidate the hearing of the two actions.

13. In *Holden & Co. v. Crown Prosecution Services* [1990] All E.R. 368, a solicitor was ordered to pay costs because a key witness was not available and a new trial was required.

12. You may be liable in damages to your client if you fail to adequately instruct counsel. Although a solicitor will not normally be answerable for the neglect of counsel where counsel is properly instructed, in *Re A (a minor)*[14] a solicitor was held to be personally liable for costs because he instructed incompetent counsel. It has also been held that a solicitor is under a duty to exercise an independent judgment after receiving counsel's advice.[15]
13. When taking over any matter from another practitioner, it is very important to satisfy yourself that at the particular stage at which you take over the wheel, all matters requiring attention have been attended to. In particular, be wary when taking over a matter shortly before the statute of limitations period is due to expire.[16] Sometimes the client may have been handling the matter on his or her own account for a time and in those circumstances it is even more important to check on the position. Backtracking on earlier work can prove costly and the client should be warned of this aspect when original instructions are received. Unfortunately, omissions by other practitioners or the client may become your own omissions simply because you failed to review the transaction and make the necessary enquiries from your client or other parties.
14. Be wary of giving gratuitous legal advice to acquaintances on social occasions. If you think that off-the-cuff advice on an informal occasion will never get you into trouble, you may be unpleasantly surprised. Acquaintances may be impressed with your advice and may act on it. If your advice turns out to be wrong, they may not hesitate to sue you. The fact that the advice was gratuitous would not protect you. You should not take the risk of being sued for negligent misstatement. It is better to make an appointment for the acquaintance to come to your office where you can be given proper instructions and you can give considered advice.

Property transactions

1. Options to renew a lease should be exercised promptly. It is common to find that solicitors for lessees and the lessees themselves are so preoccupied in negotiations for a fresh

14. (1988) N.L.J.L. 79.
15. G. R. Masel, *Professional Negligence of Lawyers, Accountants, Bankers and Brokers* (2nd edn, CCH Australia Ltd, Sydney, 1989), p. 179.
16. *Lee v. Mogg* (1989) Aust. Torts Reports 68,836.

lease that the necessity of duly exercising an option to renew is completely overlooked. If you exercise the option and a fresh lease is not concluded, you have done your duty to protect your client; if a fresh lease is concluded, then the renewed lease resulting from the exercise of the option can simply be cancelled.

2. Always do a check-search of a relevant certificate of title at the Titles Office immediately before a settlement in order to verify that no encumbrances were created in respect of the land since you last searched the certificate of title.[17]
3. If you are acting for a purchaser of a business, do not proceed to final settlement without first having obtained written approval from the landlord to the assignment of an existing lease or to the grant of a new lease. Settlement should not be effected unless an executed assignment is handed over or a fresh lease is produced at settlement. In most cases the goodwill of a business is valueless without security of tenure. Furthermore, where a lease or assignment of a lease is to be entered into, you should search the relevant certificate of title to ascertain whether there are any registered mortgages and (if there are) you should insist on the landlord obtaining the consent of any mortgagee before allowing your client to enter into the lease or assignment and complete the purchase.
4. When acting for a purchaser, always pay careful attention to the results of searches made on title. All aspects should be explained carefully to your client, particularly restrictive covenants limiting the number or type of dwellings which can be built or which may otherwise restrict development. As encumbrances can interfere with, or even frustrate, a purchaser's aspirations for a home and other developments such as garages, carports, outbuildings and leisure uses, they are obviously of great importance to your client. Remember to confirm in writing any advice you give.
5. When accounting to joint owners following sale or realisation of assets, particularly in the case of husband and wife, it is prudent to obtain a distribution statement from both of them which outlines how the funds are to be distributed. You will thus avoid an incorrect distribution and will not be involved in a belated attempt to correct the distribution or find yourself liable personally to meet any shortfall caused to one of the parties.

17. *Halsbury's Laws of England* (4th edn), Vol. 44, para. 135, n. 8.

6. Failure to account promptly to the parties entitled to money in your trust account may give rise to a claim on you for any interest lost due to delay on your part. If money is likely to be held beyond what would be regarded as a reasonable period without earning interest, obtain instructions to invest in an appropriate form of income-producing investment pending distribution.
7. Unless you are experienced in the inspection of general law or unregistered chains of title, you should not accept a retainer involving investigation of a general law title. You should either refer the client to another practitioner or else obtain the assistance of another practitioner experienced in the area. Inspection of a chain may appear easy but there are hidden traps. The fact that all the deeds are there and the dates match is not conclusive; the absence of a seal or a failure to use the appropriate words of conveyance in an old deed may cause the title to be defective. We have seen certificates from solicitors given to banks stating that a general law chain represents a good selling title when in fact the relevant chains contained over a dozen defects. If you do accept the responsibility of investigating title and you have any doubts on the chain, then you should obtain the opinion of counsel before recommending acceptance of the title.

Commercial transactions

1. Be careful that you do not hold yourself out as having expertise on commercial and financial issues, as distinct from legal issues, in case your client relies on you and later sues you if the transaction in question, while correctly documented as a matter of law, was a commercial disaster. Stick to your knitting and leave the commercial decisions to your clients and their financial advisers.[18]
2. Banks and other institutions increasingly require solicitors to sign certificates that certain steps have been taken or that certain documents are legally effective. Do not treat such certificates as mere formalities that have to be completed because as sure as night follows day you will be sued if something goes wrong with the transaction. Do not sign the certificate unless you are satisfied it is accurate. If the certificate contains matters which are outside your personal

18. See below, Ch. 46.

knowledge then delete the relevant parts or otherwise qualify what you are certifying.

3. Be particularly careful when explaining the effect of a guarantee to a client. Many banks now require guarantors to acknowledge that they have obtained independent legal advice before executing a guarantee. If you are consulted to give such advice, make sure you explain the contents of the guarantee in detail to the guarantor and if it is not in the guarantor's interest to sign the guarantee then advise accordingly, preferably in writing.

Interstate and overseas considerations

1. If you accept a retainer to act in a matter which will involve the institution of proceedings or the taking of some other action in an interstate or overseas jurisdiction, you should use interstate or overseas agents rather than trying to ascertain the law of the other jurisdiction yourself, or assuming that there are no material differences in the law of your home jurisdiction and the other jurisdiction. You should obtain immediate advice on the local requirements, in case time limits or other prerequisites exist. If you decide to do the work yourself, make sure you confirm its correctness with experienced practitioners in the other jurisdiction. Where documents (such as leases or mortgages) are involved, ensure that they are vetted by a practitioner in the other jurisdiction to ensure compliance with the law there.
2. When paying any overseas agents for work that they have done on your behalf, make sure you make proper currency calculations to avoid overpaying or underpaying them. It is easy to forget exchange rate differences, particularly where both jurisdictions use the dollar currency.
3. Before employing interstate or overseas agents, obtain an estimate from them as to what they will charge for their services and ensure your client is informed of such estimate before you obtain instructions to employ the agents. The method of fixing remuneration for legal practitioners differs among jurisdictions and accordingly you may find that legal work that in your own jurisdiction would cost approximately A$1,000 may cost the equivalent of A$4,000 in another jurisdiction. Your client is unlikely to be amused by a disbursement of A$4,000 in your bill of costs.

Office systems[19]

1. No matter how similar the interests of a group of clients may appear, always open a separate file for each client. Often the interests of one client in a group can so overshadow the interests of others that there is a danger that the latter will be neglected and even overlooked altogether. This danger should be watched for, especially in common law matters where a number of clients have personal injury claims arising from the same accident.
2. Whenever possible, avoid accumulating large files. Keeping separate files for clients' separate transactions is conducive to better organisation and efficiency. Large files are difficult to control and make it difficult to locate a particular document amongst the mass of papers on the file. Separate files help avoid the risk that you may overlook some transaction, a risk which is not uncommon with multi-transaction files.
3. It may be a pious hope but in an ideal world you should have only the file on which you are currently working on your desk. If the telephone rings and the ensuing conversation is likely to be lengthy and require reference to another file, put the current file away and get the file that the call relates to from your filing cabinet. If you have many files on your desk, particularly if they are all open, it is highly probable that you will put documents in the wrong file. When those documents are needed, it may take several hours before they are located and sometimes you may not be able to locate them at all. Depending on the nature of the documents, the consequences of misfiling can be disastrous.
4. Review all your files constantly with a view to quickly refreshing your memory as to what stage each matter has reached and what further steps need to be taken and when. It is prudent to prepare a daily list of "Things to Do" in order of priority and to cross off each item once it is completed. Items not completed at the end of the day should be carried forward to the next day. When you are working on a file and you can foresee the steps you will need to take sometime in the future, you should list these in your diary and also on a file memo to be kept at the front of the file so that, when the time comes, you will remember to take those steps.

19. See also below, Ch. 43.

5. Have an efficient diary and recall system. Enter in your diary all critical time limit dates for the issue and service of process, hearings, and also dates for exercise of options in leases and other future obligations accepted on behalf of clients. It is advisable to note reminders for major events one or two weeks before they arise. Make sure your client's cause of action does not become statute barred or your client's lease expire through the absence of an adequate office system to safeguard against this.
6. Where possible, devise instruction sheets or checklists for the various areas of your firm's practice. This will reduce the incidence of errors or omissions.
7. If you work in a large firm, discourage clients from marking correspondence to you "personal and confidential". If you are absent from the office for any reason and no one dares to open personal correspondence which may contain urgent instructions, the result could be disastrous. Alternatively, if you must receive personal and confidential correspondence from a client, then before going on holidays or absenting yourself from the office for any other reason, you should either advise your client to refer correspondence to another practitioner in the office, or alternatively, give another practitioner authority to open your personal and confidential correspondence.
8. If you work in a large firm with an "unclaimed mail" basket, ensure that the basket is checked every day and appropriate inquiries are made to clear the basket as soon as possible to ensure that correspondence—which may contain urgent instructions or cheques etc.—does not lie around idly. One way of preventing the "unclaimed mail" basket from becoming cluttered is to put your reference on every letter or document that leaves your office, in the pious hope that your reference may reappear on incoming letters or documents.
9. Place valuable items—such as title deeds and settlement cheques—in safe custody. Do not leave them on desks or in files overnight even if they will be exchanged at settlement the next morning. A break-in overnight is not an impossibility. In accordance with general principles of law, you will be liable to your clients if you fail to exercise due and reasonable care for the safety of their documents.
10. If you have custody of a client's will, you should ensure that the testator has given notice to the executor of his or her

appointment and also the whereabouts of the will. It may be prudent to obtain a written acknowledgment from the testator confirming that such action has taken place in light of the decision in *Hawkins v. Clayton*[20] where the High Court held that a solicitor owed a duty to an executor named in a will to take reasonable steps to ensure that the executor was informed of all relevant facts.

11. Unless a client is personally known to you, insist on proper identification when a person claiming to be a client, or the authorised agent of a client, comes to your office to collect title deeds or other important documents held by you. This should be done also when you receive instructions over the telephone to despatch documents.
12. It has been suggested that solicitors may be negligent if they fail to make use of reasonably available information technology tools to carry out research and inquiries. Reports on attorney research malpractice in the United States suggest that negligence concepts can be readily applied to information technology.[21] The impact of technology on legal practice is discussed below in Chapter 45.

General

1. When circumstances exist in any file which may give rise to a claim against you and you are instructed to hand over your file to the client or another practitioner, you should retain a complete copy of the file for your own use and protection.
2. Do not leave files and other documents unattended in court over luncheon adjournments or in public libraries. Similarly, do not leave a briefcase containing files, legal papers or documents of any kind in a motor car parked in the street overnight even though it may be locked.
3. Take detailed diary notes of all telephone conversations and discussions in conference with clients, witnesses, opposing practitioners and counsel. In addition, you should also confirm discussions by letter. A diary note is merely a record made by one person and might not necessarily accord with

20. (1988) 164 C.L.R. 539; G. R. Masel, *Professional Negligence of Lawyers, Accountants, Bankers and Brokers* (2nd edn, CCH Australia Ltd, Sydney, 1989), p. 176; F. Riley, "Holding a Client's Will? Consider the Duty of Care" (1988) 26 (June) *Law Society Journal* 47.
21. "The Information Age, Lawyers and Negligence" (1992) 66 *Law Institute Journal* 138.

another person's version of the same conversation or situation. Confirmation by letter is the only sure way of avoiding disputes. All file and diary notes should be clearly handwritten or, if possible, typed. A useful guide in preparing a file note is to assume that the file may be transferred to another practitioner so that you ensure that the file note is as detailed and legible as you would wish if you were the recipient of the file.

4. Make sure that you observe your client's instructions. An unauthorised deviation from the terms of your client's retainer may make you liable in damages to your client even though you act in accordance with prevailing professional practice.[22]

5. When you receive instructions by telephone involving sums of money—such as amounts owing to your client—you should not rely on the telephone conversation alone but should confirm in writing to your client the details recorded by you before taking any further steps in correspondence or otherwise with third parties. Failure to do so may leave you exposed to an allegation of mistake as to amount, leaving it to a court to determine who, between you and the client, is to be believed.

6. It is wise to decline to act for a client who places unfair pressure on you to prepare documentation or finalise matters within an unreasonable time. However, if a retainer is accepted then any advice should be confirmed in writing immediately. This is particularly important where you advise caution in relation to such things as the premature giving or taking of possession of chattels, the payment of money prior to execution of security documents or the entering into binding contracts where obtaining the consent of third parties should be made a condition precedent. If you do not adopt these precautions, you may find that the clients who pressure you for quick results will turn on you when their own judgment is later found to be at fault. Above all, do not act for pushy clients in any area of practice in which you are not experienced.[23]

7. Do not sign as a witness to a document unless you in fact saw the person whose signature purports to be on the document sign it. Signing in the absence of the signatory is

22. *Cordery on Solicitors* (8th edn, Butterworths & Co. (Publishers) Ltd, London, 1988), p. 95.
23. See also below, Ch. 46.

dishonest and may amount to unprofessional conduct and possibly a crime.[24] It may also result in a claim being made against you by a person who suffers loss. This is especially so for documents such as mortgages and transfers of land under which assets are transferred or interests in property encumbered.

8. Do not fall for the fallacy that it is acceptable to have a "too hard basket" in which you place all your difficult files. You will soon find yourself postponing attention to these files time after time, and this may irretrievably prejudice your clients.[25] The position is well summarised by Templeman L.J. in *McVeigh v. Tarmac Roadstone Holdings Ltd*:[26]

   > "One moral to be drawn was that it did not suffice to have a good excuse or reason for each day of delay. Fairly soon after the issue of the writ in a case where issues of fact were involved, there came a time when the red light ought to glow in the solicitor's office and he ought to say to himself: 'I must press on with this action; I must take it by the scruff of the neck and get on with it or I will be in trouble.' "

9. Inordinate delays in litigious matters can lead to default judgment being entered against a defendant or a plaintiff's action being dismissed for want of prosecution. The consequences of delay are also disastrous in many other areas of practice. Delay is a common complaint levelled against the profession and you should always strive to avoid it. Clients expect that their matters will be attended to with reasonable expedition, will be kept moving and will be concluded within a reasonable time. Do not disappoint them. Also remember that the sooner a matter is completed, the sooner your fees will be paid.

10. Do not try to be all things to all people.[27] You are not expected to be an expert in all areas of the law. If a matter is within your area of practice but it involves complex issues, it is proper, with your client's consent, to refer it to experienced counsel. However, if a relatively simple matter

24. Compare *Brott v. The Queen* (1992) 173 C.L.R. 426. This case involved a solicitor who purported to witness the signature of a client who was dead at the time of execution.
25. See below, Ch. 42.
26. (1981) 78 *Law Society's Gazette* 633.
27. See below, Ch. 43.

is completely outside your field, it is not fair to make your client incur counsel's fees simply because of your ignorance. In such a case the more appropriate step is to refer the client to another solicitor with experience in the relevant matter. Alternatively, if you wish to acquire experience in the relevant matter then it might be appropriate for you to brief counsel and not charge the client for counsel's fees.

11. If a client, a witness or an opponent needs to stay in your office for some time in order to attend to matters such as inspection of documents, do not leave that person in your office unsupervised, particularly if you have confidential documents relating to other clients on your desk or in full view in other areas of your office. The best course is to organise for the relevant activity to be conducted in an empty conference room. Inspection of documents by an opponent should always be supervised.
12. Ensure that all your staff (including casual staff such as students on work experience) are instructed to maintain strict confidentiality in relation to clients' affairs. Having regard to their inexperience, you should be selective about what information students on work experience are given access to.
13. Do not conduct confidential discussions over the telephone with a client if another client or some other third party is in your office. Say to the client that you will call back after you finish your meeting.

The trend towards conservative and preventative legal advice and the increasing expectations of the community in relation to the performance, standard and roles demanded of lawyers are likely in the future to broaden the accountability of lawyers and raise the requisite standard of care demanded of them.[28]

28. M. Mills, "Professional Negligence: The Expanding Liability of Lawyers" (1992) 9 *Australian Bar Review* 1.

Chapter 22

Unprofessional Conduct[1]

> "A lawyer is to do for his client all that his client might fairly do for himself, if he could."
>
> Dr Johnson, quoted in J. Boswell, *A Journal of a Tour of the Hebrides* (P. Fitzgerald (ed.), 1888), p. 212.

You must be a fit and proper person in order to be admitted to the legal profession and as a condition of continued membership. Sometimes the expression "a person of good fame and character" is used instead of the expression "a fit and proper person".[2] Both expressions obviously require that you must not do anything that is illegal, fraudulent or dishonest. But they go further than that: you must refrain from conduct that would cause you, and the profession through you, disrepute.

In *Ex parte Meagher*[3] Gordon J. stated that "fit and proper persons" are "persons who have been proved to the satisfaction of the court not only to be possessed of the requisite knowledge of law, but above all to be possessed of a moral integrity and rectitude of character, so that they may safely be accredited by the court to the public as fit, without further inquiry to be entrusted by that public with their most intimate and confidential affairs without fear that that trust will be abused."

1. Unlike some textbooks and authorities, this book does not draw a distinction between unprofessional conduct and professional misconduct. The expression "unprofessional conduct" in this book refers generally to all conduct which falls short of the standards expected of the profession and which might justify disciplinary action being taken against the practitioner concerned.
2. *Re Foster* (1950) 50 S.R. (N.S.W.) 149 at 151.
3. (1919) 19 S.R. (N.S.W.) 433 at 442.

Most jurisdictions have statutes, subordinate legislation and professional rules which provide guidelines as to what amounts to unprofessional conduct and prescribe procedures and sanctions for disciplining the profession. The ultimate sanction is to be struck off the roll of practitioners so that you cannot practise law.

It is your duty to be familiar with and abide by all statutes, subordinate legislation and professional rules which prescribe or prohibit conduct for members of the profession in your jurisdiction. These will not be discussed in this book. Rather, we shall concentrate on the standards of professional conduct demanded by the common law.

Negative duty

The common law prescribes an essentially negative duty. You must always refrain from conduct which would be reasonably regarded as disgraceful or dishonourable by your professional colleagues of good repute and competency.[4] The duty is formulated in terms which are general and flexible. As change and development occurs within the community and the legal profession, the parameters of what is or is not acceptable conduct by practitioners will also change and develop. As was stated by the Supreme Court of Queensland in 1953, the categories of unprofessional conduct are not closed.[5]

At any given time it is impossible to define exhaustively what amounts to conduct which would reasonably be regarded as disgraceful or dishonourable by members of the profession of good repute and competency. All one can do is to seek guidance from more experienced practitioners, from the relevant Law Society and from the decided cases. If you ever have any doubt as to whether what you are about to do is proper, it is better not to do it. You should avoid the possibility of an accusation of unprofessional conduct, even if ultimately it is unjustified.

Uphold the law

Because you, as a practitioner, are associated with the administration of the law, you are under a positive duty to maintain the law at all times.[6] This obviously means that you must not break the law. Being convicted of a criminal offence

4. *Re a Solicitor* [1912] I K.B. 302 at 312.
5. *Re a Solicitor* [1953] Q.S.R. 149.
6. *Halsbury's Laws of England* (4th edn), Vol. 44, para. 298.

(other than merely trivial offences such as minor traffic infringements) usually amounts to unprofessional conduct even if no dishonesty is involved because it may indicate that you have a disrespect for the law.[7] Even if no conviction results from the commission of an offence, you may still be held to be guilty of unprofessional conduct.[8] A verdict of "not guilty by reason of insanity" may disclose that the practitioner concerned is not a fit and proper person to practise law.[9]

A solicitor who deliberately infringes an injunction and is found to be in contempt of court is guilty of unprofessional conduct and will normally be struck off the roll.[10] So will a barrister who accepts instructions direct from a lay client and lies to the court.[11]

Your duty to uphold the law also requires that you must not assist a client to break the law. If a client proposes to break the law, you must alert your client to the consequences of such action and seek to dissuade him or her. However, it is not improper for you to advise a client on how to take advantage of a loophole in the law.

Your responsibilities towards your client can never override your duty to uphold the law.[12] Accordingly, you must not do anything that is dishonourable even if it is in the interests of your client and you are pressed to do it. To quote the Law Society of England, "A solicitor must not act dishonourably, degrade himself, fight unfairly, lend himself to underhand or criminal activity or descend to sharp practice in order to benefit his client or win his case."[13]

The position of barristers is very similar:

> "As an advocate [a barrister] is a minister of justice equally with the judge.... [He must] do all he honourably can on behalf of his client. I say 'all he *honourably* can' because his duty is not only to his client. He has a duty to the court

7. *Re Weare* [1893] 2 Q.B. 439 at 445.
8. *Re Crick* (1907) 7 S.R. (N.S.W.) 576 at 590.
9. *Re B (a solicitor)* [1986] V.R. 695.
10. *Law Institute of Victoria v. Little* (unreported, Vic. Sup. Ct, Tadgell J., 11 June 1991).
11. *New South Wales Bar Association v. Smith* (unreported, N.S.W. C.A., 9 May 1991).
12. *Halsbury's Laws of England* (4th edn), Vol. 44, para. 299.
13. The Council of the Law Society, *A Guide to Professional Conduct of Solicitors* (Law Society, London, 1974), p. 17. See also Law Society, *The Guide to the Professional Conduct of Solicitors* (Law Society, London, 1990).

> which is paramount. It is a mistake to suppose that he is the mouthpiece of his client to say what he wants: or his tool to do what he directs. He is none of these things. He owes allegiance to a higher cause. It is the cause of truth and justice. He must not consciously misstate the facts. He must not knowingly conceal the truth. He must not unjustly make a charge of fraud, that is, without evidence to support it. He must produce all the relevant authorities, even those that are against him. He must see that his client discloses, if ordered, the relevant documents, even those that are fatal to his case. He must disregard the most specific instructions of his client if they conflict with his duty to the court. The code which requires a barrister to do all this is not a code of law. It is a code of honour. If he breaks it, he is offending against the rules of the profession and is subject to its discipline".[14]

If your client has acted illegally, such as deliberately swearing a false affidavit of documents or answers to interrogatories or has suppressed material facts when under an obligation to disclose them, you should immediately request your client to rectify the situation. If your client refuses, you should withdraw from the case and, if your client's actions would tend to corrupt the administration of justice, you should also inform the court.[15] If you knowingly allow your client to swear a false affidavit, you may be guilty of unprofessional conduct.[16]

However, you should bear in mind that you have a duty to fully explain to your clients their obligations in relation to matters such as answering interrogatories and preparing an affidavit of documents. If you do not do so and your clients, because of inexperience, make errors, you may be held to have acted improperly.[17]

Abuse of process

You have a duty not to abuse the process of the court or, by dishonest means, hamper your opponents in the conduct of their case. It is an abuse of process to institute proceedings if you know that your client's case is false or on the basis of receiving a proportion of the amount recovered or a higher fee if the client wins the case. To launch a prosecution against someone for the

14. *Rondel v. Worsley* [1967] 1 Q.B. 443 at 502.
15. *Swinburne v. David Syme & Co.* [1909] V.L.R. 550 at 570-571.
16. *Re Thom* (1918) 18 S.R. (N.S.W.) 70.
17. *Myers v. Elman* [1940] A.C. 282 at 293, 304.

purpose of intimidation in relation to other proceedings involving your client amounts to unprofessional conduct.[18]

You should never allow your name to be put on a statement of claim without reasonable belief in its contents.[19] Nor should you make any statement of fact you know you cannot support by evidence or which is based on evidence which you know is inadmissible. You should never directly or indirectly suggest that a witness give evidence which you know to be false. This does not apply, however, where you merely suspect its falsity because it is up to the court to decide the truth.

When appearing in court, you should refrain from needless and unjustified attacks on your opponent or a witness and you must never allow yourself to be made a channel for questions intended merely to insult or annoy. Further, you have a duty to conduct yourself with dignity, propriety and courtesy towards the occupant of the Bench.

False statements

Unprofessional conduct may be constituted by a lack of complete candour in any statement you make to the court. Your duty of absolute honesty and integrity to the court precludes not only deliberate lies but also misleading statements. Unless courts can have complete confidence in the honour of practitioners and are able to accept unreservedly any statements made by them, the administration of justice will be seriously impaired.[20]

It is thus unprofessional conduct for a barrister to mislead the court while giving evidence,[21] for a solicitor to make a false declaration in registering a business name, allowing clients to use false names and operating in a fictitious name himself[22] and for a solicitor to cover up misconduct by making a false and misleading statement to the Law Society.[23]

Plagiarism may also amount to unprofessional conduct.[24]

18. *Clyne v. Bar Association of New South Wales* (1960) 104 C.L.R. 186.
19. *Gazley v. Wellington District Law Society* [1976] 1 N.Z.L.R. 452.
20. *Re Foster* (1950) 50 S.R. (N.S.W.) 149 at 152.
21. *New South Wales Bar Association v. Thomas (No. 2)* (1989) 2 N.S.W.L.R. 193.
22. *Prothonotary of the Supreme Court of New South Wales v. Chapman* (unreported, N.S.W. C.A., 14 December 1992).
23. *Adamson v. Queensland Law Society Inc.* [1990] 1 Qd R. 498.
24. A Melbourne solicitor was struck off the roll in 1992 after being found guilty of three charges of plagiarism.

Witnessing affidavits

It is improper for you to sign as a witness to an affidavit when you did not witness the affidavit or to alter an affidavit after it is sworn without arranging for it to be resworn.[25] It is also improper for you to sign as a witness to an affidavit when you saw the deponent sign but did not administer an oath or affirmation.[26]

Trust funds

If you hold funds on behalf of a client, you should keep them in appropriate trust accounts and should not mix them with your own funds.[27] Failure to maintain proper trust accounts or to account to clients for money collected on their behalf amounts to unprofessional conduct.[28] So does using trust funds belonging to a client for your own purposes or for the purposes of another client.[29]

Knowingly permitting your trust account to be used for money laundering or other unlawful purposes is obviously unprofessional conduct.

Defrauding your partners

It is unprofessional conduct to defraud your partners.[30]

Supervision of staff

A solicitor who fails to supervise law clerks and other staff may, in some circumstances, be guilty of unprofessional conduct.[31]

Conflict of interest[32]

Borrowing from clients may constitute unprofessional conduct.[33] Professional practice rules often prohibit borrowing

25. *Re a Barrister and Solicitor* (1984) 58 A.C.T.R. 1.
26. *English v. Legal Practitioners Complaints Committee* (1986) 41 S.A.S.R. 217.
27. *Halsbury's Laws of England* (4th edn), Vol. 44, paras 303, 328-331.
28. *Re a Practitioner* [1942] S.A.S.R. 188.
29. *Johns v. Law Society of New South Wales* [1987] 2 N.S.W.L.R. 1.
30. *Re a Practitioner* (1984) 36 S.A.S.R. 590.
31. *Law Society of New South Wales v. Foreman* (1991) 24 N.S.W.L.R. 238.
32. See above, Ch. 6.
33. *Re Fabricius and McLaren and Re Legal Practitioners Ordinance 1970* (1990) 91 A.C.T.R. 1.

from clients.[34] A solicitor who enters a transaction with a client or former client in circumstances of unacceptable conflict between his or her interests and duty may be guilty of professional misconduct.[35]

Not honouring obligations

Failure to meet an obligation which a practitioner is honour bound to perform may amount to unprofessional conduct. For example, in some circumstances, failure to pay counsel's fees may amount to unprofessional conduct.[36]

Similarly, the giving of a cheque by a solicitor in the knowledge that there are insufficient funds to cover it may be unprofessional conduct in circumstances where it will tend to reflect on solicitors generally.[37]

Conducting another business

A solicitor may engage in the conduct of another business concurrently with his or her practice as a solicitor where that other business is of a respectable character and is not one that would be likely to bring the profession into disrepute. If you do engage in another business, you must always observe your fiduciary obligations to your client and avoid any conflicts of interest from arising.[38]

Improper intermingling of your personal affairs and the affairs of the practice you conduct on behalf of your clients may amount to unprofessional conduct.[39]

Tax advice and defrauding the revenue

If you provide advice on tax issues, you must bear in mind the critical distinction between advice on tax minimisation and advice on tax evasion. In recent years practitioners have faced charges of attempting to defraud the Commonwealth based on

34. See, for example, *Solicitors' (Professional Conduct and Practice) Rules* 1984 (Vic.), r. 8.
35. *O'Reilly v. Law Society of New South Wales* (1988) 24 N.S.W.L.R. 204.
36. *Carver v. Legal Profession Disciplinary Tribunal* (unreported, N.S.W. C.A., 27 September 1991).
37. *Re Oakley* (unreported, A.C.T. Sup. Ct, Full Ct, 10 September 1992).
38. Rules of professional practice often require other businesses to be kept distinct from the legal practice. See, for example, *Solicitors' (Professional Conduct and Practice) Rules* 1984 (Vic.), r. 14.
39. *Law Society of New South Wales v. Foreman* (1991) 24 N.S.W.L.R. 238.

tax advice they provided. One practitioner who devised and engaged in a scheme contravening tax laws was found guilty of unprofessional conduct.[40]

Solicitors who were paid their fees in cash and who understated their income have been struck off the roll.[41]

Delays

Neglect or delay in the transaction of a client's business may amount to unprofessional conduct.[42]

Breach of undertaking

If you breach an undertaking to a court or another practitioner, you may be guilty of unprofessional conduct.[43] Breach of an undertaking to a court may also constitute a contempt of the court.

Ignorance is no excuse

Ignorance of what is appropriate professional conduct is no excuse. In fact a misconception of your duty as a barrister or solicitor could itself amount to disgraceful or dishonourable conduct.[44]

Dishonesty not required

There may be unprofessional conduct without positive dishonesty. If a solicitor, by what he or she has done, evidences that he or she does not understand the nature and extent of the obligations to clients which the profession imposes or does not observe them, then, given the sufficient gravity of the impropriety, he or she may be held guilty of unprofessional conduct.[45]

Similarly, the fact that no client or other person actually suffers loss due to the practitioner's conduct does not prevent a finding of unprofessional conduct. That fact, however, may tend to

40. *Re Maidment* (1992) 23 A.T.R. 629.
41. *Re Milte* (1991) 22 A.T.R. 740.
42. *Re Moseley* (1925) S.R. (N.S.W.) 174 at 178; *Halsbury's Laws of England* (4th edn), Vol. 44, paras 303, 328-331.
43. *Keppie v. Law Society of the Australian Capital Territory* (1983) A.C.T.R. 9; *John Fox v. Bannister, King & Rigbeys* [1987] 3 W.L.R. 480 at 483; *Udall v. Capri Lighting Ltd (in liq.)* [1987] 3 W.L.R. 465. See also above, Ch. 20.
44. *Re a Barrister and a Solicitor* (1984) A.C.T.R. 1 at 8.
45. *Law Society of New South Wales v. Foreman* (1991) 24 N.S.W.L.R. 238.

explain the nature and extent of the misconduct, and is clearly relevant to the question of penalty.

Personal life

The standards of behaviour expected of you are very demanding and extend not only to your professional life but also to your personal life. The rationale is that if you do something which brings you into disrepute then the profession will be brought into disrepute and, further, the administration of justice—of which members of the profession are an integral part—will be brought into disrepute.

Accordingly, even though personal misconduct may have less weight than professional misconduct, it may still be a ground for striking you off the roll of practitioners because it may show that you are not a fit and proper person to practise law.[46]

You must adhere to the standards of behaviour expected of you in everything you do. Some of the obvious things you should not be doing in your private life are: associating with known criminals;[47] accepting a bribe;[48] embezzling funds received by you for a specific purpose;[49] allowing houses of which you are landlord to be used by the tenants as illegal brothels;[50] putting up money that does not belong to you to bail a friend;[51] and being intoxicated and using insulting, obscene and threatening language to a public official in a public place.[52]

However, not all behaviour which may be subject to criticism amounts to unprofessional conduct. For example, having extra-marital intercourse with a client may fall short of constituting unprofessional conduct[53] and the same applies to regular betting at racecourses and failure to pay debts to bookmakers.[54]

46. *Ziems v. Prothonotary of the Supreme Court of New South Wales* (1957) 97 C.L.R. 279 at 290.
47. *Re Foster* (1950) 50 S.R. (N.S.W.) 149.
48. *Re Crick* (1907) 7 S.R. (N.S.W.) 576.
49. *Re Daly* (1896) 17 L.R. (N.S.W.) 169.
50. *Re Weare* (1893) 2 Q.B. 439; compare *Prothonotary of the Supreme Court of New South Wales v. Chapman* (unreported, N.S.W. C.A., 14 December 1992).
51. *Re B* [1981] 2 N.S.W.L.R. 372 at 394-395.
52. *Re a Practitioner* [1942] S.A.S.R. 188.
53. *Bar Association of Queensland v. Lamb* [1972] A.L.R. 285. See above, Ch. 11.
54. *Re a Solicitor* [1933] V.L.R. 103.

Likewise, breach of duty as a director or as a trustee is not necessarily unprofessional conduct.[55]

Discourtesy to members of the public

Arrogant or discourteous conduct towards members of the public can bring you and the profession into disrepute even if it does not amount to unprofessional conduct.[56] One example relates to the summoning of witnesses to give evidence. Members of the medical profession frequently complain that they are not given adequate notice of when they will be required in court and consequently have to cancel a day's appointments at very short notice. Other witnesses sometimes complain that they spend hours in corridors outside court rooms before someone informs them that the relevant case was settled the previous day.

The reputation of the profession suffers because of the cavalier treatment of doctors, police and civilian witnesses who are summoned to give evidence. It is unfortunately not infrequent that witnesses are summoned to give evidence in a case which does not proceed, or in which they are unlikely to be called for several days. Often, witnesses do not know where the court is and no arrangements are made to assist them.

You should never do anything that would attract an accusation that you have been discourteous to witnesses and members of the public in general.

55. *Re Wheeler* (unreported, Qld Sup. Ct, Full Ct, 26 April 1991).
56. *Halsbury's Laws of England* (4th edn), Vol. 44, para. 304.

Part 4

Relationship with the Courts

Chapter 23

Introduction

> "A judge is not supposed to know anything about the facts of life until they have been presented in evidence and explained to him at least three times."
>
> Lord Chief Justice Parker, *Observer*, 12 March 1961.

Although not all barristers and solicitors appear in court every day, it is rare for any practitioner not to have some contact with the court system during his or her professional life.

The courts are the fulcrum of the legal system and you, whether as a barrister or solicitor, have a recognised place there. Indeed, in some jurisdictions, solicitors are officers of the court. The courts confer certain privileges upon you by virtue of your membership of the profession and in turn impose some obligations.

Some of the obligations that courts impose—such as the duty of complete candour—have already been discussed in Part 3 of this book. In Part 4 we shall examine how you should conduct yourself towards court officials, judges and witnesses as well as some basic aspects of presenting a court case.

Chapter 24

Relationship with Court Officials

> "Sometimes it's who you know rather than what you know."

As a young practitioner you will probably find that your initial contact with the courts will not be glamorous at all. Rather than either presenting a case or instructing in court, you are more likely to be assigned responsibilities such as issuing and filing court documents. The only way you will get anywhere near a real-life court hearing will be if you deliberately digress from your less salubrious chores in order to spend some time in a courtroom.

Although chores such as issuing or filing court documents may appear boring, you should not avoid them altogether in your early years but should undertake them even if it is just for a week and even if there are experienced clerks in your office who normally do them. Such chores will give you an insight into the legal "machinery" and will expose you to the officials in charge of tasks such as issuing writs, subpoenas, summonses, warrants of execution and so on. While waiting in the queue you may even get a chance to read documents such as subpoenas which you may have heard about but had no idea of what they actually looked like.

You should always be courteous to court officials, irrespective of their seniority. Such officials are part of the court system and therefore there is no room for arrogance or discourtesy. On the contrary, you should attempt to foster a friendship with all court officials. They know the court procedures backwards and will readily assist you when you run into problems. They will obviously be less willing to co-operate with you if you have not treated them with respect.

Remember that even the most junior court clerk may one day become a prothonotary, registrar or the holder of some other responsible position. It is better to have such a person onside rather than offside. One day an emergency may arise and your friendship with court officials may not only be handy but also save you from a negligence suit.

Remember also that in some circumstances insulting or obstructing a court official may amount to contempt of court.[1]

1. *Halsbury's Laws of England* (4th edn), Vol. 9, para. 31.

Chapter 25

Contempt of Court

> "Justice is not a cloistered virtue: she must be allowed to suffer the scrutiny and respectful, even though outspoken, comments of ordinary men."
>
> *Ambard v. Attorney-General (Trinidad and Tobago)* [1936] A.C. 322 at 335.

Courage and courtesy

Courage by an advocate in the face of a hostile Bench is praiseworthy. However, it is a fine line between being a fearless advocate and a noisy troublemaker, intent upon preventing the court from carrying out its proper judicial functions. If you overstep that line, you may find yourself cited for contempt of court which carries serious penalties.

From time to time, you will be confronted by a magistrate or judge who interferes constantly with the presentation of your case, or who appears to have prejudged the issues. Pressure being exerted from the Bench, particularly when you suspect that the Bench does not really know what it is talking about, can be an emotional and vexing experience. The challenge is to act courteously to the tribunal before which you are appearing, and yet to fearlessly and vigorously represent your client. Courage and courtesy must go hand in hand.

Contempt in the face of the court

For words or actions used in the face of a court or in the course of proceedings to be a contempt, they must be such as would interfere, or tend to interfere, with the course of justice.[1] Contempt in the face of a court includes:

(a) assaulting or threatening a judge;

(b) insulting or showing disrespect to a judge;

(c) wilfully interrupting or disturbing court proceedings;

(d) defying a judge's directions or rulings.[2]

However, mere discourtesy such as shouting at a judge does not of itself amount to contempt in the face of the court.[3]

Laughing gas

If you like cases to be interesting, the law of contempt of court is a fruitful area. There will probably never be another case to match *Balogh v. St Albans Crown Court*.[4] The facts are, to say the least, extraordinary. During the hearing of a pornography trial a law clerk seated in court was finding the proceedings more and more tedious. He decided to do something about it and one night, after procuring a supply of nitrous oxide (laughing gas), he climbed onto the roof of the courthouse and worked out how to inject the laughing gas into the air conditioning system the next morning.

Unfortunately for him, he was apprehended the next day before executing his daring plan. The mind boggles at what he might have done if the case had been an equity matter, or even a simple running down case. In any event, when formally charged with contempt he remained defiant to the last. When the judge sentenced him to six months in prison for his efforts with the laughing gas, he responded, "You are a humourless automaton. Why don't you self-destruct?"

Those who applaud efforts to make court proceedings more lively will be pleased to know that on appeal it was held that the law clerk had not been guilty of contempt of court because he had not succeeded in completing the act which he had planned

1. *Parashuram Detaram Shamdasani v. King-Emperor* [1945] A.C. 264 at 268.
2. In *Re Prior; Ex parte Bellanto* (1963) 63 S.R. (N.S.W.) 190, a lawyer's refusal to abandon a line of questioning was held to constitute contempt because it was deemed by the judge to be damaging to the trial.
3. *Toner v. Attorney-General (New South Wales)* (unreported, N.S.W. C.A., 19 November 1991). See also *Re Prior; Ex parte Bellanto* (1963) 63 S.R. (N.S.W.) 190; *Lewis v. Ogden* (1984) 153 C.L.R. 682.
4. [1975] 1 Q.B. 73.

to carry out. One judge, Stevenson L.J., queried if an attempt to commit contempt of court was punishable as such.[5]

United States courts

The courts of the United States of America have been remarkably aggressive in dealing with trial lawyers who have been found guilty of contempt in the face of the court.

The transcript of the proceedings that resulted from the riots during the 1968 Democratic National Convention in Chicago (better known as the "Chicago Seven Trial") makes lively reading. One of the lawyers, Leonard Weinglass, was cited for refusing to sit down immediately after being ordered to do so, for asking questions in cross-examination beyond the scope of the direct examination, for repeating citations of legal authorities, for continuing an argument after the judge had ruled on it and for making disrespectful remarks about the prosecution. Another lawyer, William Kunstler, was cited for arguing about the time of recess and for expressing his approval of disapproving groans from the spectators in court. Weinglass was sentenced to 20 months imprisonment on 14 charges of contempt and Kunstler received four years imprisonment on 24 charges of contempt. All the contempt convictions were quashed on appeal.[6]

In California a lawyer was convicted of contempt and sentenced to a period of imprisonment. Apparently the contempt related to his dress because the judge said that his hair "looked like a cross between an Angora goat and a baboon". An appeal was lodged and ultimately it was argued that the comments were unfair because the hair of one of the Presidents of the United States resembled a koala and the hair of Justice Holmes "was a cross between a moose and a yak and a European oaudad". As an oaudad is a North African wild sheep, one can only wonder what it was doing in Europe in the first place.

Examples of contempts of court by litigants

Most lawyers are familiar with the occasion in 1631 when at Salisbury an accused threw a brickbat at a judge. The half brick narrowly missed. What is not quite so well known is that the accused's throwing arm was promptly amputated and nailed to

5. [1975] 1 Q.B. 73 at 87.
6. J. Disney and others, *Lawyers* (Law Book Co. Ltd, Sydney, 1977), pp. 726-728.

a gibbet in the court. The judge must have received a considerable fright because to underline his sense of outrage the prisoner was himself immediately thereafter hanged from the same gibbet.[7]

The 19th century must have been a period of relative gentility for there is an instance cited of a disgruntled litigant in the County Court who, dissatisfied with the result of the proceedings, removed a dead cat from a paper parcel and hurled it inaccurately at the judge. To the judge's credit, he responded by saying, "I shall commit you for contempt if you do that again." As the disgruntled litigant did not have any more dead cats at hand, she obeyed the judge's direction.[8] Another litigant who threw an egg at a judge was not so lucky.[9]

Modern litigants have had their fair share of trouble with the courts. In 1964 a litigant who threw off his clothes and made himself comfortable on a bench in court was found guilty of contempt of court.[10] The same fate befell a Canadian litigant who, after attending court in the morning and finding that his case would not be called until the afternoon, spent the interval drinking and consequently was unable to instruct his counsel or fully understand the proceedings.[11]

Different judges, however, take a different view of when to cite someone for contempt. Lord Denning, for example, did not seek to cite for contempt a disappointed litigant who threw two heavy law texts at him, whereas a defendant was convicted of contempt in Canada for refusing to stand when the magistrate entered the court and contempt proceedings were threatened in a Victorian court in 1983 against a woman barrister who appeared wearing trousers.[12]

Lord Erskine's noble stand for the independence of the Bar[13]

One of the most celebrated cases of a barrister courageously upholding the interests of a client in the face of threats from the

7. (1631) 2 Dyer 188b n; 73 E.R. 416.
8. R. E. Megarry, *Miscellany-at-Law* (Stevens, London, 1955), p. 295, n. 19.
9. *Re Cosgrave* (1877), referred to in *Halsbury's Laws of England* (4th edn), Vol. 9, para. 6, n. 1.
10. *Gohoho v. Lintas Export Advertising Services* (1964), referred to in *Halsbury's Laws of England* (4th edn), Vol. 9, para. 6, n. 8.
11. *R. v. Perkins* [1980] 4 W.W.R. 763.
12. Australian Law Reform Commission, *Contempt*, Report No. 35 (1987).
13. The discussion under this heading is adapted from C. J. Miller, *Contempt of Court* (Clarendon Press, Oxford, 1989).

Bench is *Dean of St Asaph.*[14] The case involved a prosecution for seditious libel in which the judge directed the jury that their sole function was to determine whether the defendant published the relevant item and that it was then his function to determine if it was libelous. The jury returned a verdict of "guilty of publishing only" which the judge was not prepared to accept, but which Erskine insisted should be recorded in that form. The following exchange took place:

Erskine: "The jury do understand their verdict."

Judge: "Sir, I will not be interrupted."

Erskine: "I stand here as an advocate for a brother citizen, and I desire that the word 'only' may be recorded."

Judge: "Sit down, Sir; remember your duty, or I shall be obliged to proceed in another manner."

Erskine: "Your Lordship may proceed in what manner you think fit; I know my duty as well as your Lordship knows yours. I shall not alter my conduct."

The judge did not carry out his threat of committal and Erskine's conduct has frequently been cited as illustrating the need for an independent and courageous Bar.

E. D. Lloyd and the Kaniva magistrate

Courage shown by counsel in the face of an interfering Bench is also exemplified by the behaviour of the late E. D. Lloyd Q.C. in the memorable case of *Lloyd v. Biggin.*[15] The case is illustrative of the problems which a competent and courageous barrister can encounter when appearing before an irascible magistrate.

Mr Lloyd had gone to Kaniva, which is a very hot part of Victoria during summer, to appear for a defendant in committal proceedings. During the proceedings, Mr Lloyd had asked the magistrate to rule whether he would determine the admissibility of some evidence of a witness then under cross-examination. The magistrate intimated that that was not for him to decide but Mr Lloyd pressed on.

Lloyd: "But your Worship must determine."

Magistrate: "Carry on with your case."

14. (1784) 21 St. Tr. 847. See J. C. Campbell, *The Lives of the Lord Chancellors* (4th edn, 1857), viii 277.
15. [1962] V.R. 593.

Lloyd: "Your Worship, with great respect, I wish your Worship to determine whether your Worship proposes to rule."

Magistrate: "Carry on with your cross-examination."

Lloyd: "I cannot carry on with any cross-examination unless your Worship informs me whether this . . ."

Magistrate: "I have had enough of your impertinence. I have put up with it for two days. You're . . ."

Lloyd: "Would your Worship just hear me?"

Magistrate: "You're fined £5 for contempt of court. If you do anything more I will commit you."

Lloyd: "Your Worship, if you will just hear . . ."

Magistrate: "You're committed. Constable, remove that man and place him in the watchhouse for three hours."

We believe that the constable, who had recently been cross-examined by Mr Lloyd to some effect, thought that that was a splendid idea, but a kindly policeman at the station (who had not been cross-examined by Mr Lloyd), brought Mr Lloyd a cup of tea. This annoyed the first constable no end, presumably because he thought the watchhouse at Kaniva, with the temperature at more than 45 degrees Celsius, was an appropriate place for his recent tormentor.

When Mr Lloyd refused to enter the cells, the affronted policeman returned and complained to the magistrate that Mr Lloyd would not do what he was told. The magistrate's response to that was to tell the policeman that unless he went about his business, he would be committed for contempt too!

Fortunately an inspector from Horsham brought sweet reason to this entire scene, and ultimately Mr Justice Smith set aside both the fine and the committal as having been wrongly imposed.

It is rumoured that at the back of the Kaniva police station there is still a small cairn of stones which bears the inscription "the tomb of the unknown barrister"!

Judges in Collingwood jumpers

More recently Mr A. R. Lewis of the Victorian Bar got himself in trouble by using the following colourful language in addressing the jury in a criminal case:

> "You normally think of a judge as being a sort of umpire, ladies and gentlemen, and you expect an umpire to be

unbiased. You would be pretty annoyed if, in the middle of a grand final, one of the umpires suddenly started coming out in a Collingwood jumper and started giving decisions one way. That would not be what we think a fair thing in an Australian sport. It may surprise you to find out that his Honour's role in this trial is quite different. That his Honour does not have to be unbiased at all except on questions of law . . . [H]is Honour has given some fairly definite views in this case. They have been pretty adverse to the accused Paul and certainly my presentation of the case on behalf of Paul."

The High Court of Australia held that while counsel's conduct was extremely discourteous, perhaps offensive, and deserving of rebuke by the judge, it did not constitute contempt. The court added that "the contempt power is exercised to vindicate the integrity of the court and of its proceedings; it is rarely, if ever, exercised to vindicate the personal dignity of a judge."[16]

Some suggestions

What should you do when you are faced with an antagonistic and antagonised Bench? We do not believe that anyone has ever tried to lay down guidelines for a potential contempt of court situation, but here goes:

1. Present your client's case fearlessly and with vigour and determination but always stop short of risking a contempt of court.
2. When you believe that the manner in which the judge is conducting the trial is preventing your client from having a fair trial for any reason—such as adherence to improper procedures, a flouting of the rules of evidence or a denial of natural justice—you should not get emotional and argue with the judge. Rather, you should ask the judge to disqualify himself or herself and if the judge refuses, have your objections noted and appeal to a higher tribunal at the conclusion of the proceedings. From your client's point of view, it may be better for the court to be allowed to behave outrageously so that you virtually have an order to review placed in your hands, than to behave outrageously yourself.
3. Irrespective of how unreasonable or provocative the court is, the transcript or record of proceedings should not contain statements or remarks by you of which a court of

16. *Lewis v. Ogden* (1984) 153 C.L.R. 682 at 693.

appeal could be critical. There is a vast difference between fearlessly adopting a course of action which you believe to be in your client's best interests and in accordance with the standards required of your profession, and entering into a slanging match with an unreasonable Bench. If you antagonise the court, you do not do yourself or your client any good, even if it does make you feel important. Remain respectful and courteous.

4. Although it is difficult to stand on principle against a magistrate or judge who is acting improperly, niggling and pettifogging to impress clients and onlookers is not the answer.
5. To be in contempt of court more often than not is an admission that you cannot cope with your job as an advocate within the established rules. It is better to let the court monopolise the misbehaviour and allow the appellate court to set it right.

Take the proceedings seriously

You should remember that, as an advocate, you must not only act courteously to the judge or magistrate but you must take the proceedings seriously and have respect for the position of all those involved in the proceedings, including the litigants, court officials and jurors. To wilfully insult, threaten or obstruct any person who is in court and whose presence is necessary may constitute contempt. But even short of contempt, you must refrain from any behaviour that may attract criticism from the Bench.

One of the authors was in court one day waiting for his client's case to commence. The previous case had just finished. The judge awarded the plaintiff damages of approximately $20,000 plus interest and costs. The defendant had appeared for himself and when the judge asked him whether he wanted a stay of execution he replied "Yes, I need a couple of years because I've got no money, your Honour." The plaintiff's instructing solicitor obviously thought this was funny because he burst into laughter. After a lecture from the judge, the solicitor apologised to the defendant and to the court.

We do not think that any discussion on contempt would be complete without reference to that classic Hollywood film *My Little Chickadee* in which Mae West clashed with an obviously corrupt judge. "Are you trying to show your contempt for this court?" asked the judge. "No," said Mae, "I'm tryina hide it."

Other forms of contempt[17]

Apart from the courtroom type of contempt discussed above, there are other types of conduct by lawyers pursuing their clients' interests which amount to a contempt of court. Some of these forms of contempt are discussed briefly below.

Abuse of process

If you abuse the process of the court, you may be guilty of contempt of court. For example, it is contempt of court to forge or alter process (such as forging counsel's signature on a pleading), to convey falsehoods or suppress facts in order to deceive the court (such as instituting proceedings where there is no factual or legal basis for the claim), to misuse process so as to prejudice others (such as issuing double process for the same debt and serving an imitation writ as a joke) and to use process for a collateral purpose (such as obtaining an ex parte injunction to damage the business of a client's competitor).

Obstruction

It is a contempt of court to interfere with the course of justice by conduct such as deliberately preventing originating process from reaching the court and threatening a witness.

In 1773 a man of "ferocious and terrible disposition" was prosecuted for contempt because he forced a process server to eat the court's subpoena. This contrasts with an incident some 200 years later in Western Victoria when a very large and very irate shearer attempted to achieve the exact opposite with a closely furled subpoena which a process server had just served upon him.

Destroying documents

It is a contempt of court to knowingly destroy documents which are relevant to court proceedings such as discoverable documents, exhibits and documents which are the subject of a subpoena.

Breach of orders or undertakings[18]

It is a contempt of court to deliberately disobey a court order or to breach an undertaking given to the court. Breach of implied

17. The discussion that follows draws upon material in M. Chesterman and P. Kearney, "Lawyers in Contempt" (1988) 26 (June) *Law Society Journal* 42.
18. See also above, Ch. 20.

undertakings is also a contempt. For example, breach of the implied undertaking that, without the leave of the court, you will not use documents obtained on discovery except for the purposes of the relevant proceeding, even after they are read out in court.[19]

In *Lewis v. Little*,[20] Young C.J. stated:

> "[O]bedience to orders of the court is essential if our system of the administration of justice is to survive. It is essential to the whole maintenance of our society. Where a solicitor of the court blatantly disobeys and without apology, an order of the court directed expressly to him, it is something that the court must, in my view, treat very seriously."

In that case, a solicitor was imprisoned for 21 days because he failed to observe an order of the court.[21]

Failure to appear in court

A solicitor may be guilty of a contempt of court if he or she deliberately fails to attend court with the intent to hinder or delay the hearing.[22]

Scandalising

It is a contempt of court to publish allegations tending to undermine public confidence in the administration of justice. An example is an allegation that all the judges of a court are corrupt.

In 1900 a newspaper description of an English judge as "the impudent little man in horsehair, a microcosm of conceit and empty-headedness" was held in contempt.

Sub judice

Sub judice is a head of contempt of court which most lawyers have heard of but few understand.

19. *Harman v. Secretary of State for the Home Department* [1983] A.C. 280. See also *Springfield Nominees Pty Ltd v. Bridgelands Securities Ltd* (1992) 109 A.L.R. 685.
20. Unreported, Vic. Sup. Ct, 21 May 1986.
21. See also *Little v. Lewis* [1987] V.R. 798; *Little v. Cornall* [1989] V.R. 811; *Little v. Law Institute of Victoria (No. 3)* [1990] V.R. 257; *Law Institute of Victoria v. Little* (unreported, Vic. Sup. Ct, Tadgell J., 11 June 1991); *Little v. Registrar of the High Court of Australia* (1991) 29 F.C.R. 544.
22. *Weston v. Courts Administrator of the Central Criminal Court* [1977] Q.B. 32. See also *McKeown v. The Queen* (1971) 16 D.L.R. (3d) 390.

In simple terms, once proceedings are commenced, any conduct which as a matter of practical reality has a real and definite tendency to prejudice or embarrass the trial of those proceedings is a contempt of court. Examples include:

(a) publicly stating that an accused facing trial is guilty;

(b) publicly stating that an accused facing trial is innocent;[23]

(c) publishing an accused's criminal record shortly before the trial;[24]

(d) publishing damaging material about a party or a witness who is giving evidence.

A court is more likely to find that the sub judice rule has been infringed where there is a trial by jury rather than by judge alone.

It is not a contempt of court to accurately report or repeat what was said in open court, unless the court has made an order restricting publication of any evidence given in court.

In some jurisdictions there is legislation which prohibits the publication of some material, such as the identity of a victim of a sexual offence.

Lawyers often face a dilemma when asked by the media to comment on a client's case which is before the court, prior to the conclusion of the proceedings. The most prudent course is not to comment at all. You should not criticise or debate the evidence given by a witness—especially if the witness has not completed his or her evidence—or any rulings made by the court. You should certainly not speculate on the result.

It is in order for you, however, to assist a journalist by clarifying who the parties are before the court and to assist the journalist in accurately quoting what was said in court (for example by reference to the transcript).

Lawyers who issue media releases with a view to advancing a client's case which is before the court risk infringing the sub judice rule. If your client employs public relations experts, you should ensure that you vet what they propose to publish.

Remember that proceedings are won or lost in court, not in the media. Therefore concentrate on winning the legal battle in court rather than diverting your energies to fight a public relations battle.

23. *Director of Public Prosecutions v. Wran* (1987) 7 N.S.W.L.R. 616.
24. *Hinch v. Attorney-General* (1987) 74 A.L.R. 353.

Chapter 26

Witnesses

> " 'Give your evidence,' said the King; 'and don't be nervous or I'll have you executed on the spot.' "
>
> Lewis Carroll, *Alice's Adventures in Wonderland*, Ch. 11.

The witness box is a desperately lonely place. Every young practitioner should be given the opportunity to give evidence early in his or her career in order to better understand the difficulties which the average lay person experiences while giving evidence. Under the spotlight of judicial scrutiny all but the most expert witnesses feel as though they are prevaricating or exaggerating while giving truthful evidence.

Indeed, all experienced advocates have had the experience of seeing a case destroyed when they know that their client is telling the absolute truth and the "other side" are lying their heads off.

Because it is the evidence of the witnesses that usually wins or loses a case, it is important for you to do your best to prepare your witnesses for the hearing. You must develop skills that ensure that you get the greatest possible value out of the witnesses' evidence.

Pre-trial conference with witness

Like other trades and professions, hard work and careful preparation normally triumph over spasmodic brilliance. If you are appearing in any court it is vital that you know in advance what a witness is likely to say. Resist any temptation to call a witness unheard, irrespective of how good you are told the evidence will be.

When the witness attends your office for the conference prior to the hearing you should provide the witness with a copy of the statement (or "proof of evidence") which was made originally and then carefully go through that statement with the witness to bring it up to date or to correct any errors that may be present.

There are several ways of holding a conference with a witness whose evidence is likely to be contentious. One is a method of careful reassurance of the witness. With this method, you laboriously go through the witness's proof of evidence and emphasise and prop up those sections which are vital to your client's case. In every proof of evidence there are certain vital points, and questioning during the conference should emphasise in the witness's mind that questions will be asked to bring out those points. The questioning should also assist the witness to decide the best way in which he should answer consistent with the truth.

Another method which is used mainly in criminal matters is to subject the witness to trial by ordeal in chambers prior to the hearing. By this method, instead of a quiet and comfortable conference which is full of reassurances, the witness is asked to stand behind a chair with his or her hands on the back of it and is then vigorously cross-examined. This method can reduce witnesses to blubbering jelly but most of them find that the cross-examination they undergo the next day is pale in comparison.

Whatever can be said for the respective merits of these two differing approaches, the worst way of dealing with witnesses in conference is to read their proof aloud to them and then ask if it is correct. The answer is invariably a nod of the head. It is better to ask the witness to re-tell the story without aid from the proof and put questions based on discrepancies to him or her during the conference. It may be that the first proof is incorrect, or it may be that the first is correct but the questions will re-alert the witness to something that was forgotten. Advise witnesses that there is nothing improper in refreshing their memories from previous statements.

Invite witness to observe other proceedings to gain familiarity

If you remember how nervous you were when you first appeared in court, then multiply that nervousness by one hundred, and, irrespective of the brave front put on by some witnesses, you will know what they are experiencing as they await the hearing. Nervousness is generally due to unfamiliarity with court procedure.

One way of putting witnesses at ease is to invite them into a court well before the case in which they are involved comes on. If they wish, they can sit there for most of the day watching witnesses in other cases being called, sworn, giving evidence-in-chief and then being cross-examined. Your witnesses will probably be more composed when they give evidence after seeing other people go through the ritual.

Some suggestions[1]

Some basic practical points to bear in mind in relation to witnesses are as follows:

1. Outline to the witnesses the basic procedure involved in giving evidence. Tell them that their name will be called, that they will have to come forward and go into the witness box and there take the oath or make an affirmation. You will avoid potential embarrassment to the witnesses if, before the hearing, you explain the difference between an oath and an affirmation. Warn the witnesses that they should not leave the witness box until directed to do so by the court.
2. Always confirm well in advance of the hearing that the witness is available and knows where and when to be at court.
3. Tell a witness that to be effective, the answers must be directed to the people who decide the facts. If you are aware of the physical set-out of the courtroom where the action will be heard, demonstrate where the witness will be required to stand, where the questions will come from and where the answers should be directed. Remind the witness to listen to questions carefully and to request that a question be repeated if he or she is uncertain about what is being asked.
4. It is a constant worry to witnesses what they should call the tribunal. We have heard "Your Worship", "Your Honour", "Your Majesty", even "Your Holiness". For simplicity and to eradicate yet another cause of stress, why not suggest the all-encompassing "Sir" or "Madam"?
5. Some witnesses clearly want to be coached. They have seen enough of Perry Mason to think that you will tell them what you think their answer to a particular question should be. It would be mealy-mouthed to say that coaching does not go

1. See also above, Ch. 16.

on, but only very few counsel will be a knowing party to perjury. The answer to a feeler from a witness as to what should be said in evidence is the time-honoured reply—"I cannot tell you anything but to tell the truth as you know it."[2]

6. Few witnesses are so willing that they will agree to attend court and give evidence to their own financial detriment. If a witness's expenses are to be claimed, then obtain details from the witness prior to the hearing and ensure there is no misunderstanding as to what will be paid. Also ensure the witness understands that it is your client, rather than you personally, who is responsible for payment of witness fees.[3]
7. If you find that a witness in conference is timid and speaks too quietly, the time to tell him or her to speak louder to be heard by the judge and jury is during your conference, not in court on the day. To coach your witness in the manner in which to give evidence in front of a public assembly is to cause embarrassment and distress.
8. If the witness is loquacious, someone who is expansive in answering your questions, try to give him or her practice in just answering the question and nothing more. If the witness is taciturn and answers have to be extracted, try to get the witness to expand the answers in the conference. Experience has shown that it is very difficult to get leopards to change their spots overnight, but at least if you can make the witness aware of what you expect, you discharge your function in trying to assist the witness to give evidence in the best way possible.
9. Try to warn your witness about the old chestnuts which are likely to be asked. A common one is "Have you discussed your evidence with A?". If the witness has, the answer should be "Yes, I have". Point out to the witness that there is nothing criminal or improper in discussing his or her evidence with another witness. If the witness has not discussed his or her evidence with another witness, so much the better.
10. Warn your witness that he or she might not have the luxury of sitting in court and hearing the evidence of other

2. Sir Gregory Gowans, *The Victorian Bar, Professional Conduct, Practice and Etiquette* (Law Book Co. Ltd, Sydney, 1979), p. 73.
3. I. Freckelton and H. Selby, "Lawyers, Hired Guns and Money—Who Pays the Experts?" (1989) 63 *Law Institute Journal* 1163.

witnesses. Also explain the likelihood or otherwise of being ordered out of court and spending a good part of the day sitting either in a draughty corridor or a barren waiting room.

11. Finally, if you have a child or young person as a witness, always conduct your conference in the absence of the parents. It was Mr Justice Darling who once said that the most truthful kind of child witness was an orphan. Interfering parents in conference prevent you getting to the truth, prevent you getting a sneak preview of what the witness is going to say, and leave the child too dependent on outside assistance that will not be available in the witness box.

Which witnesses to call and in what order

It goes without saying that a few good witnesses are far better than a multitude of prevaricating, unimpressive, shuffling and vague witnesses. One of the true measures of counsel is how courageous he or she is prepared to be in evaluating the likely worth of a witness and electing to call one in preference to another. It is just too tempting at times for you to think that your case is being strengthened by having a procession of witnesses.

Sometimes you will be faced with the dilemma of whether or not to call your own client to give evidence. Fortunately, the dilemma seldom arises because invariably you have no choice because you cannot win the case without your client's evidence. Where there is a choice, not to call your client is risky and requires considerable courage. If you feel that your client will make a poor witness and do more harm than good to the case by giving evidence, then you may be tempted to rely only on the evidence of other witnesses.

If you succumb to the temptation and your client loses the case then you will almost certainly have on your hands a bitter and angry client who believes that you cheated him or her because you allowed the other side to win without giving him or her the opportunity of giving his or her side of the story. On the other hand, if you do call your client and lose the case, you may not be able to dispel the thought that the case might have been won if you had been firm and refused to call your client.

Another decision that you must make is the order in which you call your witnesses. Is it a case of best first, or do you leave your best till last? Ideally, if you have two impressive witnesses, a strong beginning and a strong finish suggest themselves. The case of one strong witness and a series of successively weaker witnesses tailing off to a fizzing finish detracts markedly from the strong evidence before the court. Similarly, an assessment of the overall case of your client can be so unimpressive to begin with that no witness has the strength to retrieve the situation.

Decisions such as these are not easy to make. Yet they are crucial because they structure your client's evidence and influence the outcome of the case. Considering the evidence that you have, discarding the rubbish and deciding in which logical sequence you should call the witnesses to prove your client's case, are decisions which can put the stamp of quality on a young advocate, as much as knowledge of the law and articulate presentation.

Chapter 27

Conducting a Case

> "The alternative would be, for example, that a three-weeks old baby . . . could conduct an appeal from its crib placed near the bar table. Perhaps its arguments would not be less persuasive than some that are heard in this place."
>
> *Wallace v. Health Commission of Victoria* [1985] V.R. 403 at 407.

Not many of us are extraordinarily intelligent or wonderfully articulate. If a survey were done of the truly great advocates of our time, it would probably be found that, although many of them have been very good lawyers indeed, the hallmark of their success has been meticulous preparation.

A colleague once said, "I will settle for 100 per cent knowledge of the facts against all the law in the world." Although that may be overstating the position, many barristers who had nothing more to offer than grinding preparation and sheer hard work have not only become silks, but have also reached the Bench.

All of us remember our first court appearance, irrespective of when or where it was. It is of concern that few solicitors, particularly young solicitors, are prepared to try their luck in the local courts. That reluctance in turn has led to few solicitors being even moderately equipped to appear in any of the higher jurisdictions in which they have a right of audience.

Let us look at a practitioner who aspires only to be an advocate in the local court. There are certain basic matters that you should bear in mind.

How to begin

To represent your client properly it is essential that you become familiar with the practice and procedure of the court and the basic rules of evidence as soon as possible, so that you are totally at home in presenting your case and are not worrying about technical matters. No textbook has yet been written which can match the value of sitting in court to watch how a case is being conducted by an experienced advocate. We know of one leading silk who spent the first six weeks of his days at the Bar firmly ensconced in the back row of a Supreme Court watching the then leaders of the Bar locked in heavy combat.

In your early days you should take every available opportunity to go to sit in court and watch how cases are presented. That way you will see diverse styles, a variety of situations encountered and different methods of cross-examination. Not all that you will see will be good. You will see shuffling, mumbling, obfuscation, prevarication and stupidity. But at the end of a few weeks you will become accustomed to some of the general pitfalls that can befall advocates.

Apart from observing trials, you should talk to judges' associates to find out what the case is about and also speak to the barristers conducting it to find out what problems they encountered with the case. Find out why they asked a particular question. Also talk to the instructing solicitors and find out why the case was being presented in a certain way.

Starting out

After you have observed a number of cases, you can volunteer for simple appearance work, for example, call-overs, directions hearings, and consent applications. This is an easy introduction to the court system, allowing you to become familiar and comfortable with court proceedings.

There are a few things to remember when appearing before a court or tribunal:

1. If the court is in session, you should bow to the court or tribunal on entering the hearing room. You should also bow when you leave the room.
2. You should note your appearance by filling in the form or slip provided by the court. Generally, practice courts will first hear applications to which both parties have consented, followed by unopposed matters, and finally opposed matters. Within these categories of cases, unless alternative

directions are given, the order of appearance before the court is determined by seniority, based on the date of admission to the profession. Although it is not a rigid rule, it is a courtesy to more senior members of the profession.

3. When introducing your matter, you should commence by saying "If it please the court (or "if the court pleases"), I appear for the" plaintiff/applicant/defendant/respondent (as the case may be). Be sure to use the appropriate appellation for your client. If you are an articled clerk, you should advise the court of this and ask the court for leave to appear. You should never hold yourself out to the court as a solicitor if you are not qualified—misleading the court about your credentials may constitute a contempt of court.
4. The correct form of address differs from court to court. In the Magistrates Court, the correct form of address is "Your Worship"; in the County, Supreme, Federal and High Courts, "Your Honour" is appropriate. You should use "Master" if you appear before a Master. If you appear before a tribunal then it is appropriate to use the term "Sir" or "Madam".
5. There are a number of rules of etiquette to observe from the bar table. You should always stand to address the court unless the court or tribunal requests otherwise. There should only be one person addressing the court at any time. If your opponent objects to a point that you are making, you should resume your seat until your opponent has finished or the court asks a question of you. As a courtesy to the court, you should not leave the bar table unattended. If you are the last person at the bar table, remain in your seat until someone else arrives.

Checklists

Irrespective of how pedestrian it may seem, if you are acting for a plaintiff in a civil matter or even as a prosecutor, it is essential in your early days that you prepare checklists of the formal matters which you have to prove to establish your case. As the formal matters are put to prosecution witnesses or witnesses for the plaintiff, tick them off. This is a guarantee against being thrown out of court on a "no case to answer" submission by your opponent as a result of some omission on your part.

Although checklists may seem to be demeaning, they are not as embarrassing as losing the case because you have failed to prove a material matter. By all means lose cases on their merits, or even because of your own inadequacies or the inadequacies of your witnesses, but never lose cases because of carelessness or lack of preparation.

Reverse checklists

When appearing for a defendant, list the elements of the case which the plaintiff or the prosecution must prove to shift the onus onto your client. As formal proof is led of each matter, cross them off your checklist. If all the essential ingredients are crossed off at the end of the plaintiff's or prosecution's case, then you have a fight on your hands. If some element has not been proved, then you can submit that there is no case to answer.

Humble cases

As a young practitioner, you should not turn up your nose at what may be considered humble cases such as appearing for a plaintiff to recover the cost of repairing a motor vehicle involved in a collision.

Humble cases they may be, but they involve all the basic elements of major litigation. There is the same analysis of what is required to be proved, the same consideration of the evidence to determine whether it is worthwhile issuing proceedings, the same awkwardness in arranging for uninterested witnesses to go to court and finally a public arena in front of the scrutiny of a magistrate and strangers where you are obliged to think on your feet and to choose the right word for the right occasion.

If you have never appeared in court before, these humble actions are good cases to cut your teeth on. They have provided the basic grounding for many advocates.

Let us look at four aspects of a motor car property recovery case in the local court:

1. You have to prove ownership and thus will need to call a witness who will swear to being the owner of the vehicle. Remember that the driver is not always the owner.
2. You must prove the cost of repairs either by the repairer giving evidence or (where permitted) by an affidavit.
3. You must prove that the defendant was the driver of the vehicle that collided with your client's vehicle and that the collision was caused by the negligence of the defendant. You may need independent evidence to establish negligence on the part of the defendant driver. Apart from asking your

own client whether the names of any independent witnesses were obtained, you should obtain the police report (if any) to see whether the police took statements from any independent witnesses. You should interview and take a statement from as many independent witnesses as possible. If your client was carrying passengers at the time of the collision, you should obviously obtain a statement from them.

4. You should know in advance what your scale costs are so that if you win the action, you will be able to seek and obtain an accurate order for costs against the defendant.

Know the magistrate

Magistrates are very much like the length of your arm. Some are attracted to fine technicalities, others reject them and put a minus against you and your client for introducing them into the argument. Some magistrates are good lawyers but others are not. Some magistrates believe that all police evidence is true, others prefer to keep an open mind. While familiarity may not breed contempt, certainly familiarity with the way in which a magistrate thinks (or doesn't think) is of great assistance when appearing in the local court.

If you find yourself before a magistrate with whom you are unfamiliar, make a point of talking to the clerk of courts and ask what sort of a person the magistrate is. Clerks of court are invariably helpful and a good relationship with a clerk can lead to preferential listing in the court. The law, unlike many other disciplines, is sometimes not a case of what you know but who you know.

A colleague used to say that the first assessment that you have to make is that of the tribunal before whom you are appearing. He saw that as taking preference over a consideration of the merits of the case!

Ordering witnesses out of court

At any stage before the proceedings commence or during them, it is open to you to apply for witnesses to be ordered out of court. The purpose of doing so is to prevent your opponent's witnesses from improving their performance in the witness box after listening to the evidence given by others. The likelihood that your opponent's witnesses will contradict each other is greater of course if they have been ordered out of court.

You should not ask for witnesses to be ordered out of court as a matter of course. Whether or not you should do so is a matter of common sense and nothing else. For example, if in a motor car case you only have the plaintiff as a witness and the other side has four or five independent witnesses, all of whom are adverse to your client, you should certainly seek an order that witnesses be sent out of court. In those circumstances you have nothing to lose. In the reverse situation you would certainly not make an application for witnesses to be sent out as this can only be to your client's detriment.

In a situation where there are roughly the same number of witnesses on either side, it really does become a case of evaluation of your own witnesses. If you believe that they are strong witnesses who are telling the truth and are clear in the presentation of their respective versions of the facts, then seek an order that witnesses be sent out of court. If, on the other hand, they tended to prevaricate in conference and to vacillate, then it would be best to leave the responsibility for the decision whether or not witnesses should sit in court to your opponent.

Opening the case

In the local court, it is essential that the magistrate be made aware as soon as possible what the case is about. The more simply you can outline on behalf of the plaintiff the circumstances of the collision or the nature of the contract, the more sympathetic the response from the magistrate. If you watch a magistrate you will see a look of relief as he or she acknowledges comprehension of what the case is about. The magistrate can then concentrate on deciding whom to believe. Too often young practitioners leave the magistrate to find out as the matter goes along what it is all about.

Of course you will not be able to assist the magistrate in understanding what the case is about unless you have a thorough understanding of the facts. Lack of adequate knowledge of the facts will invariably lead to confusion at the hearing and will give the impression that you did not prepare your case properly.

Remember that cases are made up of facts as well as law. It is like university examinations: there is no point in presenting a brilliant treatise on a particular area of the law if it has no relevance to the question being asked or the case being argued.

You should strive to use simple language and speak slowly. Usually nervousness causes rapid speech. If you have just started appearing in court, deliberately speak slower than you think necessary. The result may then be about right.

Examination-in-chief

Many practitioners find examination-in-chief very difficult. Cross-examination may be glamorous but the competent conduct of examination-in-chief is the foundation upon which cases are won. It is a wonderful facility to be able to take pressure off your own witnesses by guiding them carefully through their evidence. You should have assisted them greatly already in conference, but now is the time to encourage any witness who is timid and to keep a garrulous witness to the point. The conference hopefully has enabled you to form an opinion as to whether your witness is obstinate, facetious, a hypocrite or a liar, and this will ultimately enable you to examine that witness best.

If you have not previously interviewed the witness in conference then your first object will be to gain the confidence of the witness and, for this purpose, it may be advisable for you to adopt a quiet and conversational tone.

The ability to cope with witnesses who do not swear up to their proofs of evidence will always be the stamp of a good advocate. If the missing evidence is important, then your whole case is in jeopardy. There are several ways of dealing with this situation. One is to indirectly suggest the forgotten evidence without asking a leading question. That is probably a delicate operation and one that would rarely succeed.

Another option is to ask the witness to repeat his or her version of what was said in the hope that, this time, the omission will be cured. A further course, which may not always be available, is to ask the witness something which is only explicable by reference to the omitted evidence to direct his or her attention to it. Sometimes, and only sometimes, a magistrate will allow you to direct a witness's attention to a matter that has apparently been forgotten. This exercise is extraordinarily unimpressive.

According to Wrottesley,[1] the whole object of your examination-in-chief is to lead the witness, but to do so imperceptibly. This involves avoidance of obviously leading questions. However, it is amazing how many practitioners really

1. F. J. Wrottesley, *Letters to a Young Barrister* (Sweet & Maxwell Ltd, London, 1930), p. 47.

do not understand what a leading question is. We have seen counsel of several years experience fumbling desperately under pressure from a judge to ask a question which is not leading. Clearly, it has been a case of bad habits developing through the tolerance either of magistrates or opposing counsel, who themselves may not be capable of phrasing a question which is not in a leading form. In any event, there is great pressure upon counsel in examination-in-chief and our suggestion of ticking off the essential elements of the witnesses' evidence is equally appropriate to this problem.

Jacobs[2] makes the following suggestions to an examiner-in-chief:

1. Let the questions be short and clear.
2. Make your examination complete. Before resuming your seat be sure that the witness has told you everything he or she knows that will help your case. Get all the flesh off the bone.
3. Be courteous to everyone—witness, magistrate, and even your opponent.
4. Summarise from the proof you hold from the witness the essential points that you must elicit in examination-in-chief. Examining from memory may be impressive on television, but it has been known to lose cases.
5. Be calm and good-tempered under all circumstances if you want to help your client and maintain your reputation.

Finally, never attempt to mislead the court. It is unprofessional conduct to allow evidence that you know to be untruthful to be placed before the court.[3]

Cross-examination

A Medico-Legal Society paper some years ago was entitled, "Is your cross-examination really necessary?". It is a good question. Whilst the mystique of court appearances seems to be built around the incisive question in cross-examination leading to the destruction of a witness, such is not always the case.

Cross-examination is both the high and the low of court appearances. We have seen remarkable incisive and inspired

2. P. A. Jacobs, *Trial of County Court Actions* (Law Book Co. Ltd, Melbourne, 1935), pp. 86-87.
3. *New South Wales Bar Association v. Thomas (No. 2)* (1989) 18 N.S.W.L.R. 193.

cross-examination win cases. Equally, and unfortunately more frequently, we have seen totally ineffective cross-examination where the witness is virtually asked all the questions that were put during examination-in-chief.

It seems that some practitioners believe that cross-examination consists of involving the witness in a dreary repetition of the evidence which was given in examination-in-chief in the hope that as a result of some mental aberration, the witness will this time say something different. The "search and destroy" approach is far more effective. You should pick out the salient points which you wish to test and direct your questioning to those.

You should bear in mind that the main objects of your cross-examination are:[4]

1. To destroy or weaken the force of the evidence given against your client by the witness. This assumes that the witness's evidence is incorrect or incomplete but not deliberately false.
2. To elicit something in your client's favour which the witness has omitted.
3. To discredit the witness by showing him or her to be unworthy of belief. This assumes that his or her evidence is deliberately false.

In achieving these objects, there is enormous scope for the exercise of judgment. Do you cross-examine savagely or gently but firmly? Some younger practitioners seem to think that it is essential to be rude and to shout at a witness in order to make an impression. However, if a witness is biased, then that bias can be exposed in the gentlest way possible. Give the witness a verbal arena in which to disclose his or her bias.

The ability to cross-examine well stems basically from experience and it is impossible to teach it in this or any other book. It is an area of rough and tumble where you have to think on your feet.

All the theory in the world cannot replace sheer experience. Indeed, someone once said that advocacy is very much like sexual intercourse: to get a real appreciation of what is required, you have to do it. It might be best not to take that analogy too far.

4. P. A. Jacobs, *Trial of County Court Actions* (Law Book Co. Ltd, Melbourne, 1935), p. 89.

Some suggestions for cross-examination

The following comments may be of assistance to practitioners:

1. Except where a case is absolutely desperate, never ask a question in cross-examination unless you believe you know the answer to it. Many young practitioners have been absolutely devastated by an utterly destructive and unexpected answer. The prospects of a shot in the dark scoring a bullseye have lured young practitioners to destructive advocacy. Always cross-examine from the foundation of your instructions and leave litigious lotto to others.
2. Cross-examination cannot be satisfactory unless, upon completion, you are at least certain that you have not strengthened the other side's case.
3. Remember that the first decision to make is whether you stand up to cross-examine at all. Some of the most effective representation on record has been associated with no questions in cross-examination. Never cross-examine for the sake of cross-examination. Always have a distinct object in mind. If the witness has said nothing which is destructive or material or relevant, why take the risk of improving on it? It requires great courage to elect not to cross-examine at all.
4. Always watch a witness's demeanour. The witness's voice, movements and physical reactions to questions are the index and barometer of his or her mind.
5. Never hesitate to allow a judge or magistrate to show how smart he or she is. Who cares who does the winning so long as you win? If the judge or magistrate wants to take over the cross-examination and tear the opposing side's witness to ribbons, so much the better. Stand aside and applaud at the appropriate times.
6. Some practitioners seem to believe that if they ask the same question often enough, they will eventually elicit a different answer. This manner of cross-examination may in fact strengthen the other side's case because as the witness becomes familiar with the question, the answer will be more robust, more certain and the constant reiteration of the answer will become more and more impressed on the minds of the magistrate, judge or jury.
7. Be courteous and do not make unjustified and unnecessary attacks on a witness's credit. The House of Lords has said

"Cross-examination becomes indefensible when it is conducted . . . without restraint and without the courtesy and consideration which a witness is entitled to expect in a court of law . . . Courtesy to the witness . . . is by no means inconsistent with a skilful, yet powerful, cross-examination."[5] Remember that the aim of your cross-examination is to destroy or undermine the witness's evidence—not his or her self-respect.[6]

8. It often helps to ask important questions as if they were unimportant and to let the witness think that you want him or her to say the exact opposite of what you really want to be said.[7]

In an entertaining article entitled "A letter in which Cicero lays down the ten commandments of cross examination", Professor Irving Younger summarised the ten commandments of cross examination as: be brief; short questions, plain words; ask only leading questions; never ask a question to which you do not already know the answer; listen to the answer; do not quarrel with the witness; do not permit the witness to explain; do not ask the witness to repeat the testimony given on direct examination; avoid one question too many; and save the explanation for summation.[8]

Re-examination

The object of re-examination is basically to enable the witness to explain answers which have been given in cross-examination, to correct any adverse impressions that may have been created by those answers.

For example, in a motor accident case, the witness may have admitted that he did not hear your client sound her horn. But he may have omitted to add that he was deaf, or so placed that it was unlikely that he would hear, or that a train was passing close by at the time. All these are matters properly put to the witness in re-examination.[9]

5. *Mechanical and General Inventions Co. Ltd v. Austin* [1935] A.C. 346 at 359, 360.
6. G. Hampel, *Aspects of Advocacy: Cross Examination and Pleamaking* (Leo Cussen Institute for Continuing Legal Education, Melbourne, 1982), p. 11.
7. P. A. Jacobs, *Trial of County Court Actions* (Law Book Co. Ltd, Melbourne, 1935), p. 98.
8. See (1987) 61 *Law Institute Journal* 804.
9. F. J. Wrottesley, *Letters to a Young Barrister* (Sweet & Maxwell Ltd, London, 1930), p. 103.

On the other hand, if the witness not only survives cross-examination unscathed but also manages to score a few points in your client's favour then there may be nothing to be served by re-examining the witness.

Interruptions and objections by your opponent

Some of your opponents in court will constantly interrupt you while you are examining a witness. Such interruptions can take many forms. The most obvious is by standing and objecting to your questions. Some practitioners see themselves as a shield for a witness, a means by which the witness can escape answering a question.

A cagey practitioner will object and make a speech heard by the witness which acts as a warning to the witness in regard to the subject matter of the cross-examination. After the objection has been heard, and presumably disallowed, you should continue, "Now that you have had time to consider your answer do you still say . . .?"[10]

When the going is tough, a cagey opponent may also seek to distract you by either a joke or a physical diversion. This has sometimes been taken to extraordinary lengths. The dropped text book, the removal of a wig, the deliberately spilt glass of water. There was one occasion when a practitioner suggested to his male opponent at the height of his cross-examination that his fly was undone. More often, distractions take the form of monotone muttering from your opponent. There is an easy solution to this. Example:

You: "Mr Smith, how far was your vehicle from the intersection when you first saw the defendant's car?"

Muttered interjection from your opponent: "How would he know? He is as blind as a bat!"

You, sitting down: "Your Worship, my friend wants to say something to the court."

Opponent: "No, I don't."

You, standing up again: "Your Worship, my friend doesn't want to say anything to the court. Now, Mr Smith, how far away was your vehicle from the intersection when you first saw the defendant's car?"

Muttering from the other end of the table: "You have already asked him that one."

10. P. A. Jacobs, *Trial of County Court Actions* (Law Book Co. Ltd, Melbourne, 1935), p. 99.

You, sitting down: "Your Worship, my friend wants to say something to the court."

Opponent: "Oh no, I don't your Worship."

Stand up again, and then so on.

This method is guaranteed to stop the distracting mutterer and allow you fluency in your examination.

All forms of diversion are usually directed to allowing the witness to gain time or to confuse the witness, depending on who called the witness. Sometimes, the sole purpose of the diversion is to distract you from your task. In whatever way you combat such diversions, you should ensure that you are able to steadfastly continue in your line of examination.

Interfering judge

All of us have been confronted by the magistrate or judge who says: "What possible use is there in asking that question?" This raises a fine question of balance, namely the difference between being overweening and being kicked around on the one hand and firmly standing your ground without being impertinent to the Bench on the other.

One temptation is to explain why you are asking the question, which will detract totally from it. It is better to respond to the inquiry from the Bench by saying: "Your Worship, not all the facts have been brought out at this stage. There are many facts in my possession which are still not before the court and the relevance of my question will become apparent as the case progresses." And then proceed with the question.

Keep awake

Finally, whatever else you do in court, remember to stay awake throughout the entire hearing. The United States case of *Favor v. United States*[11] involved an attorney who slept through a substantial portion of the trial. The Court of Appeals' North Circuit held that sleeping counsel was no counsel at all. Judge Ferguson said that although the attorney might have presented an adequate defence while he was awake, his "partial absence" prejudiced the defendant as a matter of law and his conviction had to be quashed. No doubt this result was good news for the defendant but one suspects that the attorney did not look upon the case as a career highlight.

11. 724 F. 2d 831 (1984).

Chapter 28

Instructing in Court

> "Lawyers are persons who write a 20,000 word document and call it a brief."
>
> Popular saying.

For many solicitors, the lead-up to a trial is a very busy, and often stressful, period. Witness statements or proofs of evidence must be finalised, subpoenas must be issued, pre-trial conferences with counsel must be held, witnesses must be notified of the likely time of giving evidence, exhibits and other important documents must be organised, legislation and case law must be photocopied for counsel and so on.

Once all these matters have been attended to, some solicitors wrongly assume that the conduct of the case from that point on is the sole responsibility of counsel and that, as instructing solicitor, he or she can relax and merely observe the trial.

This is a fallacy. As instructing solicitor, you owe a continuing duty to your client to ensure that the client's interests are advanced as well as possible at the trial.

While the actual presentation of the client's case at trial will be the responsibility of counsel,[1] as instructing solicitor you have more than a nominal role. In the true sense, your role is to instruct counsel about the conduct of the case and, where relevant, its settlement.

It is best to see yourself and counsel as members of a team whose energies and skills complement each other in the best interests of the client.

1. See above, p. 86.

Before arriving at court

In order to instruct properly in court, you should obviously be familiar with the facts of the case and the issues that will be argued in court. You should be organised so that you can hand up to the court or to counsel documents that may be required, such as affidavits, exhibits, legislation or reports of cases.

Explain to your client what will happen during the hearing and how it will be conducted. Explain to the client where you will be sitting, where counsel will be sitting and where you would prefer the client to sit. Explain to the client that if he or she wishes to speak to you during the course of the trial, a signal should be given for you to leave the bar table to speak to the client or alternatively the client should pass a written message to you.

Sometimes statements are made by witnesses, opposing counsel or even your own counsel which the client knows are wrong and the client has a burning desire to let you know the true position. The client will be very unhappy if he or she is not afforded the opportunity of being able to communicate with you until the luncheon or afternoon adjournment.

At the start of the trial

On the first morning of the trial, you should contact counsel and the client to ensure that there are no last minute tasks that you should attend to. Sometimes, counsel prefers you to attend chambers to discuss the trial and to then accompany counsel to court. In large matters, counsel will have many books and documents and assistance will need to be provided to counsel to take these to the court.

If the client is inexperienced with court procedures and is nervous about the trial, suggest to the client that he or she attend your office before the trial so that you can attend court together. This is often a reassuring gesture for clients.

You should arrive at the court well before the judge is due to arrive so that you can set up your law reports, exhibits and other documents to have ready access to them when required.

You should also complete any formalities, such as filling in appearance forms or slips and last minute filing of court documents with the judge's associate.

In the unhappy event that your counsel does not arrive before the judge arrives, do not panic. Inform the court that you are the instructing solicitor and that counsel has been delayed. Request that the matter be stood down for a short period while you attempt to contact counsel.[2]

Instructing

Often you are more familiar with the facts of the case than counsel, particularly if you have had to brief new counsel urgently because the original counsel that you had briefed became "jammed" at the last minute with another case. Because of unfamiliarity with the facts, sometimes counsel make statements which are inaccurate. You have a responsibility to inform counsel of the error so that counsel does not mislead the court.

When counsel is examining a witness, a relevant question may occur to you which may not have occurred to counsel. In such a situation, you should discreetly inform counsel of the proposed question. In doing so, you should be careful not to interrupt counsel and disturb the flow of counsel's submissions or questions. The best approach is to write a message for counsel and to signal to counsel to look at the message at the first available opportunity.

During the hearing, take detailed notes of the evidence given by all witnesses, the submissions made by counsel and any remarks made by the judge. Also keep a separate record of all exhibits as they are tendered.

You should record the time the case starts, when it is adjourned for lunch, when it resumes and when it concludes for the day. You should also record the relevant times of any adjournments and the beginning and end of each witness's evidence. These times may be relevant for costing purposes, including calculation of counsel's and witnesses' fees.

Discuss with counsel whether a transcript should be ordered (if transcript facilities are available in the court). Often, transcripts are very expensive. Discuss with counsel whether the benefit of having the transcript justifies the substantial costs that will be involved.

Settlement discussions[3]

It is a fact of life that many cases settle. Some settle at the door of the court just prior to the commencement of the trial. Some

2. Litigation Lawyers Section, "Essential Litigation Skills" (1991) 65 *Law Institute Journal* 1072.
3. See also above, pp. 18, 85.

settle during the course of the trial, particularly after evidence has been given which is damaging to one of the parties or after the judge has made some remarks which may indicate the result of the case.

As we stated in Chapter 15, you should not leave settlement negotiations entirely to counsel. You should actively participate in settlement discussions because your client will be looking to you to ensure that the settlement is in the best interests of the client in all the circumstances.

Drafting terms of settlement

Once agreement in principle is reached to settle a proceeding, it is usual for counsel to draft the terms of settlement.

Solicitors sometimes fall into the error of not vetting the terms of settlement. They authorise counsel to sign the terms of settlement on the assumption that all relevant matters are covered by the terms of settlement and that appropriate releases are contained in the terms of settlement.

While in many cases the drafting of terms of settlement is a routine and uncomplicated matter, inadequate attention to detail may cause enormous problems for you and your client later.

A classic trap for solicitors acting for defendants is the inadequate release. If the plaintiff had a choice of several causes of action but sued only in respect of one cause of action and the release covers only that cause of action, what otherwise seemed a good settlement may turn out to be a disaster if the plaintiff is not precluded from suing on the other causes of action. If you act for a defendant, you should ensure that the release is drafted in the widest possible terms to eliminate any further rights the plaintiff may have against your client arising out of the subject matter of the proceeding.

The drafting of terms of settlement is also important from a taxation perspective. Often, the type of document used to effect a settlement may have stamp duty implications and the description of the payment to be made pursuant to the settlement or the method of payment may have income tax implications for the plaintiff or the defendant or for both. Make sure that you turn your mind to these taxation issues and if you are not familiar with the area, seek assistance from colleagues in your firm who are.

Above all, do not forget your client when finalising terms of settlement. Everyone is usually relieved when a proceeding settles and attempts are made to document the settlement and conclude the proceeding as a matter of urgency. Notwithstanding the desire to effect settlement quickly, you should provide to your client a copy of the proposed terms of settlement and seek confirmation that the client is happy with the terms of settlement.

Do not rely on the fact that the client approved in principle the agreement that was reached; make sure the client agrees with the actual wording of the terms of settlement. This will avoid arguments later that the client was misled about the settlement and did not agree to the settlement actually reached.

Make sure that your client understands the effect of the settlement. In the case of the payment of an "all in" amount to your client, make sure the client understands that no separate amount will be recovered in respect of legal costs and that legal costs will be deducted from the settlement amount. It is important that the client is informed of the approximate net amount that will be paid to him or her.[4]

4. Some Law Societies require that advice be provided to a client who is a natural person of the minimum net amount payable to the client. See, for example, *Solicitors' (Professional Conduct and Practice) Rules* 1984 (Vic.), r. 12(2)(b). See also above, pp. 18-19.

Chapter 29

"From the Bench"

> "Ladies and gentlemen of the jury, I am going to concentrate on the facts. I won't confuse you by trying to explain the law: His Honour will do that later."
>
> New Zealand barrister.

In an effort to obtain another slant on how to appear in court effectively we spoke to several judges who had retired in recent years and requested constructive suggestions for a young advocate. The comments we received were remarkably similar. Although court procedures differ from State to State in Australia and of course from country to country, we suspect the following guidelines might be endorsed by judges sitting in any jurisdiction, anywhere.

Be Punctual

The best way to get a judge offside is to arrive late. To be told by an Associate that "we are waiting for Mr X or Ms Y" is irritating and likely to put counsel at a disadvantage when the case commences. Similarly, for a judge to walk into court to find that the bar table is empty or only partially occupied does nothing to engender warmth from the judge towards the absentees.

One judge likened a young lawyer arriving late in court for his or her case to parking in the boss's car park on your first day at work. If you are asked for an explanation for your tardiness, tell the truth. The "crowded lift" explanation is only effective for one outing.

At least know your name and the name of your client

If instructions are dumped into your lap literally minutes before the case is due to commence, you owe it to your client and the court to seek an adjournment rather than fumble for the facts. Lengthy pauses, fumbling with papers and stuttered misstatements quickly create an atmosphere in which your client could be prejudiced. It is no fault of yours that you have been made a scapegoat for judicial irritation. An adjournment with costs is preferable to wasting the court's time and making a fool of yourself into the bargain.

Know the facts

There are few Clarence Darrows or Patrick Hastings practising at any bar. Initially focus your attention on the facts and know them backwards and forwards. One judge told us of a prosecutor who had appeared before him on a criminal plea who was incapable of telling him which of the circumstances surrounding a series of offences related to which particular charge. In short she was asking the judge to take a guess at the basis for each charge and hence the justification for each sentence. The charges were serious ones and likely to result in lengthy periods of imprisonment. To describe such conduct as unbelievably sloppy is to choose judicially neutral terms.

Don't guess

Young counsel seem to assume that judges know everything. All judges we spoke to conceded how dependent they were on reliable assistance both from the prosecutor and defence counsel in criminal trials and from opposing counsel in civil litigation. If a judge seeks clarification of the case law or relevant statutes and you are not sure, say so. Better irritation from the bench than disastrous reliance upon unstable authority and repealed or amended legislation resulting in an expensive appeal with red faces all around.

Shut up

If it is not your turn to address the bench, shut up. Interjections from the side of your mouth while opposing counsel is on his or her feet or audible conversation with your instructor while your opponent is addressing the court, does nothing to promote your cause. This sort of behaviour annoys the fairest judge.

Know what the point is

In even the lengthiest cases there is a central point. It stands out like the centre of an amoeba. From the moment that you are first instructed to appear you should seek to identify the point or points upon which the case will be decided. All judges we spoke to commented on how often even in the most voluminous material it is possible to identify issues which can be stated on one piece of paper. That identification is the first part of the process of assisting the court to focus upon what the case is all about.

Get to the point quickly

Minimise the preliminary palaver and seek to assist the court or tribunal to understand as quickly as possible what you say the principal point or points are. Once you have focused the court's attention on what you consider to be the live issues you can broaden the scope of your submissions to encompass less important peripheral matters. However your first challenge is to attract the court's attention to a central issue.

The more quickly you can give the court the simplest outline of what a case is about, the more readily you will get the court's interest. Judges pay attention to what they think they can understand.

Stick to the point

Having identified the principal issue or issues and having focused upon them initially it is essential that you not be distracted from them. All judges criticised counsel who ramble on with a prolix argument or submission which relates to a matter which is not in issue or, if it is relevant to the dispute, is so peripheral that it can be conceded by the other side without destroying their defence. From the moment that you are on your feet you should be honing the facts and directing the evidence to the issues as you identify them.

The length of a submission or the duration of the evidence influences only members of the judiciary who suffer from mental anorexia. The KISS principle ("keep it simple stupid") applies equally to advocacy. Remember it is your job to help the judge come to a conclusion, preferably one that is favourable to your client.

Don't tilt at windmills

As a corollary to the above, you should avoid setting up arguments to knock them down. Demolition of these legal windmills is time-consuming and unproductive. Whilst your knowledge of the law might be impressive, what is ultimately relevant is whether this line of argument advances your case in that it is relevant to the principal issue or issues as you identify them.

Minimise the codswallop

There is a fine line between courtesy and sycophancy. A rambling submission liberally sprinkled with "If your Honour pleases", "May it please the court" and similar expressions is both distracting and unproductive. All judges demand courtesy not so much for themselves but for the court as an entity but that can be achieved with the minimum of flourish if indeed that courtesy exists.

Lip-licking subservience from the bar table can prove a significant irritant whilst quiet courtesy can promote a rapport between the Bench and the Bar which can react favourably to the advocate.

Keep control

Screaming, shouting, ranting and histrionics went out with button-up boots. Avoid creating a situation which embarrasses everyone. Except in the case of witnesses who are arrant liars most judges will jump to the defence of a witness who they see being bullied. Once a judge finds himself or herself in a position of protecting a participant in the court process, unconsciously there is an identification with the interests of that witness.

Look like a lawyer

Even where you are ill-prepared or inexperienced, it is essential that you look like a lawyer. In jurisdictions where wigs and gowns are still worn, to look like a drunken reveller from the age of Charles I does nothing for your case. Sadly, a sloppy appearance often signifies a sloppy mind. In those jurisdictions where street dress is worn, regard yourself as part of the court process and adopt a standard of dress which you consider signifies your respect both for the court and for your own client.

Stick up for yourself

Faced with an unsympathetic, antagonistic, even bullying judge, the answer of young counsel is neither abject surrender or an undignified slanging match. The true test of able counsel is to exhibit grace under pressure. This does not mean meek subservience in the face of a belligerent bench. Rather, it means stout resistance but always with a mental eye being kept on the transcript which will ultimately finish in the hands of the Court of Appeal. Let that transcript show that all the outrageous, prejudiced and ill-considered utterances emanated from the judge. Let the transcript show that counsel's responses were courageous but always considered and courteous.

Keep it clean

John W. Davis, in his famous article "The Argument of an Appeal", put forward ten basic propositions. One of these was to avoid personalities. That advice is applicable to any court anywhere. As Davis put it:

> "Rhetorical denunciation of opposing counsel, litigants or witnesses may arouse a measure of sympathy for the persons so denounced. Controversies between counsel impose on the court the wholly unnecessary burden and annoyance of preserving order and maintaining the decorum of the proceedings. Such things can irritate: they can never persuade. Avoid the temptation to translate vehemently opposed legal argument into personal vendettas against everyone including counsel, opposing parties, witnesses, and even the judge who threaten to frustrate your purpose. An advocate who is personally involved is a poor advocate."

Be courteous

Even when things aren't going your way don't resort to discourtesy. Remember that there will be other cases to fight. Judges talk amongst themselves and a reputation earned for irascible and rude behaviour, while easily acquired, tends to attach itself like an albatross to your professional career.

In a nutshell

Be punctual.
Be courteous.
Be relevant.

Be prepared.
Be succinct.
Be honest.

The next time you stand up in court and look towards the judge you might be dismayed to think that all these matters are going through his or her mind as the judge assesses your performance and considers your submissions.

Part 5

Mistakes and Misapprehensions

Chapter 30

Introduction

> "Lawyers, unlike doctors, are unable to bury their mistakes."

Part 5 of this book identifies some of the more common mistakes and misapprehensions that bedevil young (and sometimes not so young) practitioners. The purpose of identifying such mistakes and misapprehensions is to assist young practitioners in avoiding them.

We believe that young practitioners should learn as much as possible from the mistakes of others very early in their career. There will be time enough for them to make their own particular mistakes, but they should not make the same mistakes that others before them have made. Otherwise, there is a risk that some mistakes and misapprehensions will be perpetuated.

Chapter 31 will deal with a wide variety of mistakes and misapprehensions. Chapter 32 will concentrate on mistakes and misapprehensions in property matters and Chapter 33 will concentrate on mistakes and misapprehensions in litigious matters.

The mistakes and misapprehensions have been collated after consulting many senior as well as junior practitioners. They are listed in point form for convenience. Whilst the lists in Chapters 31, 32 and 33 do not purport to be exhaustive, they encompass the mistakes and misapprehensions that frequently recur among junior practitioners.

Chapter 31

General Mistakes and Misapprehensions

> "The English have a low opinion of lawyers until they become judges."
>
> Lord Devlin, *The Judge* (1979).

Clients

1. Giving advice to strangers over the telephone. This is usually unremunerative because you may never hear from the person again and any bills you send to the address given may be returned unclaimed. It is also dangerous because the stranger may sue for negligence if, as a result of instructions being incomplete, your advice turns out to be wrong. The only people you should give advice to over the telephone are established clients.
2. Making an appointment to see a new client and forgetting to take down the client's name, address and telephone number. This is very embarrassing if you unexpectedly have to cancel the appointment but have no way of contacting the client. Alternatively, you will feel foolish if you spend a few hours researching the problem that the new client outlined briefly to you over the telephone only to find that the new client not only breaks the appointment but never contacts you again.
3. Believing that a solicitor is bound to accept as a client any person who consults him or her. This is not the case. However, a barrister is bound to accept a brief in the courts in which the barrister professes to practise if it is marked with a proper professional fee, unless there are special circumstances to justify refusal to accept a particular brief.[1]

1. *Rondel v. Worsley* [1969] 1 A.C. 191.

4. Becoming so personally involved in your client's case that you take all points and matters offensively and aggressively. This "overkill" attitude is unprofessional and may do more harm than good to your client's case by annoying the opposing practitioner and removing the spirit of compromise. You should at all times retain your professional objectivity and detachment.

Family law[2]

1. Using affidavit and other documentary material as weapons for the purpose of insulting the opposing party. Such tactics might win immediate adulation from your client but will not assist your client's case or assist the long-term relationship between the parties and their children.
2. Enlisting neighbours to form part of your client's armoury. While some situations may demand evidence from neighbours, you should always consider whether the value of the neighbours' evidence is outweighed by the deterioration in relations between the neighbours and one or both of the parties to the marriage that might result if neighbours are required to give damaging evidence. You should also take into account whether any children of the marriage would be adversely affected.
3. Failing to warn your client against being over-emotional and placing emphasis on petty complaints when giving evidence. Courts are not impressed by inflammatory, irrelevant and repetitious evidence or affidavit material. You should alert your client to the fact that it is always counterproductive to be overcome by anger, frustration and a desire to get vengeance or inflict harm on the other party to the marriage when giving evidence, especially if questions of custody are involved.

Affidavits

1. Using affidavits to advance arguments rather than present facts. In affidavit material, one paragraph of helpful facts is worth a dozen of argument.

2. The points under this and the next heading have been adapted from J. Myers, "Twenty Common Mistakes Made in the Preparation and Filing of Documents" (1983) 57 *Law Institute Journal* 549.

2. Drafting an affidavit which uses complicated and esoteric language when it is to be sworn by a deponent who, because of lack of education or difficulty with the English language, cannot understand such language. Although it is proper for you to prepare an affidavit for your client, it is your client who has to swear it and accordingly you should use language that your client will understand.
3. Drafting an affidavit which overstates your client's case. This is counterproductive because if your client is cross-examined on the affidavit, it will become clear that it is pitched beyond the truth and this will harm your client's credibility.
4. Not advising your client to check through an affidavit that you have prepared for your client to swear. Apart from problems of perjury and unprofessional conduct, it is obvious that your client's case will be damaged if under cross-examination your client is forced to admit that parts of the affidavit are inaccurate. You should always insist that your client is satisfied of the accuracy of any affidavit you prepare for your client. You should not discourage any suggested changes by your client, even if this might result in inconvenience to you or your typist.
5. Unbinding an original affidavit or exhibits for the purposes of photocopying. Some courts will not receive such documents in evidence because they have been "tampered with" after swearing. You should therefore make copies before binding these documents, whether with a stapler or otherwise.

Guarantees

1. Releasing the principal debtor from a debt when you still intend to sue the guarantor for the debt. By operation of law, a discharge of the principal debtor automatically discharges the guarantor also.
2. Giving a release to one guarantor when you still intend to sue a co-guarantor for the debt. By operation of law, a discharge of one guarantor may be held to automatically discharge all other co-guarantors. Instead of a release, you should execute a covenant not to sue in favour of the first guarantor so as to preserve the liability of the co-guarantors.
3. Believing that if you want to sue a guarantor you need to either sue the principal debtor first or join the principal

debtor in the action against the guarantor. This is not so. However, you will need to satisfy the court that the principal debtor has defaulted in his or her obligations to you before the guarantor becomes liable.

Wills

1. Sending a will to a client for execution without proper advice as to the way in which the will should be executed and witnessed so that it complies with the requirements of legislation relating to wills. There are many pitfalls involved in relation to wills and unless you warn your client what these are, the consequence might be that the will is invalid. Some of the matters you should point out to your client include the desirability of the testator and the witnesses using the same pen and the undesirability of stapling or pinning other documents to the will. You should also warn your client that the beneficiaries in the will should not be witnesses and that no alterations should be made to the will without first consulting you.
2. Preparing a will for a client who proposes to leave part of the estate to a fiancee without warning the client of the danger that the will may be revoked automatically by operation of law upon marriage.

Criminal law

1. Believing that if a client in a criminal matter confesses guilt to you, but insists on pleading not guilty, you should automatically cease to act for the client. The fact that your client has confessed to you does not mean that you cannot defend him or her any longer. You can still present evidence and make submissions urging the court to find your client not guilty. However, the confession imposes some limitations on how you conduct your defence. Whilst you can test the evidence of prosecution witnesses and argue that the prosecution has not discharged its onus of proof, you cannot make positive assertions (such as setting up an alibi) which you know are untrue having regard to the confession. You should certainly not inform the court of the fact that the defendant confessed to you.[3]

3. *Tuckiar v. R.* (1934) 52 C.L.R. 335 at 346.

2. Believing that a client who is on bail need not attend court where it is intended to adjourn the hearing. When bail is granted the accused is released on condition that he or she attends court at the specified time; the fact that an adjournment will be sought does not excuse non-attendance.

Costs

1. Failing to obtain costs in advance from clients you have not dealt with before. The risk is that you will do the work for which the client will get the benefit but the client will not pay your bill. The result will be either that you will have a bad debt on your hands or you will have to sue the client for your costs. Both results are obviously undesirable.
2. Underestimating the amount of legal costs when asked by a client to give a quotation. Estimating costs is not always easy and it may be prudent to give an approximate figure rather than a firm quotation.[4]
3. Failing to take into account disbursements such as stamp duty and bank charges when you cost a file.

Irrevocable authorities

1. Accepting at face value that an irrevocable authority is truly irrevocable. An example of an irrevocable authority that solicitors are accustomed to is a letter from a new client stating "out of the net proceeds of sale of my house, I irrevocably authorise you to pay $2,000 to my former solicitor in respect of outstanding legal costs." What happens if, on the day of settlement, the client gives you written instructions that notwithstanding the previous "irrevocable authority", the entire net proceeds of sale are to be paid to the client?
2. The situation posed in the preceding paragraph gives rise to apparent competing duties on your part. On the one hand, you are obliged by legislation or rules of professional conduct to disburse your client's funds as directed. On the other hand, the latest instructions from your client seek to

4. The rules of professional conduct and practice in your jurisdiction may require you to provide your client with an estimate of costs and disbursements or the method of calculation of such costs. See, for example, *Solicitors' (Professional Conduct and Practice) Rules* 1984 (Vic.), r. 12.

revoke a previous authority which was described as "irrevocable". The question that arises is whether irrevocable authorities are irrevocable as a matter of law.

3. The Law Institute of Victoria takes the view that an irrevocable authority is legally irrevocable only where it constitutes an assignment of the relevant chose in action to the relevant assignee (the former solicitor in the above example). If there is an assignment, your client does not have the right to deal with the relevant funds contrary to the wishes of the assignee. If there is no assignment, however, then your client is entitled to change his or her prior instructions in relation to the fund.
4. The Institute recommends that if the position is unclear in a particular case and you are faced with competing demands from your client and the alleged assignee, you should pursue interpleader proceedings in the appropriate jurisdiction.[5]

General

1. Assuming that there is something unethical about submitting an argument to a court when you believe it is wrong in law. You must obviously advise your client of your opinion on the question but if instructed to put the argument, you should do so unless the case is so hopeless as to amount to an abuse of the process of the court.[6]
2. Researching an area of law you have not dealt in before and acting on your findings without first consulting an experienced practitioner in the area who can give you assistance with the "practical aspects" of that area of law. Often the practice differs from the strict theoretical position. It is sound policy always to obtain a second opinion in your early years of practice. If you think you know the answer to a problem but have some doubt, it is better not to take the punt; you should seek the views of more experienced practitioners before taking any action.
3. Failing to obtain appropriate searches—such as company searches, business name searches and title searches—immediately after instructions are received. Such searches are essential to verify vital facts. For example, if you receive instructions to sue "Mean Machine Pty Ltd", you should not assume that your client has got the name of the company

5. See "Irrevocable Authorities" (1992) 66 *Law Institute Journal* 122.
6. *Abraham v. Jutsun* [1963] 1 W.L.R. 658.

correct or that the potential defendant is in fact a company. If you do a search you may find that the correct name is "Mean Machine" which is a business name owned by "Motorcycles Pty Ltd". Alternatively, you may find that the company is in liquidation. In either of these circumstances you would be negligent if you instituted proceedings against "Mean Machine Pty Ltd" without conducting proper searches. It is better to delay issuing proceedings for such time as it takes to conduct proper searches rather than to issue immediately and then either have to withdraw the proceedings or seek leave to amend if you discover that you have made a mistake.

4. Acting as a post office for a client, in the sense of sending things to your client without adequate explanation or comment. Do not assume that your client understands clauses in documents, such as leases, mortgages and guarantees which you consider to be standard. You have an obligation to adequately explain the provisions of documents you prepare or peruse on behalf of your client before allowing your client to sign them.
5. Forgetting to advise clients who are in partnership that it is necessary for them to notify suppliers of goods and services whenever any partner leaves the firm. Such notification is necessary to protect remaining partners from the possibility of being liable for any future debts incurred by the departing partner purportedly on behalf of the partnership. Such notification could also protect the departing partner from being liable for future debts of the firm. Legislation relating to partnerships prescribes a procedure for notification of changes in the membership of a firm. Business names legislation also makes provision for notification of changes in the ownership of business names.
6. Believing that if you obtain advice from counsel and act in accordance with that advice, you cannot be held liable for negligence. This belief leads to a false sense of security. The fact that you have obtained counsel's advice does not automatically relieve you from your normal duty of care to your client.[7]
7. Failure to recite the Australian Company Number (ACN) or Australian Registered Body Number (ARBN) in all public documents of a corporation as required by the Corporations Law.

7. *Halsbury's Laws of England* (4th edn reissue), Vol. 3(1), para. 424; Vol. 44, para. 136; see also above, Ch. 21, p. 115, para. 12.

Chapter 32

Common Mistakes in Property Matters

"The law the lawyers know about
Is property and land;
But why the leaves are on the trees,
And why the waves disturb the seas,
Why honey is the food of bees,
Why horses have such tender knees,
Why winters come when rivers freeze,
Why Faith is more than what one sees,
And Hope survives the worst disease,
And Charity is more than these
They do not understand."

H. D. C. Pepler, *The Devil's Devices* (London, 1915), p. 38. Quoted in R. E. Megarry, *Miscellany-at-Law* (Stevens & Sons Ltd, London, 1955), p. 54.

Acting for a purchaser of land

1. Forgetting to do a "check-search" at the Titles Office just prior to settlement. You should never rely on an old search but must ensure that no unexpected dealings affecting the land have taken place since your original search.
2. Forgetting to ensure that the purchaser executes the transfer of land before you send it to the vendor's practitioner. This may cause delay in settlement. Make sure not only that your client signs the transfer but also that you send it to the vendor's practitioner several days before settlement, so that arrangements can be made for the vendor to sign it in time for settlement.

3. Failing to lodge a caveat promptly to protect the purchaser's equitable interest in the land prior to registration of the transfer. You should always give careful consideration to whether a caveat is needed. If there is any doubt, lodge a caveat. If your client is reluctant to pay the costs of a caveat, advise him or her in writing of the consequences of not lodging a caveat.
4. Failing to obtain an assignment of the benefit of any guarantee that is associated with a lease over the land your client is purchasing. Often leases have annexed to them a guarantee of the lessee's obligations. If your client is purchasing the land subject to the lease then it is important that your client obtains the benefit of the guarantee. If the benefit of the guarantee is assigned to your client, written notice of the assignment should be given to the guarantor.
5. Failing to advise your client in writing to measure the land being purchased. Your client should also measure the distance to the nearest intersection to ensure that it corresponds to the title plan. Ensure that your client has a copy of the the title plan.
6. Failing to apply to relevant authorities for information about restrictions affecting the land or to explain these to your client.
7. Failing to advise your client about the implications of planning restrictions or requirements affecting the land.

General

1. Accepting a personal cheque instead of a bank cheque or cash at settlement. You must never take the risk that a cheque you accept will be dishonoured. Similarly, when something which is essential remains outstanding when the time for settlement arrives, do not settle on the basis of an undertaking that the outstanding matter will be attended to. It is always wiser to defer settlement until the outstanding matter is actually completed. For example, if you act for a purchaser and there are unpaid rates or other taxes affecting the property, you should not accept an undertaking from the vendor that these will be paid because the relevant legislation normally provides that such rates are a charge on the property and therefore if the vendor breaches the undertaking, your client will be prejudiced.

2. Believing that, as between lessor and lessee, the lessor is entitled to possession of the original stamped lease. In fact, the lessee is entitled to the original lease during the continuance of the term of the lease.[1]
3. Being inconvenienced. If you act for a vendor or a first mortgagee and hold the duplicate certificate of title, you should not agree to settlement being held away from your office. The rule is that settlement takes place at the premises of the person who holds the title. You should not inconvenience yourself out of ignorance.

1. *Hall v. Hall* (1841) 3 Man. & G. 242 at 253; 133 E.R. 1133 at 1138.

Chapter 33

Common Mistakes in Litigious Matters

" 'Let the jury consider their verdict,' the King said, for about the twentieth time that day. 'No, no!' said the Queen. 'Sentence first—verdict afterwards.' "

Lewis Carroll, *Alice's Adventures in Wonderland*, Ch. 12.

Client

1. Failing to communicate adequately with your client. It is very easy to become so involved in an action that you forget that you are acting on behalf of someone else. You should always obtain proper instructions for the steps you take and should give progress reports to your client at regular intervals. It is also advisable to send copies of relevant correspondence to your client so that he or she has a clear idea of what you are doing. Your client may be more willing to pay your bill if you have kept him or her up to date during the course of the action instead of keeping him or her in the dark until the end.

2. Failing to obtain a written authority from your client before commencing proceedings. Although the old view that you are under a positive duty to obtain such written authority is no longer fashionable, it is in your interests to ask your client to give you written authority instead of being satisfied with oral instructions to sue.

3. Failing to obtain written instructions from your client concerning settlement. You should not invite disputes as to whether a particular settlement was authorised. Such disputes are completely avoided if you insist on precise written instructions.[1]
4. Neglecting to advise your client promptly that the case has been settled and to provide details of such settlement. What may be just another settlement to you may have far-reaching consequences for your client and accordingly you should not keep the client in suspense.
5. Forgetting to obtain instructions from your client on unusual expenses or disbursements before incurring them. Failure to take this precaution may mean that you must bear such expenses yourself.[2]
6. Failing to explain adequately to your client the steps that need to be taken and the delays that will be experienced before the case will come on for trial.
7. Neglecting to obtain receipts from your client for documents or other items that you send to your client. Whenever you send important documents to your client, you should list them in your covering letter and enclose an additional copy of your covering letter to be signed, dated and returned to you by your client as evidence that they have been received. Clients sometimes lose documents and then accuse you of misplacing them. A simple acknowledgment of receipt will avoid disputes with your client. The same approach should be adopted whenever you release important documents to other people. In addition, you should keep diary notes of where important documents go whenever they leave your office. In large firms, such diary notes are just as important when the documents are given to a colleague for a specific purpose as when they are given to an outsider.
8. Unreservedly believing clients who at the first interview declare that they will fight the case all the way to the highest appellate court and will insist on having only the best silk to argue the case. You should not be surprised if after further reflection such clients tell you that they do not want to institute proceedings at all, let alone appeal to a superior court.

1. See above, Ch. 4, pp. 18-19.
2. See above, Ch. 7, p. 43.

9. Expecting thanks from your client. Generally speaking, clients involved in litigation fail to respond even to the most brilliant result. Don't be disappointed or disgruntled if you think you have done an extremely good job but your client does not acknowledge it. In most litigation, neither party wins completely. The plaintiff usually receives less than he or she seeks (even if the differential is in the costs recovered) and the defendant usually has to pay something when he or she would prefer not to pay anything at all.

Costs

1. Failing to explain the difference between party/party costs and solicitor/own client costs to your client. Such failure is bound to cause confusion and complaints from your client. The distinction between party/party costs and solicitor/own client costs should be explained to your client at the earliest possible opportunity.[3]
2. Charging a client a full fee for instructing in court when you attend court for only a short while every day that the case is being argued. If you practise as a solicitor, you are only entitled to charge your client for such part of the day as you are actually in court on behalf of your client.
3. Omitting to make an agreement as to costs with the practitioner acting for the other party whenever a case is settled. If you act for the plaintiff and are instructed to file a notice of discontinuance, you should obtain an express acknowledgment from the defendant's practitioner that any agreement reached as to costs is in lieu of the defendant's right to taxed costs pursuant to the rules of court.
4. Believing that if you write a letter of demand on behalf of a client you are entitled to your costs from the other party even though no proceedings have been issued.[4] Generally speaking, costs are not payable unless a court makes an order as to costs. Accordingly, if you write a letter of demand to Jo Bloggs on behalf of your client and Bloggs pays the amount demanded, Bloggs is not obliged to pay you for the costs of the letter of demand. Your client will have to bear that cost.

3. See above, pp. 40-43.
4. See below, pp. 220-221.

Counsel[5]

1. Forgetting about a case once the trial has commenced, on the premise that counsel will take care of everything and your only remaining task is to find out what the outcome is and to send a bill to your client.[6] In very minor cases your absence from court may be excused but, generally speaking, your client can legitimately expect that you will attend court to assist counsel. Unless counsel has been involved with the case during the interlocutory stages, it is unlikely that his or her knowledge of all the relevant facts is as good as yours.
2. Not marking a fee on briefs delivered to counsel. You should always mark fees on briefs. Such fees should not exceed the fee (if any) prescribed by a scale unless you have express authority from your client.[7]
3. Not preparing briefs to counsel adequately to ensure that counsel is given all the facts and documents that counsel needs to complete the task assigned to counsel.
4. Being reluctant to pressure counsel to expeditiously complete work. Remember that your client will hold you responsible for any delays that prejudice his or her case.[8]
5. Not checking documents, such as statements of claim, drafted by counsel prior to filing or serving them. Not infrequently, counsel make mistakes because they have misunderstood the facts. They also get the law wrong from time to time. More commonly, however, there may be typographical errors that should be corrected. Such errors can be critical. A simple perusal of documents drafted by counsel may avoid delays or the need for amendment at a later date.
6. Making substantial alterations to documents such as pleadings that are drawn by counsel and which bear counsel's name without prior consultation with counsel. As a matter of courtesy, if nothing else, you should ask counsel's permission before altering such documents.

5. The comments under this heading are relevant for jurisdictions that have a separate Bar.
6. See above, Ch. 28.
7. See above, pp. 82-83.
8. See above, p. 87.

Court documents

1. Failing to serve copy documents on the practitioner acting for the other party after filing the originals, and failing to file an affidavit of service (where necessary). It should be a standing instruction to your secretary that whenever any documents are served by post, an affidavit of service should be prepared in case it is needed later. If it is too inconvenient to prepare an affidavit of service on every occasion, your secretary (or the person who posted the documents) should at least make a file note of the time, date and place of service by post.
2. Not drafting or completing court documents in compliance with all applicable rules of court.
3. Drafting pleadings in haste without a full consideration of the legal principles involved in the particular case. Too often, this is done in the knowledge that in most cases, errors can be rectified by applying to the court for permission to amend the pleadings. However, you must bear in mind that errors in pleadings lead to expense and inconvenience, even if amendment is permitted. Where amendment is not permitted, the result may be disastrous both for you and your client.
4. Failing to serve a sealed copy appearance on the plaintiff's practitioner. This is discourteous because it puts the plaintiff's practitioner to the inconvenience of having to search the court file with a view to ascertaining whether a default judgment can be entered.
5. Failing to fill in the plaint number of the action on the copy summons or writ being served on the defendant. This causes inconvenience to the defendant's practitioner because he or she will have to make enquiries about the number of the action when filing a document or when contacting the court in relation to the action. When a copy document is "marked up" for service, every detail on the original document must be transcribed on the copy so that in fact it is a true copy of the original.
6. Neglecting to give your client the opportunity of checking documents before they are filed or served. Documents, such as answers to interrogatories, which are sworn by your client should definitely be read by your client. The same practice should be followed for other documents, such as further and better particulars, which you sign on behalf of your client.

7. Failing to ask for further and better particulars when your opponent's pleading is vague and uninformative.

8. Basing your client's claim on one cause of action and not relying on alternative causes of action that may be open. If there is doubt, you should always plead in the alternative. The same applies for the relief sought in the pleading.

9. Failing to ensure that all file copies of important documents are complete. Too often, file copies are made before the original is signed, dated, filed and served. This may mean that you will not be able to determine when a particular document was signed unless you inspect the court file or ask your opponent. Although the phrase "the blank day of blank" is honoured by usage in the drafting of documents, to be obliged to put to a witness that he or she swore an affidavit on the "blank day of blank" is an unforgettable experience!

Interrogatories

1. Sending an opponent's interrogatories to your client and asking your client to supply you with answers without previously checking through the interrogatories to determine, firstly, whether there are any interrogatories which are improper and need not be answered, secondly, whether your client will be able to understand the interrogatories and, thirdly, whether your client can answer them. The covering letter by which you send a copy of the interrogatories to your client should explain what they are and why they must be answered. The letter should ask your client to read the interrogatories and then telephone you to arrange an appointment to discuss them and to formulate answers to such of them as need to be answered. At the interview you must alert your client to the fact that the answers will be in the form of a sworn affidavit and that the truth must be told even if the truth is damaging to the case. You should also inform your client that if he or she is called to testify and gives evidence which is inconsistent with the answers to the interrogatories, then adverse inferences will be drawn against him or her.

2. Assuming that all interrogatories sent to you by an opponent are relevant and proper without verifying that they actually are. This mistake may lead to the consequence that your client will answer questions which he or she is not bound

to answer and thereby provide the opponent with admissions that need not have been made.

3. Sending interrogatories to an opponent before discovery and inspection of documents is completed. Inspection of documents should precede interrogation because the documents may contain information about which you may wish to obtain details by appropriate interrogatories. Alternatively, the documents may give you a more complete picture of the facts which may lead you to suggest answers to some of your opponent's interrogatories which differ from those you would have suggested without the benefit of the inspection.

Discovery

1. Failure to explain properly to your client that all relevant documents in his or her possession or power must be preserved and must be given to you for the purposes of discovery. Clients do not fully appreciate their responsibilities in relation to discovery and the consequences of deliberately or inadvertently omitting a relevant document from the affidavit of documents. These matters must be explained to them. You cannot allow your clients to make whatever affidavit of documents they think fit nor can you escape the responsibility of careful investigation and supervision.[9]
2. Delegating the task of preparing an affidavit of documents to be sworn by your client to an employee who is not familiar with the rules governing discovery. The employee will probably list every document on file without regard to questions of relevance or privilege and this has obvious dangers for your client's case.
3. Using documents obtained on discovery for purposes unconnected to the relevant proceeding. Practitioners are subject to an implied undertaking to the court that, without the leave of the court, they will not use an opponent's discovered documents for any purpose other than the proper conduct of the proceeding on behalf of their client. The implied undertaking subsists even if the documents in question have been read out in open court and have been admitted in evidence. Breach of the implied undertaking

9. *Myers v. Elman* [1940] A.C. 282.

constitutes a contempt of court.[10] The same principle applies to answers to interrogatories, witness statements and affidavits filed or given in a proceeding.[11]

Hearing

1. Attending "callovers" without having all the information required by the court in order to fix a date for the hearing of the case.
2. Not checking the court list regularly in order to keep abreast of the progress of cases and to have adequate warning as to when any of your cases is likely to come on for trial.
3. Not properly co-ordinating the availability of your client and all the witnesses in anticipation of trial.
4. Adopting the attitude that if you act for a defendant, it is proper to allow the plaintiff to unduly delay interlocutory procedures. The view that it is against the defendant's interest for the case to come to trial speedily is not always sensible when you bear in mind that if the plaintiff ultimately succeeds, interest may be awarded from the date of the issue of proceedings on the amount awarded by the court.

Office

1. Not using diary and other follow-up systems to guard against unexpected expiration of time limits for the taking of relevant steps in the litigation process.
2. Failing to retain file copies of all letters, memoranda to counsel and other documents that leave your office.
3. Failing to keep adequate file notes. Notes that you leave on file should be as legible and as detailed as possible. This will make it easier to resolve disputes as to precisely what was said or done on a particular occasion. File notes sometimes are so important that they are used as exhibits in court proceedings. You should also bear in mind that at some stage in the future someone else may be handling the file. That practitioner will not know what is going on if you keep everything in your head instead of preparing informative file notes.

10. *Harman v. Secretary of State for the Home Department* [1983] A.C. 280.
11. *Springfield Nominees Pty Ltd v. Bridgelands Securities Ltd* (1992) 109 A.L.R. 685.

General

1. Guessing what the correct court procedure is instead of checking the rules of court to make sure. Adopting the wrong court procedure will not only lead to personal embarrassment but will cause extra costs and delay for your client.
2. Forgetting to read "practice directions" which are issued from time to time by the various courts and tribunals. These supplement and give practical meaning to the ordinary rules of court. Familiarity with practice directions makes court work more efficient and less frustrating.
3. Failing to verify that the court in which your client is being sued has jurisdiction in relation to the matter before taking any step—such as entering an appearance—which would constitute waiver of any jurisdictional problem.
4. Serving a company with writs and other documents personally. Corporations legislation usually provides that documents may be served on companies by being posted to their registered offices.
5. Taking all threats by other practitioners seriously. In the context of negotiations for settlement, a lot of threats are mere bluff. Over time, you will be able to detect what is bluff. Even if you perceive that another practitioner intends to carry out a threat—such as issuing proceedings—you should let him or her go ahead if you think the action is misconceived because that practitioner will ultimately pay for his or her error.
6. Being diffident about bringing proceedings against another practitioner. If your client has a valid cause of action against some person, the fact that that person is a practitioner should in no way colour your advice to your client. Similarly, if a former practitioner of your client should pay particular costs—such as the cost of an application to have a necessary defendant joined—because they are occasioned by that practitioner's negligence, you should inform your client that he or she can insist that the former practitioner pay those costs.
7. Failing to consider a payment into court or an offer of compromise (where applicable) as a means of inducing a plaintiff to settle an action. These are valuable tactics to consider whenever you are acting for a defendant.

8. Making incomplete disclosure of facts in an application to the court without notice to the other party (ex parte application). Care must be taken when preparing such an application because you are obliged to make full and frank disclosure of all relevant facts to the court.

Part 6

Communication and Drafting

Chapter 34

Introduction

> "Only the law insists on making a 'party' out of a single person."
>
> F. Rodell, *Woe Unto You, Lawyers*. Quoted in E. Kahn, "The Seven Lamps of Legal Humour" (1984) *De Rebus* 251.

Communication is the name of the game so far as practitioners are concerned. Almost every minute of your life as a lawyer will be spent communicating with someone, whether a client, another lawyer, a court official or a government department.

Few occupations stress the need for effective communication as much as law. A surgeon can operate on a deaf mute in the middle of a desert island and the patient will live. A plumber might advise you that your water pipes need replacing and can then proceed to replace them in splendid isolation. But for you, words will be your tools.

You can know all the law there is to know but unless you can effectively communicate it, you will not be a successful practitioner.

You will be a more successful communicator, and hence a more successful practitioner, if the purpose of every word you utter or write is to convey a message rather than to impress or confuse.

Part 6 of this book looks at some aspects of the art of effective communication. The relevant chapters emphasise that the use of clear and simple language, whether in telephone conversations, letters or drafting, is always preferable to technical and esoteric terminology.

Chapter 35

Correspondence

> " 'When I use a word,' Humpty Dumpty said in rather a scornful tone, 'it means just what I choose it to mean—neither more nor less.' 'The question is,' said Alice, 'whether you can make words mean so many different things.' 'The question is,' said Humpty Dumpty, 'which is to be Master—that's all.' "
>
> Lewis Carroll, *Through the Looking Glass*, Ch. 6.

One of the first tasks that you will be required to perform when you commence work in a legal office is to write a letter. It sounds easy but at first even the simplest letter is likely to take you several hours to write. You may know exactly what you want to say but, somehow, the right words will not come to you.

When you finish your first letter and nervously take it to your principal for approval, the chances are that he or she will shake his or her head and tear up your letter. As if to underline his or her disgust, your principal might "show you how it is done" by picking up the dictaphone and dictating "the perfect letter" in no time at all.

You should not get too depressed if most of your early letters end up in the rubbish bin or are radically amended. The fault usually lies with your university course for failing to train you to write effectively. Your task is to educate yourself to write letters that you and your principal will not be ashamed of and the recipients will understand.

Remember that clients and other practitioners will judge your competence by how well you can compose a letter.

Examples of sloppy letters

The following is a letter written by a New South Wales solicitor to an expert who had furnished a report.

> "We thank you for orally telephonically communicating to us epitome of your instant report on Monday 24th August 1981. As predicated to you then, we have pleasure in furnishing herewith our client's cheque in your favour of $250, your nominated relevant fees.
>
> We shall accordingly be appreciative of your provision to us at your early convenience of your engrossed report, together with your receipt pertaining to the said cheque."

Funny? No, sad, if you consider that that solicitor is writing similar letters to members of the public throughout New South Wales.

Particular care is necessary when you are drafting letters to clients who have difficulty with the English language. A thought-provoking example is a letter written by a solicitor to his Vietnamese client whose ability to steer his car fell far short of his skills with the boat that brought him to Australia. The letter was as follows:

> "I refer to my letter of 26th ultimo wherein I enclosed interrogatories for your examination together with draft answers for your perusal, consideration and return. This matter is now one of extreme urgency as the plaintiff's solicitor has threatened to take out a summons to enforce delivery of answers. Please deal expeditiously with this matter."

Presumably the solicitor has still not heard from his client who is no doubt overcome by perusement.

Another problem is that the language used by practitioners in letters does not always measure up to professional standards. A Victorian solicitor once wrote a letter to a debtor who owed his client money which began, "You rude illiterate Teutonic peasant."

Perhaps one up on even that effort was a letter by an English solicitor to his client which said, in part, "You are a sinister little creature, a poisonous creature—an offensive little wretch." The English solicitor was held to be guilty of conduct unbefitting a solicitor.[1]

1. The Law Society, *A Guide to the Professional Conduct of Solicitors* (The Law Society, London, 1974), p. 81. See also Law Society, *The Guide to the Professional Conduct of Solicitors* (Law Society, London, 1990).

Clinging to literary lifebelts

Almost as a response to an uncertainty in expression, some practitioners tend to rattle off meaningless pieces of jargon, and sentences choked to death by cliches.

Because of their inexperience, many young practitioners tend to follow closely precedents for correspondence. They tend to treat precedents as literary lifebelts to which they cling desperately when trying to think of a way of communicating. The unfortunate result is that the errors and pomposity of the past go on from one generation to another without any real questioning of the necessity of the language or the meaning intended.

More experienced practitioners will not look upon unsatisfactory letters with much favour. A practitioner once responded to an overlengthy letter putting an offer of settlement on behalf of a client with the following:

> "Dear Sir,
>
> *Smith & Jones*
>
> NO
>
> Yours truly,"

Cut out unnecessary verbiage

If you take a little care in choosing your words you will probably realise that many words which are fashionable in the profession are merely surplusage. Let us look at an example:

> "Dear Sir,
>
> *Re Smith ats Jones*
>
> I acknowledge receipt of your letter of 26th instant. I wish to advise that I have this day prepared draft answers to interrogatories, a copy of which is enclosed herewith for your perusal and return.
>
> Yours faithfully,"

But why not:

> "Dear Mr Smith,
>
> *You and Jones*
>
> Thank you for your letter of 26 June. Enclosed is a copy of the draft answers to the questions you were asked, which I

prepared today. Would you please check them and send them back soon?

Yours sincerely,"

Let us look at the first letter in detail:

1. "Re Smith ats Jones". Why "Re"? The word is superfluous when followed by "Smith ats Jones". If the letter is headed with the title of its subject matter, surely that is what it is about. Give your typist a break and leave out "Re". "You" is more personal than "Smith": your client already knows his name!
2. "ats"—Is this part of a lawyer's secret code? There is no need to resort to secret codes. Use words that the recipient of your letter will understand.
3. "I acknowledge receipt of your letter." One wonders at the cost to the legal profession of secretaries in legal firms typing "I acknowledge receipt of". If you are acknowledging the document, surely then you must have received it. "I acknowledge" is right, "receipt of" is unnecessary. "Thank you for your letter of 26 June" is not only more personal, but probably gives the recipient the impression that a person is writing the letter and not a machine. Of course "thank you" is not always appropriate. For example, it would be inappropriate to write "Thank you for your letter of 26 June demanding $20,000 from me". In that case, try "I have", "I acknowledge", "I refer to" or "I received".
4. "26th instant"—This is formal and stiff. "26 June" is clearer and simpler.
5. "wish to advise"—This is mere verbiage. If you did not wish to advise you would never have written in the first place.
6. "this day"—This is pompous and stilted and more suitable for an age of high stools and quills. Why not "today"?
7. "enclosed herewith"—Where else would the document be enclosed?
8. "for your perusal." Who peruses these days? "Perusal" lends itself to legal posing, not easy communication. There are simpler words that can be used in its place.

Some suggestions

1. Think before you write. Organise the structure of your letter before you start writing.

2. Accept the challenge of writing in plain English by finding simple alternatives to the jargon and cliches that have been used in legal offices for years. Compare the following alternative letters which are used as examples in a booklet on plain English that was published by the Victorian government:

   "Sir, it is desired to acknowledge receipt of your letter of the 4th August, in which you requested advice of the progress of the consideration of your application for the issuance of a licence under section 40A of the regulations administered by this Department. It has been ascertained that consideration of the application has not been finalised; however it is anticipated that advice of the decision reached will be despatched to you not later than seven days after date hereof.

   Yours faithfully,"

   "Dear Mr Watson. You wrote to us on 4 August about your licence application. We have a little more work to do but expect to let you know the result within a week.

   Yours sincerely,"

3. If you are writing to a client, write the type of letter that you would like to receive if you were the client. For the preservation of a good practice it is essential that you minimise the frustration, dissatisfaction and unease that you can cause to your client by cumbersome legalistic letters. You will also reduce the number of telephone calls you get from clients asking you to explain what your letters mean!
4. A good example of a letter that practitioners often send is: "We have searched the title and found that it is unencumbered, save for a mortgage to the X Bank which will be discharged at settlement." Even the most junior practitioner would understand such a letter but are you sure that your client knows what the words "searched", "title", "unencumbered", "discharged" and "settlement" mean?
5. Remember that a letter is a permanent way of communicating a view, a fact or a suggestion. Make the letter say exactly what you want to convey to the recipient. Once a letter is written and sent, you cannot change it. Therefore get it right.
6. Apart from increasing your client's confidence and satisfaction, writing clearly and simply may also protect you

from professional negligence. In England, a firm of solicitors was ordered to pay around $220,000 to a client because of a "disastrous" letter of advice that the judge described as written in "very obscure" English.[2]

7. Wherever possible use short sentences and paragraphs. Experts suggest that 20 to 25 words is a good sentence length,[3] although some flexibility is required. Keep one idea to a sentence. Write as briefly as the material will allow, and where appropriate, use paragraph headings. Remember that people associate a muddled letter with a muddled mind.

   One of the authors still has a letter from a practitioner which contains the longest sentence that he has ever encountered. The sentence, which is 347 words long, demonstrates the love affair which existed between the practitioner and his dictaphone. His secretary was not heavily into full stops and the result was that nine similar sentences would have constituted an essay for university purposes in any faculty. However, this example pales in comparison to the unpunctuated sentence of over 450 words referred to by Stephen J. in *National Bank of Australasia Limited v. Mason*,[4] and the single sentence of 722 words found in a covenant by the Law Foundation Centre for Plain Legal Language.[5]

8. Wherever possible, use the active voice rather than the passive voice. It helps you to be far more positive, definite and specific. It is better to write "The cow jumped over the moon" than "The moon was jumped over by the cow"!

9. Use simple words: "buy" not "purchase"; "sign" not "affix your signature"; "if" not "in the event of"; "allow" not "afford an opportunity"; "because" not "by virtue of the fact that"; "second last" not "penultimate"; "about" not "in relation to" or "in respect of"; "near" not "imminent"; "use" not "utilise"; "happen" not "eventuate". In particular, the phrase "in relation to" must win the prize as the most overused in legal correspondence.[6]

2. P. Macalister, "Eliminating Legalese—New Body to Clear the Fog from Legal Documents" (1992) 30 (February) *Law Society Journal* 77 at 80.
3. E. Kerr, "Plain Language: Is It Legal?" (1991) 29 (June) *Law Society Journal* 52 at 55; M. M. Asprey, *Plain Language for Lawyers* (The Federation Press, Sydney, 1991), p. 75.
4. (1975) 133 C.L.R. 191 at 203.
5. P. Macalister, "Eliminatng Legalese—New Body to Clear the Fog from Legal Documents" (1992) 30 (February) *Law Society Journal* 77 at 79.
6. M. M. Asprey, *Plain Language for Lawyers* (The Federation Press, Sydney, 1991), provides a useful chapter on plain language vocabulary.

10. Even when working under pressure, you should resist the temptation to use familiar phrases unless you are sure they mean exactly what you want to say. It is a great discourtesy to send a precedent letter that is inappropriate to the person to whom it is sent.

11. Write as directly as you can. It is better to say "I am sorry" than "It is regretted".

12. Write as accurately as possible. Make sure that you have checked all the facts. Simplicity is a desirable quality but you should not take it to such an extent that your letter becomes inaccurate or misleading.

13. On the quarantine list of words which should never be touched are, "aforesaid", "albeit", "before-mentioned", "said", "hereintofore" and "hereinafter".

14. Never write a letter in anger and post it on the same day. Some of the best (or worst) letters we have ever written never saw the inside of a letter box. If you are so angry that you feel you will burst if you do not write something down, put something in writing and then leave it aside for a couple of days. It is odds-on that when you again look at the letter you will be embarrassed by its contents and a much more conservative form of letter will be sent.

15. Slanderous statements, no matter how justified in your belief, usually aggravate rather than improve a situation. They may also constitute unprofessional conduct.[7] We recommend that you seek advice from a dispassionate colleague before launching a brilliant offensive or sending an acrimonious reply.

16. The actual style of a letter to a client should take into consideration the ethnic background, education and intellect of the particular client. The tone and formality of the letter should be specifically geared to the client.

17. If you must use standard letters which are spat out by a word processor, make sure that they are informative and are suitable to the circumstances of the particular client. If, for example, after winning a case for a client you are advised that the client does not wish to enforce the judgment, there is no point in sending a standard letter to the effect:

7. See, for example, *Horak v. Secretary of the Law Institute of Victoria* (unreported, Vic. Sup. Ct, Phillips J., 18 October 1991).

> "Now that judgment has been entered in your favour, the following options are open to you in enforcing judgment . . ."

18. Similarly, if you write a lengthy letter of advice to one client and then discover that other clients require the same advice, you should make sure that the name and address of the first client is changed not only on the envelope and first page, but also on the top of each subsequent page and elsewhere in the body of the letter. It will be extremely embarrassing for you if client X receives a letter commencing with "Dear X" and halfway through the letter the client is referred to as "Y", particularly if "Y" is a competitor.
19. Never sign a letter you have dictated without first reading it. Unfortunately, the foibles of secretaries are not limited to embarrassing spelling mistakes: sometimes they leave out words or even paragraphs, or do something else to a letter that completely alters its intended meaning. A common mistake made by secretaries is to omit the word "not"—an omission that can be disastrous. Similarly, "not" is sometimes supplanted by its mischievous third cousin "now". If confusion or misunderstanding or even litigation arises from your letter, you will not be able to hide behind your secretary. The alternative to reading your letters is to provide a standard last paragraph. "Dictated but not read or signed by the writer" and to instruct your secretary to sign your letters. However, this is no solution at all. Apart from the discourtesy which can be involved to a recipient of such a letter, the dangers of such a practice are obvious. We have all come across letters signed by secretaries in the practitioner's absence which contain hidden pearls such as "our client claims the sum of (Julie please look up this amount and insert)"!
20. Be polite and, where appropriate, pleasant in your correspondence. It is rare, if ever, that an abusive letter is called for. Whenever you write, you should bear in mind the following words of Lord Denning:

> "It [is] unbefitting conduct for a solicitor to write offensive letters to clients of other solicitors, to government departments and to the public. The use of insulting language and indulging in acrimonious correspondence is neither in the interests of the client nor conducive to the maintenance of the good name of the profession."[8]

8. *Weston v. CCC Courts Administrator* [1977] Q.B. 32 at 43.

21. Do not resort to Latin or other foreign phrases in your correspondence. You will not impress anyone, and will probably cause confusion and misunderstanding. It is also more likely than not that your foreign phrases will be inappropriate in the context of your letter so that you will embarrass yourself. As Fowler puts it: "The display of superior knowledge is as great a vulgarity as the display of superior wealth."
22. Although formal references to judicial decisions may be appropriate in correspondence to other lawyers, it is often not appropriate to send to clients letters containing extensive case citations.
23. Writing in plain English can also save you money. Writing simply often means fewer words which means less for your secretary to type and less for you to proofread. Moreover, there is evidence to suggest that the time taken to comprehend documents written in plain English is much less than that taken to read traditional legal text. The results of a study commissioned by the Law Reform Commission of Victoria demonstrated that lawyers were able to comprehend more quickly plain English versions of legislation than the original legislation.[9]
24. There are many advantages in plain English writing. You will deliver better service to your clients. Your clients and colleagues will respect your communication skills and will be better able to appreciate your legal skills. And you will assist in demystifying a profession that has long been unintelligible to the general public.

The above suggestions are simple and sensible. You should adopt them very early in your career, otherwise you will fall into the habit of using jargon like many practitioners before you. Eventually, it may become too late for you to change your ways and write simply and directly.

9. Victorian Law Reform Commission, *Plain English and the Law*, Report No. 9 (1990 reprint), pp. 69-70.

Chapter 36

Letters of Demand[1]

> "Woe unto you also, ye lawyers! for ye lade men with burdens grievous to be borne, and ye yourselves touch not the burdens with one of your fingers."
>
> *The Holy Bible*, Luke, Ch. 11, v. 46.

Letters of demand before the commencement of proceedings create two main problems—first, whether you should write one at all, and secondly, if you do write one, how much you should say.

Is a letter of demand necessary?

There was a time when a letter before action was regarded as essential, almost a work of art. The past 20 years have seen its gradual decline. More and more, letters of demand are treated as unnecessary formalities and are restricted to cases where it is hoped that the letter itself will "do the trick" and that litigation would become unnecessary.

There are, however, some areas where letters of demand are very useful. For some types of personal injuries claims, insurers are often willing to negotiate with an injured claimant on the basis of a letter of demand, a tendered medical report and a medical examination by a doctor nominated by the insurer.

In deciding whether a letter of demand is necessary, ask yourself: "In this particular matter, is it reasonable to think that some practical benefit can be gained for my client if a letter of demand is written?" You should also ask yourself whether your letter of demand is designed to induce a settlement, or whether it is a preliminary to litigation and nothing else.

1. Some parts of this chapter are adapted from P. A. Jacobs, *Trial of County Court Actions* (The Law Book Co. Ltd, Melbourne, 1935), pp. 12-14.

Some reasons for not writing a letter of demand could be:

1. The history of the matter indicates that the letter will be pointless.
2. The nature of the action—such as an action for serious and unprovoked assault and battery—renders the letter inappropriate.
3. The letter will waste time by committing you to await an answer for a fixed period, when time is important.
4. The letter will disclose your client's hand.
5. The letter will be seen as a sign of weakness.
6. Because of urgency, there is no time to send a letter of demand.
7. Where prior notice would enable the defendant to take such steps as would render the action useless.[2]

Arguments in favour of sending a letter of demand could be:

1. The letter may bring about a speedy resolution of the dispute.
2. The absence of the letter may affect your client's entitlement to costs if proceedings are issued.[3]
3. The letter is a relatively inexpensive way of achieving a basis for negotiations.

Some practitioners believe that it is always advisable to send a letter of demand because the response you get to it may disclose deficiencies in your instructions. For example, you may discover that the potential defendant is dead, or is not incorporated, or has been wound up, or has a different name to the one your client told you, or has permanently gone overseas, or has changed address and his or her whereabouts are now unknown.

Such information would obviously be useful in advising your client about the available options. Issuing proceedings without first sending a letter of demand may prove embarrassing for you and costly for your client.

In a libel action, it is generally advisable before issuing proceedings to write a letter giving the defendant an opportunity to withdraw and apologise for the defamatory statement.

2. *Walter v. Steinkropff* [1982] 3 Ch. 489.
3. *Re the Estate of Lucas (dec'd)* (1895) 1 A.L.R. 61. See also S. Williamson "Initiating Proceedings without Notice to the Defendant" (1990) 64 *Law Institute Journal* 914.

Whether or not you will ask for damages as well depends upon the circumstances. The letter will show that the plaintiff does not aim solely at making money out of the libel but seeks vindication of his or her character. There is also the advantage that if the defendant refuses to accept an olive branch, his or her conduct may aggravate the damages to be awarded.

Threats in a letter of demand

You must be careful about what you say in a letter of demand. For example, it is unethical for you to threaten that criminal proceedings will be taken if civil redress is not obtained: *Re Chubb.*[4] In that case, Mr Chubb, a solicitor, was censured by the court "for his foolish and ignorant conduct" in writing a letter to a person who was indebted to his client in which he threatened that criminal proceedings would be instituted if the debt was not paid.

Similarly, a practitioner named Swanwick was struck off the roll of practitioners for writing a letter on behalf of a client in which he threatened to prosecute the addressee for selling adulterated flour and to "advertise" what the addressee had done throughout the colony of Queensland.[5]

In another case, a solicitor wrote to his client's opponent and threatened to have him attached if his costs were not paid. The solicitor was not only censured by the court but was also fined and suspended from practice.[6]

The Law Society of New South Wales ruled in 1991 that in connection with the recovery of moneys or damages it will regard as unsatisfactory professional conduct the sending of a letter by a solicitor to a third party on behalf of a client which threatens criminal proceedings as an alternative to available civil redress. The Law Society has also held that it is improper to threaten someone with no legal liability to pay an alleged debt, such as the spouse or parent of an alleged debtor.[7]

Stories abound about letters of demand. One of our favourites is about the articled clerk who, when told to write a letter by his principal, and given a rough precedent, wrote:

4. (1887) 3 Q.L.J. 35.
5. *Re Swanwick* (1883) 1 Q.L.J. 117.
6. *Re Fanker* (1913) 30 W.N. (N.S.W.) 39.
7. "Letters of Demand Threatening Criminal Proceedings" (1992) 30 (February) *Law Society Journal* 37.

"We have been consulted by Mr X of . . . who is owed $1,000 by you in respect of goods sold and delivered. Unless we receive the sum of $1,000 together with our costs within 14 days, we will take such action as will amaze you."

Do not take letters of demand too lightly. The receipt of a letter of demand is often a person's first contact with the profession, the law and the legal system. Ensure that your letters of demand are reasonable and do not become the subject of a complaint to your Law Society. Such a complaint will distract you from representing your client properly. The allegations against you may put you on the back foot and make it more difficult for you to negotiate a good settlement for your client if your own conduct is under a cloud.

Make your letters of demand brief, courteous and temperate. It is seldom necessary to go into any details. There is no need to disclose names and addresses of witnesses. Why submit your brief to the other side?

Claiming costs in a letter of demand

In the absence of a contractual right, there is no basis for enforcing payment of legal costs in addition to the amount owing to the client without the issue of proceedings. Notwithstanding this principle, it is not uncommon for letters of demand to contain a claim for costs.

There are differences of opinion on whether a claim for costs in a letter of demand is proper. Several Law Societies have ruled that a solicitor should not claim the costs of a letter of demand.

In 1973 the English Law Society ruled that a solicitor should not demand costs in a letter of demand because "it cannot be said the costs of the letter are properly recoverable in law".

The Law Society of New South Wales has ruled that in circumstances where there is no contractual obligation on a debtor to pay the legal costs of the creditor before action, no demand, request or application for payment shall be made.[8]

Similarly, the Law Society of Western Australia has ruled that it is not in the interests of the profession or proper that a solicitor should claim costs in a letter of demand.

A claim for the costs of a letter of demand has always been accepted in Victoria. The Law Institute of Victoria maintains the

8. *New South Wales Solicitors Manual*, para. 12191.

view that damages include the costs (such as costs of a letter of demand) expended by a proposed plaintiff in asserting his or her right to compensation. In an article in January 1993, the Institute stated:

> "Solicitors must take care in the manner in which costs on the letter of demand are claimed having regard to the best interests of the client.
>
> A solicitor must be careful not to:
>
> 1. ask for costs that are unreasonable or excessive in the circumstances;
> 2. frame the letter in terms that might be considered threatening or otherwise unlawful, deceptive or misleading within the meaning of the *Crimes Act* or the *Trade Practices Act*; or
> 3. allow the letter to be in an inappropriate form.
>
> Without in any way seeking to be definitive, suggested versions of a claim for costs in a letter of demand might be:
>
> (a) ". . . together with legal costs of $. . . occasioned by your default";
>
> (b) ". . . together with $. . . legal costs occasioned by your failure to pay the said sum"; or
>
> (c) ". . . our client's legal costs to date which we assess at $. . .".
>
> Care should be taken not to imply that proceedings will be issued if the costs claimed in the letter of demand are not paid.
>
> Therefore it is better for a solicitor to say "If my client's claim is not satisfied within seven (7) days, I am instructed to issue proceedings claiming the amount owing to him and costs," rather than to say ". . . should your total payment of $1,100.00 (which sum includes the legal costs requested) not be received at this office within seven (7) days, legal proceedings will be issued without further notice and at your expense."[9]

An interesting question arises if the costs claimed are excessive or unjustifiable on any view. A situation could possibly be reached where a letter of demand amounts to a form of extortion.

9. See (1993) 67 *Law Institute Journal* 146-147.

Without prejudice

Never head a letter of demand "without prejudice" because if proceedings ensue, you may need to rely on it. The consequence of heading the letter "without prejudice" is that neither the letter nor the answer to it can be used in evidence. Letters of demand provide an opportunity for creating evidence in your own favour; you will be defeating their purpose if you head them "without prejudice".

The words "without prejudice" are discussed further below, in Chapter 39.

Replying to a letter of demand

If your client receives a letter of demand, your response to it will obviously depend on your instructions. Sometimes it is advisable not to do anything in order to see whether any threats contained in the letter of demand are actually carried out. Often, letters of demand are written on the off-chance that your client will pay, without any intention of commencing proceedings if no payment is made.

You should note, however, that in certain circumstances the failure to answer a letter of demand may amount to an admission of its correctness.[10]

If your client intends to defend any proceedings that are issued it is better not to give too much away; an appropriate letter might say tersely "In reply to your letter of . . . my client denies liability."

On the other hand if your client intends to admit the claim, you should send a reply to that effect as soon as possible before any proceedings are commenced. You should seek to take advantage of the rule that where a defendant has offered to the plaintiff the substance of the relief sought before proceedings are issued then the plaintiff may be deprived of the right to costs.[11]

10. See *Thomas v. Hollier* (1984) 156 C.L.R. 152 at 157 per Gibbs C.J.; "Effect of Failure to Reply to a Letter of Demand" (1986) 60 *Australian Law Journal* 194.
11. *Jenkins v. Hope* [1896] 1 Ch. 278.

Chapter 37

Telephone

> "Once there was an elephant
> Who tried to use the telephant
> No! No! I mean an elephone
> Who tried to use the telephone."
>
> Laura Elizabeth Richards. Quoted in J. Bartlett, *Familiar Quotations.*

The telephone has come to tyrannise practitioners and one wonders whether somewhere in a law course there should be some rudimentary instruction in its use.

Some suggestions

Rudimentary instruction in the use of the telephone would include the following points:

1. When making a call, announce who you are, where you are from and in relation to what matter you are calling. Do not go to the substance of your call without introducing yourself first.
2. If you instruct your secretary to call someone for you, make sure you are immediately available to take the call when the other person answers. As you are the caller, it is discourteous to keep the other person waiting. It may well be more efficient for you to make all your own telephone calls.
3. You should never begin another call whilst waiting for the telephonist to connect you with a number you have requested.
4. If you are in the office but unable to take a telephone call, try to encourage your secretary or receptionist to avoid phrases such as "He is unavailable" or "She is too busy".

Within reasonable bounds, encourage your secretary to give the true reason why you cannot take the call at that time. However, the line must be drawn somewhere and we suggest that a day at the races or a quick eighteen holes should remain confidential information!

5. As the receiver of calls, try to ensure that your staff only ask for information about the incoming call when the information is useful and relevant. For a caller to be asked his or her name, address, telephone number and reason for calling on three separate occasions—first by the receptionist, then by your secretary and finally by you—is both time consuming and discourteous.

Rudeness over the telephone

Some practitioners are offensive, bullying and generally unpleasant over the telephone. They may be called "telephone heroes". It is interesting that although this group exists in the metropolitan area, its numbers are almost non-existent in the country. Does this mean that country practitioners are more gracious and accommodating? Probably not.

The real reason for the rudeness stems from the anonymity of it all. In the city, names are just names and practitioners can deal with each other almost daily without ever meeting. Behind that sort of anonymity, rudeness is easy. It is a totally different situation when practitioners have to meet in the street and confront one another eyeball to eyeball.

You should always resist the temptation of becoming angry or abusive during telephone conversations.

Winning a case over the telephone

You will no doubt be confronted from time to time by practitioners who endeavour to win their cases over the telephone by attempting to bludgeon you into submission. Such practitioners will argue forcefully that your client's case has no merit and will expect you to capitulate immediately.

Our experience has been that practitioners who wish to prolong conversations about the merits of their case usually have plenty to worry about. When a practitioner tends to enthuse too much about a client's cause of action, it is best to respond by saying: "Well, since your case is so strong, you obviously don't want to negotiate so I will see you in court". The reply is often interesting.

The converse situation, when you are confronted by a practitioner acting for a defendant who virtually accuses you of maintenance in pursuing a worthless cause of action is not much different. Faced with a verbal battering from the practitioner on the other side, a brisk, "Well, we'll let the court decide" is usually effective.

Without prejudice

Whether or not conversations by telephone are without prejudice has led to a number of disputes between practitioners. Often the problem arises as a result of a "mixed conversation", that is, a conversation which is partly an open conversation and partly "without prejudice". The ideal is to make a conversation by telephone either one thing or the other.

Just as it is advisable not to write a letter which is partly without prejudice and partly open, so it is better to separate your telephone calls, one totally protected with the words "without prejudice", the other an open discussion. If a telephone conversation is to be without prejudice, the words should not be used as an almost apologetic aside, but they should preface in the clearest terms any offer to settle or negotiate.

A note should always be made of telephone conversations; in the case of "without prejudice" conversations, this is imperative. Both the fact that it is without prejudice, and the amount of an offer or counter-offer should be recorded carefully.

The words "without prejudice" are discussed further below, in Chapter 39.

Office systems gone mad

Some zealots streamline their office systems to an extent that they create more difficulties and inefficiency than they avoid.

Some practitioners have boasted that they organise their day so that they never take telephone calls between certain times, say 10 a.m. and noon. Similarly, others say that they only make telephone calls between 10 a.m. and noon! A thought-provoking question is what happens when a practitioner who only makes telephone calls between those times wants to deal with one who is never available then.

Don't call me, I'll call you

Unfortunately you will have to put up with the discourtesy of some practitioners who never return calls and who are "not in" or "unavailable" whenever you telephone them. Perhaps the only solution is to put everything you want to say in a letter.

Some years ago there was a practitioner who believed he had another answer to the problem. Confronted by a constantly "unavailable" practitioner (Mr X), he had his receptionist put through a call to Mr X's office. She said it was Tattslotto[1] and that she had some very good news for Mr X. Mr X, who had always been unavailable, was suddenly on the line waiting with breathless anticipation. Not nice, but frustration can drive the most proper practitioner to desperate remedies.

Speaker phones

Many practitioners use speaker phones. A speaker phone permits you to locate documents or flick through file papers while talking. Speaker phones are also useful for telephone conferences between more than two people, often in several different locations.

There are, however, some problems with speaker phones. One problem is that the voice quality is often inferior to a conventional telephone. The caller sometimes fades in and out—particularly if he or she is pacing up and down the room while talking!

Another problem is that you can never be sure who else is listening on the other end of the line. If you are discussing confidential matters, request the person using the speaker phone to identify who else is present and if you object to their presence, request that the loudspeaker function be turned off.

If you wish to use the speaker phone during a discussion you should, as a matter of courtesy to the person on the other end, ask whether you may use the loudspeaker and introduce anyone who is present in your office and who will be listening to the discussion.

If you are considerate when using a speaker phone it will assist you in being efficient. But if you abuse a speaker phone, it will be a source of resentment and friction when dealing with other practitioners.

1. Tattslotto is a lottery game based in Victoria.

Chapter 38

Faxes

> "When Armageddon does come I hope that God will have the decency to send me a fax first to prepare me."
>
> Anon.

In the last ten years or so, facsimile machines have become standard office equipment in most law offices and barristers' chambers. They have brought about significant improvements in efficiency and client service. They have also brought about their own set of problems for practitioners.

Instantaneous communication

The key advantage of facsimile machines is obviously their ability to transmit letters and other documents instantaneously. This is an enormous benefit for lawyers operating under time constraints. Where a client wants a letter of advice by a particular time, if you have a fax machine you can work on the letter until approximately ten minutes before the deadline and then send it by fax. In the past you would have to finish the letter at least the day before the deadline if the letter was to be posted.

The fax has become an indispensable part of legal practice for practitioners who work regularly on transactions which have an interstate or overseas component. If you are receiving instructions from an overseas client, you can prepare drafts of documents, fax them to your client and then receive the client's comments in a few hours.

In some jurisdictions, court rules enable court documents to be filed and served by fax. This is a considerable advantage in matters of extreme urgency where there are tight timetables for the preparation, filing and serving of court documents.

Overuse of faxes

Some practitioners have been so taken by faxes that they tend to send virtually all their correspondence by fax and rarely use the post or other forms of delivery.

Overuse of faxes is becoming a problem in legal practice.

Before sending a document by fax, ask yourself whether your client will gain an advantage if you send it by fax as distinct from other modes of delivery, such as the post, document exchange facilities or courier. In many cases, there is no particular urgency about the document which would justify use of a fax.

The cost of sending documents by fax should always be borne in mind. If all documents are sent by fax as a matter of routine, you may find that the client will complain about the large facsimile charges.

Practitioners who post the original of every document sent by fax are imposing an extra cost burden upon their clients.

In the case of bulky documents which need to be sent to someone in the metropolitan area, facsimile transmission may not only be more expensive than a courier, but it may well be slower. The courier may be able to deliver the whole document well before the last page of the document arrives at the recipient's facsimile machine.

Do not get into bad habits with faxes. Only send documents by fax if it is necessary.

Increased time pressures

Although faxes assist practitioners in meeting deadlines, they also significantly add to the time pressures that practitioners operate under.

In the days when most correspondence was sent by post, a letter of instructions would arrive from the client in the post, a letter of advice would be prepared and this would be sent by post. The client had an expectation of a reasonable delay before receiving the letter of advice.

Now, however, the client is able to send a letter requesting advice by facsimile and will expect a response by facsimile very promptly and, in many cases, on the same day! If all clients had the same expectation, then a busy practitioner could simply not cope with client pressures.

The best way to deal with such situations is to telephone the client as soon as a fax is received and inform the client of when you are likely to respond. Hopefully the client will be understanding and will modify his or her expectations about your ability to perform miracles.

Confidentiality

Faxes have created enormous difficulties with confidentiality.

One problem is the loss of privacy when personal letters are sent by fax to a central fax machine. The fax machine operator and the despatch clerk, and possibly others, will be able to read private correspondence before it is delivered to the intended recipient.

To overcome this problem, many senior executives in various organisations have their own private facsimile machine. Where this is the case, you should send all personal or confidential documents to the private facsimile machine rather than the central facsimile machine.

Where the recipient does not have a private fax machine, you should telephone him or her when you are about to send a document in order to enable the recipient to go to the fax machine and receive the document personally.

Another way of dealing with the problem is to be old fashioned and send the document by post or by courier in an envelope clearly marked "personal and confidential". It is only in situations of extreme urgency that the post and courier delivery will not be suitable.

Another serious confidentiality problem with fax machines is the sending of a fax to the wrong fax number. In the case of sensitive and confidential documents, a serious breach of confidence may take place which may entitle your client to sue in negligence.

In the United States, a large scale trial had to be abandoned because a sensitive document was erroneously transmitted to the attorneys for the opposing party.[1]

Sending a fax intended for your client to an opposing solicitor is not necessarily a rare occurrence. If you are working on a matter where you are constantly sending documents by fax to your client as well as the opposing solicitor, it would be

1. "Misfaxed Papers Stop Asbestos Trial" (1991) (August) *American Bar Association Journal* 22.

relatively easy for the wrong fax number to be typed on the document or for the wrong fax number to be dialled at the time of transmission. Irreparable harm can be done to your client's case if such an error is made.

One way of dealing with the problem of misdirected faxes is to always check the confirmation of transmission sheet that is normally printed when a document is sent by fax. Most of these confirmation sheets record the recipient fax number as well as the time of transmission and the number of pages transmitted. If the recipient fax number printed on the confirmation sheet does not correspond with the intended fax number, then immediate steps should be taken to identify the recipient number and to make arrangements for the recipient to return the document to you.

Many practitioners have standard form "confidentiality clauses" in their facsimile cover pages which basically alert the recipient to the fact that the document transmitted is confidential and request that the document be returned immediately if it is transmitted in error.

Such "confidentiality clauses" are obviously prudent. The difficulty with them, however, is that often the recipient will not realise that the document was not intended for him or her until after reading at least part of the document. The recipient obviously cannot erase from his or her mind what has already been read.

Confidentiality clauses, of course, are no substitute for proper training of staff to ensure that documents are always sent to the correct facsimile number.

Counsel

Many barristers share fax machines. Often, there is only one fax machine for all barristers having chambers on a particular floor. In such situations, you should avoid using faxes because of the danger that another barrister on the same floor may be acting for the other side and may have access to your confidential documents.

If you must send a document to counsel by fax, telephone counsel first and request that he or she attend the fax machine to receive the document personally. Your documents should not be left sitting in a fax machine in full view of anyone who may be passing.

Proof of receipt

Many fax machines print on the top of each page that is received the details of the sender, the date and time of receipt and the number of pages received. Make sure that you keep the originals of the fax documents as they are received in case there is a dispute later as to the time and date of receipt.

Always retain confirmation sheets which indicate when a document was transmitted. Such confirmation sheets will become useful evidence if a dispute arises over whether a particular document was received by the intended recipient.

Invisible ink

The paper used in some facsimile machines is very flimsy and fades over time. In some cases, after only a few months, the document fades to such an extent that it is not possible to read what is printed on it.

You should obviously not use such paper. If you are forced to do so due to reasons of cost, you should immediately make a photocopy of incoming faxes so that you have a more durable record of documents that are sent to you.

Chapter 39

Without Prejudice

> "A man, having eaten his cake, does not still have it, even though he professed to eat it without prejudice."
>
> *Haynes v. Hirst* (1927) 27 S.R. (N.S.W.) 480 at 489.

There seem to be many inexperienced as well as experienced practitioners who really do not understand what the words "without prejudice" mean. They are probably the most misused words in legal jargon.

There is story of a law student who was having a raging love affair with a mild-mannered accountant. The student always put "without prejudice" on top of the love letters to avoid any further commitment and the chance of future litigation!

General rule

The general rule is that communications—whether oral or written—which are made during a dispute between parties and which contain a genuine offer for the purpose of settling the dispute, are privileged and are not admissible in evidence. Any admissions made in such a communication cannot prejudice the party making them because they cannot be given in evidence if the negotiations for settlement break down and the case goes to court.

Thus, if the defendant writes to the plaintiff and offers, without prejudice, to pay half of the plaintiff's claim, the plaintiff cannot rely on that offer as an admission of having a right to some payment. The plaintiff cannot give evidence of the letter or tender it or use it as an exhibit to an affidavit.

The underlying philosophy of the rule is that parties should be encouraged so far as possible to settle their disputes without resort to litigation and should not be discouraged by the knowledge that anything that is said in the course of negotiations may be used to their prejudice in the course of the proceeding.[1]

The rule enables litigants to engage freely in discussions or correspondence for the purpose of negotiating a settlement. Such communications are protected by the principle whether they are made before the commencement of proceedings or after the trial commences. They remain privileged even after settlement is achieved.[2]

The rule does not extend to every word spoken during settlement negotiations. It is restricted to admissions and excludes assertions made during the negotiations which are not connected with the subject matter of the negotiations.[3]

Use of words "without prejudice" not conclusive

In practice, letters containing offers of settlement are headed "without prejudice". These words have been interpreted to mean "without prejudice to the position of the writer of the letter if the terms proposed are not accepted".[4]

These words need not be used. If a letter is clearly part of the negotiations for a settlement then it will not be admissible even if the letter is not headed "without prejudice". Conversely, merely putting the heading "without prejudice" on top of correspondence, or prefacing discussions with another practitioner with the words "this conversation will be without prejudice", cannot make the document or conversation privileged from disclosure to the court, if the correspondence or discussions do not form part of settlement negotiations.

The rule looks not to whether the words "without prejudice" are used, but whether the statements made form part of genuine negotiations between the parties for the purpose of settling the dispute.

1. *Cutts v. Head* [1984] 2 W.L.R. 349 at 360; *Rush & Tompkins Ltd v. Greater London Council* [1988] 3 W.L.R. 939.
2. *Rush & Tompkins Ltd v. Greater London Council* [1988] 3 W.L.R. 939 at 943.
3. *Quad Consulting Pty Ltd v. David R. Bleakley & Associates Pty Ltd* (1991) A.T.P.R. 41-065.
4. *Walker v. Wilsher* (1889) 23 Q.B.D. 335 at 337.

Even though use of the words "without prejudice" is not conclusive, they are useful because they provide evidence that the parties intended that if negotiations fail, nothing that has passed between them during the negotiations will be disclosed at the trial.

In *Rush & Tompkins v. Greater London Council*[5] Lord Griffiths stated:

> "A competent solicitor will always head any negotiating correspondence 'without prejudice' to make clear beyond doubt that in the event of the negotiations being unsuccessful they are not to be referred to at the subsequent trial. However, the application of the rule is not dependent upon the use of the phrase 'without prejudice' and if it is clear from the surrounding circumstances that the parties were seeking to compromise the action, evidence of the content of those negotiations will, as a general rule, not be admissible at the trial and cannot be used to establish an admission or partial admission."

In effect, when you state in a letter that it is without prejudice, you are saying: "I want to make it quite clear to you that I am making this offer in an endeavour to settle this dispute without prejudice to my client's claim. Should you reject the offer, then the very fact that this offer is being made shall not be led in evidence against my client if this matter proceeds to hearing."

All related communications protected

Generally, the whole of the negotiation is protected if its commencement is without prejudice and thus all documents and discussions which form part of the negotiation are covered.[6] For example, a reply to a letter headed "without prejudice" is protected whether it is headed "without prejudice" or not.[7]

If in the course of without prejudice negotiations one of the parties wishes to make an "open" offer, that party must make it clear to the other party that the basis of the negotiations is to change.[8]

5. [1988] 3 W.L.R. 939.
6. *South Shropshire District Council v. Amos* [1986] 1 W.L.R. 1271.
7. *Paddock v. Forrester* (1842) 3 Man. & G. 903; 113 E.R. 1404.
8. *Cheddar Valley Engineering Ltd v. Chaddlewood Homes Ltd* [1992] 4 All E.R. 942.

Third parties

In *Rush & Tompkins Ltd v. Greater London Council*[9] the House of Lords rejected a claim by one of the defendants to discover details of the without prejudice negotiations that led to settlement between the other defendant and the plaintiff. The House of Lords held that:

> "as a general rule the 'without prejudice' rule renders inadmissible in any subsequent litigation connected with the same subject matter proof of any admissions made in a genuine attempt to reach a settlement. It of course goes without saying that admissions made to reach settlement with a different party within the same litigation are also inadmissible whether or not settlement was reached with that party."[10]

It would seem that the privilege is not available against third parties unconnected to the litigation in question.[11]

Communications which are not protected

Some communications are admissible even if they are made on a without prejudice basis. They are:

1. Communications which are not made bona fide for the purpose of negotiating a settlement. Thus, if your house is compulsorily acquired and you lodge a claim for compensation it would be meaningless to write "without prejudice" on the claim form; you either intend to make a claim or you do not.
2. Communications which are not referable to a dispute of any kind. Thus, a notice of intention to suspend payment which is sent to creditors on a without prejudice basis may be used in evidence in bankruptcy proceedings.[12] Similarly, you cannot prevent your client from submitting your bill to the Taxing Master by merely heading it "without prejudice".[13]

9. [1988] 3 W.L.R. 939.
10. *Rush & Tompkins Ltd v. Greater London Council* [1988] 3 W.L.R. 939 at 943-4.
11. *Hawkesbury Two Pty Limited v. Kelly* (unreported, N.S.W. Sup. Ct., Young J., 16 April 1987 unreported); P. George and M. Green "Without Prejudice Communications" (1990) 29 (December) *Law Society Journal* 63 at 64; A. R. N. Cross, D. Byrne and J. D. Heydon, *Cross on Evidence—Australian Edition* (Butterworths, Sydney, 1991), para. 25375.
12. *Re Daintrey; Ex parte Holt* [1893] 2 Q.B. 116 at 119.
13. *Ex parte Levy* (1902) 19 W.N. (N.S.W.) 252.

3. Communications which both parties agree should be admissible. Without prejudice communications cease to be privileged if both parties agree to waive the protection.
4. Communications whose "without prejudice" privilege is waived expressly or impliedly by both parties.[14]
5. Communications that contain an offer and an acceptance and which thereby create a contract. If proceedings for breach of the contract are taken, the communications would be admissible in evidence in such proceedings to show the existence of the contract. When an offer is accepted, a contract is complete and the acceptance of the offer cannot be made without prejudice to its legal effect.[15]
6. Communications which constitute criminal conduct. Accordingly, a letter by which someone is seeking to blackmail another would not be rendered inadmissible on a charge of blackmail if it is headed "without prejudice".
7. Communications the disclosure of which will prevent a party from misleading the court.[16]
8. Communications which constitute tortious conduct. Accordingly, a defamatory letter headed "without prejudice" would be admissible in defamation proceedings.
9. Assertions made during negotiations which are not connected with the subject matter of the negotiations.[17]

The "without prejudice" privilege protects admissions. It does not protect facts learned by you with your own senses during the course of negotiations and which can be proved by direct evidence.

Admissibility of without prejudice offers on the question of costs

Assume that A sues B for $10,000 and that B makes a written without prejudice offer of $8,000. If A rejects the offer and when the case goes to trial the court awards A $5,000, should the court take into account the without prejudice offer so as to award A less costs than A would otherwise have been entitled from B?

14. *Trade Practices Commission v. Arnotts Ltd* (1989) 88 A.L.R. 69.
15. *Walker v. Wilsher* (1889) 23 Q.B.D. 335 at 337.
16. *Kurtz & Co. v. Spence & Sons* (1887) 58 L.T. 438.
17. *Quad Consulting Pty Ltd v. David R. Bleakley & Associates Pty Ltd* (1991) A.T.P.R. 41-065.

The answer is no. There are two reasons for this. Firstly, by using the words "without prejudice", B impliedly intends that the offer should not be disclosed to the court for any purpose. Secondly, if B wanted to put A on risk in relation to costs, B could have made a payment into court or offer of compromise pursuant to the rules of the court.

The position is different, however, in cases where the payment into court or offer of compromise procedure is not available and A qualifies the without prejudice nature of the offer by express words such as "in the event of this offer being unacceptable to you, I reserve the right to bring this letter to the notice of the court on the issue of costs."[18]

In such a case the letter is inadmissible on the question of liability but if the court finds that B is liable to A for $8,000 or less, then the court may refer to the without prejudice letter with a view to deciding what an appropriate order as to costs would be. The court would probably order B to pay A's costs up to the date on which A should have made a decision to accept the without prejudice offer and would then order A to pay B's costs after that date.

The English Court of Appeal has said that although this principle places at risk plaintiffs who reject without prejudice offers, this was consistent with the underlying philosophy of without prejudice offers which is to encourage out of court settlements. The court said that a plaintiff would be more willing to accept a without prejudice offer if the plaintiff had something to lose in the event of a court awarding less than the defendant had offered.[19]

Whenever you receive a without prejudice offer on behalf of a client, you should immediately ascertain whether a right is reserved to refer to the offer on the question of costs and, if so, whether the payment into court procedure is available. The payment in procedure is generally not available in actions where equitable relief—such as an injunction—is sought. In such cases you should treat very seriously all without prejudice offers which contain a reservation as to costs. You should carefully advise your client on the consequences of not accepting such an offer.

18. This is known as the *Calderbank* letter or offer, after *Calderbank v. Calderbank* [1976] Fam. 93. See *Messiter v. Hutchinson* (1987) 10 N.S.W.L.R. 525.
19. *Cutts v. Head* [1984] 2 W.L.R. 349 at 368.

Do not mix communications

In order to prevent complications from arising, it is advisable to avoid mixing "open" and "without prejudice" material in the same letter or conversation. You should prepare separate letters and separate file notes dealing exclusively with one or the other.

"Off the record"

From time to time another practitioner will invite you to take part in an "off the record" discussion. You should immediately seek clarification of what is meant by "off the record" because this expression does not have a fixed legal meaning. If what is meant is simply "without prejudice" then use this expression rather than "off the record". If what is meant is that you should not disclose the discussion to your client then, in our view, you cannot agree to this prior to knowing the subject matter of the discussion and without instructions.

As a general rule, you are obliged to disclose to your client all information available to you about your client's case and it is therefore difficult to envisage situations where it would be proper for you to withhold "off the record" information from your client.

Chapter 40

Drafting

> "Layman to lawyer: "I think legal documents contain too many big words, they should use shorter words." Lawyer's reply: "Oh! you think we should be eliminating polysyllables."
>
> Anon. Quoted in (1978) 52 *Law Institute Journal* 513.

Drafting is a skill that is developed through experience and is not something that can be acquired easily through reading textbooks.[1] Drafting an agreement or even a legal letter[2] for the first time is often one of the most difficult tasks for a young practitioner.

Basic principles

1. Before putting pen to paper, make sure that your client's instructions are clear and that you know precisely what your client wants. Do not hesitate to involve your client in the revision of drafts. The client's opinion should be sought if there is any doubt as to whether the draft reflects his or her instructions.
2. Never draft a legal document without being familiar with the law that governs the subject matter of the document.
3. Remember that there is no such thing as "legal English". The language of the law is ordinary English. Therefore, use plain words and keep your sentences as short as possible. Beware of legal cliches and avoid technical terms unless you understand them thoroughly.

1. There are, however, a number of very good texts and manuals on drafting skills. Your Law Society library should have these. For example, the Law Institute of Victoria has recently published *Legal Writing for Good Business*.
2. See above, Ch. 35.

4. Develop a mental picture of the structure of your draft before you put pen to paper. Remember that there must be some order in your draft. Begin at the beginning and end at the end.
5. Clarity must always take precedence over style.
6. You must not vary words but must always use the same word when the same meaning is intended. You must never use the same word with different meanings.
7. Use definitions if they will save a great deal of repetition. However, use your discretion. Definitions should be used to assist comprehension of the document but should not be required to carry too much of the active purpose of the document. Be sure to provide a definition at the beginning of the document when using abbreviations and acronyms.
8. Always use the active voice, the indicative or imperative mood and avoid the subjunctive.
9. Avoid words such as "heretofore", "hereinafter", "said", "aforesaid", "same" and other such legalese.
10. Use punctuation but do not rely on punctuation to make a word clear.
11. Use headings, particularly in large letters or documents.
12. Avoid provisos.
13. Draft in the singular.
14. Beware of rushed jobs. There is an irreducible amount of time and thought required for any drafting job. To skimp on either may lead to real disasters.
15. If the document you are drafting is based on specific provisions of an Act then you should adhere closely to the wording of those provisions.
16. Be as brief as possible and avoid lengthy, repetitive drafting.
17. Keep in mind principles such as the ejusdem generis rule so that such principles do not lead to unintended interpretations.
18. Date and number successive drafts of a document.

Legal precedents

In many cases, frustration and desperation cause young practitioners to rely excessively on precedents. When using precedents, bear in mind the following:

1. Use precedents with great care and thought.
2. Do not assume that a precedent is correct or up-to-date. Find out who was the author of the precedent, when it was drafted and when it was last revised. If the author is an articled clerk who was dismissed for incompetence, then obviously you should throw the precedent away. The same applies if the author is an experienced partner of the firm—if that partner drafted the document in 1910 and died soon after! Most areas of the law do not remain static but change and therefore precedents over time become out of date and worthless.
3. Ensure that the precedent you rely on suits your client's requirements. A precedent may be well drafted and up-to-date, but it cannot help you if it does not fit your client's instructions. Beware of taking a precedent into a completely different area from that for which it was developed.
4. Never use a precedent unless you have first read it in full. This is especially so for standard documents on a word processing system which only contains a few variables. At first sight you may think it is easy to fill in the variables and out will come your new agreement. However, unless you read it, you cannot be sure that the standard provisions are the ones your client wants. We have, for example, seen a lease for a 200 hectare farm which required the lessee to keep the lifts and escalators in working order!
5. Do not be fooled by the heading of a particular precedent. If you want to draft a mortgage, do not use the first document with the heading "mortgage" that you come across in the office. There are many different kinds of mortgages with many different kinds of provisions.
6. Even if a precedent is suitable for your purposes, do not automatically plagiarise it. See if you can improve it, for example, by redrafting ambiguous or prolix provisions and removing archaic language.
7. Even if your office has a comprehensive and refined system of precedents to meet most requirements of clients, do not allow any agreement to be executed by your client unless you have first checked it. This is so even if the agreement is so standard that only the name and address of your client needs to be filled in by your secretary. Things can still go wrong. For example, a page may be missing which alters the whole thrust of the agreement. Alternatively, your secretary

may misspell the name of the client and a doubt may later arise as to who are the parties to the agreement. This will be a problem especially where your client belongs to a group of companies with similar names.

8. Never rely on any provision in a precedent unless you understand what it means and why it is there. Do not assume that any particular provision is either necessary or desirable.
9. Never alter a part of a precedent without ensuring that there are no adverse effects on the remainder of the document. Failure to do this may lead to inconsistencies and ambiguities in the document. For example, if a particular word is defined to mean something quite specific in the precedent then you should not, in ignorance, add a new clause which uses that word in a different sense.

Client alterations

Once you have drafted an agreement and you receive it back from a client duly executed, before stamping or registering the agreement, check to see whether your client has altered any of the clauses without your knowledge.

Frequently, agreements are the subject of negotiation between clients and alterations often result from such negotiations. What may seem to be a sensible alteration to a lay person may have serious legal consequences. If you come across such alterations, you should alert your client to the consequences. In any event, you should write to your client pointing out the alterations that were made without your advice and ask whether the client wishes the alterations to stand.

Part 7
Practice Management

Chapter 41

Introduction

> "A place for everything and everything in its place."
>
> Everybody's mother.

From the time that you commence your life as a lawyer, whether you opt for life at the Bar or as a solicitor, you will quickly realise that organisation is one of the critical keys to success.

With the competing demands on your time brought about by court timetables, over-zealous clients and energetic colleagues, it becomes obvious at a very early stage that a lack of organisation on your part will hamper your ability to use effectively your legal or practitioner skills.

If you are disorganised, you will be quickly put on the back foot and will find that most of your energies will be directed towards damage control. You will often be in the position of merely being able to react to the demands of clients and other practitioners. This will limit severely your effectiveness as a lawyer and reduce your ability to act in the best interests of your client.

The simple fact is that to be a successful practitioner you must be in control of your practice. You must get organised. Once you do, you will immediately remove a potentially large source of stress from your practice.

Chapter 42

Prioritising

> "Everything should be made as simple as possible but not simpler."
>
> Albert Einstein.

In order to conduct a successful legal practice, you must have the ability to prioritise work.

Some priorities will be obvious, for example, where a deadline is imposed by a court for the completion of an interlocutory step in a proceeding. Other deadlines are not so clearly defined. The priority that these matters are afforded often depends on a combination of how vocal your client is together with the level of aggression of the solicitor acting on the other side.

Where there is no externally imposed deadline, the client is sheepish and the opposing practitioner uninterested, you may be tempted to drop the matter down the list of "things to do" time after time. This is dangerous. You must give these matters appropriate priority otherwise the stage may be reached where your client is prejudiced, for example where the matter is struck out for failure to prosecute, and you are sued for negligence.

Be realistic

No matter how well intentioned you are or how good you are at devising systems to prioritise your work, it is simply not possible to conduct an effective practice if you take on more work than you can possibly handle. This will result in a feeling of being totally out of control with the consequence that you will miss deadlines, be tardy in responding to clients and be completely unable to take a pro-active role in the conduct of any file.

If overwork becomes a habit, your clients will be dissatisfied and there will be unhappiness and friction in your relationship with colleagues and opposing practitioners. You will also be inviting an action in negligence against you.

As tempting as it is for a young practitioner to take on all work that is offered, this is often professionally disastrous. It is most important in the early stages of your career to handle a file competently, in a timely manner and to the best of your ability. Neither your clients, principals or colleagues will thank you if the price of never saying "no" to a new matter is the loss of a client or a suit for negligence against the firm.

Communication

Fortunately for practising lawyers, most people are reasonable. You will find that if you explain to a client or a practitioner for the other side that you will not be able to respond until a particular date, most people will accept that, even if the date is somewhat further away than they had hoped. The key is to keep people informed and explain your circumstances.

Of course, there are exceptions and some clients will steadfastly refuse to accept any delay even though you may be in court, on leave or otherwise occupied. Obviously these clients need to be accommodated and are entitled to have their expectations met, provided these expectations were reasonable in the first place.

Office systems

It is essential that you adopt some sort of office system to assist you in prioritising your work. It is not necessary, however, that the system be high tech or complicated. The most important thing is that it is simple to use, you do use it, your secretary uses it, and it works. These are the only rules and the rest is up to you.

Be flexible

It is impossible to have rigid priorities when practising law. Clients' demands change, as do the priorities and timetables of the courts and other practitioners. These changes in themselves may either inject new urgency into a matter or remove it. Accordingly, you must be flexible. The ability to change course and respond quickly to new or altered priorities is essential.

You will be involved in a continuing process of taking stock and assessing what needs to be done in order that the interests of all your clients are met. It is often not easy and the demands of competing priorities are bound to cause stress at some stage. The need to consistently reassess circumstances and note the change of priorities is important and will be one constant throughout your legal career.

Some suggestions

1. Plan your day. This is often optimistic because on many occasions nothing at all that you plan to achieve gets done. Nevertheless persevere and set your goals each day.
2. Keep lists of things to do. There are many computer based diary planners that you can use. The humble pen and paper, however, are quite adequate and user-friendly. The list of things to do should differentiate between long-term and short-term deadlines. You should be realistic about the amount of work that is able to be completed.
3. Involve your secretary or assistant in your system for prioritising work. This is particularly useful when court deadlines are imposed or when critical dates pursuant to agreements or contracts need to be met. The system should be designed so that your secretary can remind you of the due date and appropriate time in advance.
4. If you know that you will require more time than usual to respond to your client or a solicitor on the other side, as a matter of courtesy let them know when you expect to respond as soon as possible after you have received their letter or request. Whilst they may not be happy with the delay, they will be far less happy if you do not advise them of the delay until several weeks after you have received the letter or request, at the time they would normally be expecting a response.
5. Do not forget to work on large tasks or tasks that have an unspecified time-frame. These tasks require self-imposed deadlines and you should adhere to them. If this is not done you will quickly find that time has elapsed whilst you have been occupied with immediate priorities. It would be embarrassing to admit to your client that the matter has not progressed in recent months.
6. Conduct a monthly audit of your files. Not only will this remind you of things that have slipped through your diary system but it will also enable you to assess whether you have the capacity to take on further work.

Chapter 43

File Management

"The leading rule for the lawyer as for the man of every other calling is diligence."

Abraham Lincoln.

Your client's problems and the resolution of those problems manifest themselves in a file. Your task is to "manage" or "run" the file by carrying out your client's instructions and doing whatever is necessary to bring your client's problem—and your file—to a satisfactory conclusion.

Common mistakes of young practitioners in conveyancing, litigious and other matters are outlined in Part 5. Apart from the legal pitfalls which you should avoid in the course of managing a file, there are certain organisational rules that you should follow.[1]

I am a lawyer, not a manager

Wrong. You did go to law school and as a result of that experience you should have a good grasp of legal principles. None of this, however, will be of any use to your clients unless you are able to manage your files in a way that gives you the opportunity to bring your skills to bear on the matter. There will be a large amount of routine correspondence and matters to attend to. If you cannot keep up with this it is unlikely that you will have the opportunity to consider and advise upon the interesting legal issues that may present themselves.

Winning the paper warfare

If you are sensitive about the destruction of forests, you will never stop weeping as a lawyer. A lawyer's office is always filled

1. See also the discussion under the heading "Office systems" above, pp. 119-121.

with paper and there is a constant stream of correspondence every day. If the paper warfare is not under control you will lose documents, fail to respond to correspondence and you will have a miserable life. It is important to involve your secretary or assistant in the process of containing the paper warfare and ensuring that all relevant documents get filed on the appropriate file. While this is perplexing at first, you will quickly get better at it. Necessity is, after all, the mother of invention.

Personal style

It quickly becomes obvious when you commence practice that the personal style or habits of practitioners vary greatly. Whilst some practitioners adhere to a clean desk policy with several documents only gracing their desks at any one time, others are less minimalist. These practitioners adopt the "volcano" approach to desk organisation, hoping that the important document will somehow erupt from the mass of papers on their desk.

While a clean desk is preferable from an organisational and aesthetic point of view, the important thing is that you know where everything is and how to access it quickly. There is nothing more embarrassing than having to rifle through a bundle of assorted documents to find a letter whilst a client is waiting on the telephone. If you regularly have clients in your office for conferences, the appearance of disorganisation in your office may concern them.

Some suggestions

1. Read correspondence and other documents as soon as you receive them, respond or take other appropriate action as soon as possible and place the relevant documents on the appropriate file at the earliest opportunity. Filing documents immediately on receipt and prior to responding has the risk that you will forget what action you are required to take. Other matters will take your attention and you may overlook the document. A record or note of the action required should be made on your list of things to do or in your diary prior to filing the document.
2. Keep files neat and ordered by filing all correspondence and documentation in chronological order so that any document may be quickly and easily located. Do not overcrowd files. If they are too full, start another file.

3. Always take proper file notes of telephone conversations. These file notes should be dated and the time noted. The file note should be filed in chronological order on the file so that you may readily consult it should there be a dispute at a later stage as to your instructions or statements made in the course of conversations.
4. Where the documentation is voluminous, keep separate files or separate parts of files for general correspondence and other documents such as contracts or court documents.
5. All original documents provided by your client should be clearly identified and placed in the office safe or other secure place. If this is not available then the document should be permanently fixed to your file in a way that preserves the document and ensures that it is not misplaced. Do not write on original documents of your client and do not retain them for any longer period than is necessary.
6. Do not retain original documents of title or security documents on your file. Whilst these documents are sometimes required for court, there are very few other circumstances where a photocopy of the document is not sufficient for your file. Such documents should be returned to your client by hand delivery as soon as you have finished with them and the client should be asked to acknowledge in writing that the documents have been received.

Chapter 44

Research

> "Necessity knows no law; I know some attorneys of the same."
>
> Benjamin Franklin, *Poor Richard's Almanack* (1732-1757). Quoted in E. Kahn. "The Seven Lamps of Legal Humour, Part 3" (1984) *De Rebus* 251.

Law school should have taught you that you must be methodical in your research. The need for efficiency in research is much more pronounced when you are in practice because pressure of other work simply does not permit you to spend all day looking up a simple point for a particular matter. You certainly cannot charge your client for your inefficiency.

The opposite of over-research is, of course, under-research. Many young practitioners suffer from the illusion that their lecture notes are the exclusive repository of all legal learning. Do not rely on cases and legal propositions contained in your lecture notes without checking whether the law has changed since your student days. The chances are that the law has changed.

When you are confronted with a problem involving an unfamiliar area of law, you should ensure that any research you undertake is done as efficiently as possible.

Looseleaf services

It is wise to use an up-to-date looseleaf service that specialises in the relevant area of law as a starting point. Look at the table of contents and the index. If something looks relevant then turn to the relevant page or paragraph. If you are lucky, you may solve your problem quickly by using this procedure.

The relevant page or paragraph may refer to a case or statute that is directly on point. It is advisable to consult the case or statute to make sure that the writer of the looseleaf service has not made a mistake. If more than one case is cited then read the case decided by the most superior court. If the cases have been decided by the same court and you cannot read them all then start by reading the most recent.

Books and articles

If there is no specialist looseleaf service, or, alternatively, you cannot solve your problem by reference to one, then you should consult recently written articles or textbooks in the relevant area of law. Once again, these should refer to relevant cases or statutes. Always check when a book or article was published and, if necessary, update the information yourself to ensure that there have not been any changes to the law since the article or book was published.

General references

If you have still not found the answer then you should look at general reference works such as *Halsbury's Laws of England*, the *Australian Digest*, *Halsbury's Laws of Australia* and *The Laws of Australia*. Also consult indexes and annotations of statutes and digests of cases.

Computer-based legal research[1]

You should also bear in mind that there are numerous computer-based legal research programs available. If you are lucky enough to have access to such a program, you should try it. By keying in the correct catchwords, you may obtain instant access to pertinent information. One drawback of some computer-based legal research programs is cost. They are generally expensive. Often the cost is a specified charge per minute for accessing information. If that is the case, you will have to weigh up the cost-effectiveness of the search against the need for thoroughness and accuracy in the information.

Opinion bank

Your firm may have an office precedent management system that stores opinions, precedents and advices prepared by the firm over time. You should check whether someone else has

1. See below, Ch. 45.

already advised on the area you are dealing with. If so, you should not re-invent the wheel at your client's expense.

Consult colleagues

If you work in a large firm, you should consult those colleagues who are likely to be familiar with the area you are dealing with before conducting independent research. They will either give you the answer you need or put you on the right track and thereby save you considerable research time.

Briefing counsel

If the problem is too complicated and outside the areas in which your firm practises, the most efficient course might be to obtain instructions from your client to brief appropriate counsel.

Legislation

Remember always that statutory provisions are often supplemented by regulations and other subordinate rules. Regulations often amplify or give meaning to general expressions found in Acts. In particular, regulations often lay down specific requirements or procedures and prescribe forms that need to be complied with.

Contact relevant officials

Sometimes the quickest and easiest way to find the answer to a problem is to pick up the telephone and talk to a person who obviously knows the answer.

For example, if you want to find out what the current fees for jurors are, rather than looking up numerous amendments to the relevant legislation, simply ring the sheriff or other appropriate court official.

Court officials can be consulted on court procedure. You must recognise that sometimes rules of court can be misleading because the practice differs from the literal wording of the rules and has probably done so for years.

If you need to know in a hurry what regulations have been passed under a particular Act then the quickest way is to telephone the department administering the Act. If that department has an in-house lawyer, you are likely to receive a very prompt and helpful answer.

You should not feel as though you are cheating or lazy if you find the answer to a question by telephoning an appropriate person rather than by resorting to books.

Your methods of research should be governed solely by the objectives of speed and accuracy.

Keep up with the law

Because the law changes so quickly, you should strive to keep up with developments. If you specialise in a particular area, you will need to follow changes in that area very closely. But you should not ignore changes in other areas altogether. You should have at least a general knowledge of key changes in core areas of the law. Such a knowledge will make it easier to research those changes in detail if it becomes necessary.

A good way to maintain an overview of change in the law is through reading legal journals, especially regular journals published by your Law Society.

Participation in continuing legal education programmes is now an essential element of legal practice and in some jurisdictions it is compulsory.

Chapter 45

Technology

"The times they are a-changing."

Bob Dylan.

The legal profession is often criticised for being slow to respond to change. This criticism is often valid. In relation to technology, however, most practitioners have embraced enthusiastically the benefits offered by technological advances.

All types of technology impact on the practice of the law. "Technology" includes tools like dictaphones and word processing packages, and more sophisticated advances such as video conferencing, on-line court transcript and document imaging.

As competition both from within and outside the profession continues to place pressure on practitioners' ability to provide efficient and profitable services, lawyers will increasingly look to technological advances to assist them to automate manual activities and improve their productivity.

The successful lawyers of the future will be those who understand and make sensible and effective use of ongoing technological advances. Those who ignore technology or fail to upgrade their skills will find it harder to compete and offer a cost-efficient (and profitable) legal service.

Listed below are a number of suggestions to assist young lawyers as they confront technology in their legal practice.

Welcome and embrace technology

Accept and embrace technology as a necessary tool that will increase your efficiency and improve the quality of the legal services you deliver. Not only will using technology make you and your firm more productive and competitive, but it will free your time to expand the number of matters you can deal with and therefore broaden your legal experience.

Dictaphones

A dictating machine (or "dictaphone") is the solicitor's most basic piece of technology.

Based on the principle that we can speak faster than we can write, the dictaphone offers the solicitor enhanced efficiency in the production of documents and the delegation of tasks.

Be careful though—having spent most of your life writing points down on paper, the transition to oral dictation is not easy, and junior solicitors often find themselves suffering from what is known as unstructured "verbal diarrhoea".

Handy lessons for learning to use the dictaphone include:

1. Speak slowly and clearly into the dictaphone and always minimise the level of background noise when dictating. Give instructions in a courteous manner rather than a peremptory manner.
2. Initially restrict yourself to using dictation for simple tasks, such as filling in variables in a precedent document or providing simple directions to your secretary. You may even find it helpful to defer using a dictaphone until you have mastered the skill of structuring letters and memoranda on paper.
3. When dictating longer letters of advice or memoranda, prepare a written plan in point form to give your work structure before you commence dictating. This will keep you on track as you dictate and will improve the quality of your dictation.

As you gradually build confidence and learn to structure your work as you dictate, you should see significant improvement in your efficiency, directly attributable to the dictaphone.

Learn how to use basic office equipment

Familiarise yourself with how to operate all basic office equipment such as the photocopier, facsimile machine and laser printers. Know how to turn them on after hours and perform simple maintenance, such as clearing paper jams and replacing toner in the photocopier.

Murphy's law ensures that these machines always break down at the most crucial times. The last thing you want at 11 p.m. on the Sunday night before your first trial is a paper jam in the photocopier or facsimile machine with no one who is "qualified" present to fix it.

Word processing packages

As soon as practicable after commencing with a firm, learn how to use the firm's word processing software package so that, at the very least, you can amend and print out documents after hours when your secretary is not available. Especially make sure that you can print out documents, as it is of little use knowing only how to amend a document without being able to produce another copy.

In the 1990s all lawyers—including partners—should be able to produce documents and facsimile cover sheets after hours using the firm's word processing system.

The firm's billing system

Most practitioners have a system of regular—often monthly—review of files and preparation of bills. It is therefore important for you to become familiar with the system that monitors your work in progress and disbursements on your files.

If your firm's billing system is computerised, make sure you and your secretary are familiar with the system and understand how to produce your own bills at the appropriate interval. If your office renders accounts on a monthly basis, do not leave your bills for the last day of the month. If a matter concludes early in the month, bill it then. If appropriate, spread your bills over the course of the month in order to avoid the end-of-the-month rush.

New frontiers

New technology is finding a place in lawyers' offices. While this technology has in the past been confined to the larger firms, the cost of equipment has decreased rapidly and thus all firms should be in a position to explore at least some of these new technological frontiers. Some of the recent innovations include:

1. Lap-top computers which can be used in court with an on-line transcript facility—that is, as witnesses speak, the text of their evidence is simultaneously typed by a court stenographer and appears on a lap-top computer, accessed by the judge, counsel and solicitors.

2. Transcript search packages which can hold over 20,000 pages of transcript and perform complicated searches of the transcript to help with the cross-examination of witnesses.
3. Document imaging and optical character readers ("OCR") which enable hard copies of documents to be scanned into a computer and reproduced. For example, while it used to take hours to have a 100 page document retyped, the same document can now be scanned into a word processing package using an OCR, and amendments made and multiple copies reproduced within a fraction of the time.
4. Mobile phones, mobile facsimile machines and lap-top computers with built-in modems which enable advances in telecommunications to be used by lawyers to enhance the service they provide. For example, statements from witnesses could potentially be taken personally in a small country town and then transferred electronically by telephone lines directly to your word processing system in a metropolitan city.
5. CD-ROM ("Compact Disc-Read Only Memory") facilities which enable large volumes of information to be stored on single compact discs. Legislation, cases and other library information that used to be stored on several bookshelves can now be accessed by a single CD-ROM disc using a CD player linked to a computer.
6. Multi-media technologies which provide exciting opportunities for the future. Multi-media combines different forms of communications technology, such as CD-ROM, word processing, computer packages and video technology. For example, a multi-media package might combine a videoed witness statement with a word processed document including notes for cross-examination. This is especially valuable if the case involves an interstate or international element. This multi-media package could be stored on video and transferred electronically via a telephone line between offices in, say, Melbourne and New York. A video or computer screen can then be used in New York to play the video, and simultaneously view the typed comments for cross-examination.

Let technology work for you

One of your first objectives when commencing legal practice should be to master the technology in your firm's office.

The dictaphone and basic office equipment should be your first priority. As your confidence grows, you should test the bounds of the "new technological frontiers".

Many sole practitioners and barristers have found that "working for yourself" is more efficient and rewarding when you have appropriate technological facilities to work for you.

Part 8

Working in the Law

Chapter 46

Back to Basics—Lessons from the 1980s

> "Entrepreneurial activity does not attract the same privilege nor the same protection as professional activity; and the promotion of a scheme in which particular clients may be advised to participate is pregnant with the possibility of conflict of entrepreneurial interest with professional duty."
>
> *Leary v. Federal Commissioner of Taxation* (1980) 80 A.T.C. 4438 at 4453 per Brennan J.

The business and commercial environment has changed dramatically in the last decade. The increased complexity of commercial transactions and the internationalisation of business have brought about significant changes in the role of lawyers. Whilst traditionally lawyers were hauled in to document deals after they were made, lawyers are now involved in large commercial transactions from the beginning.[1]

Ironically, the increasing complexity of commercial matters has been coupled with shorter time-frames for completion. The impact of technology has meant that clients often have the expectation that large and complex negotiations or deals may be closed in a very short space of time.

The increasing participation of lawyers in these types of transactions, possibly as a member of a multi-disciplinary team working on the commercial transaction, means that the lawyer

1. S. Fisher, "Lawyers in the Money", *Business Review Weekly*, 11 August 1989, p. 56.

may run the risk of being indistinguishable from the other professionals involved. It is therefore important for a lawyer to maintain sufficient distance from the transaction and the client in order to preserve professional independence and carry out his or her duties with appropriate care and skill.

Lawyer not financial adviser

As a lawyer your role is clear. You have duties to the law and to your client. Your expertise is in the law and it is legal advice that you are retained to give to your client. Whilst you may gain some commercial and business experience in the course of your practice, you are not a financial or business adviser. It may be necessary for you to make certain observations on the business or finance related aspects of a transaction, but these observations should be restricted to how these factors impact on your legal advice. Your client's business adviser or accountant is the appropriate person to give financial advice. Decisions on the commercial viability of any proposal should be left to clients and their financial advisers.

Stopping the clock

In some instances, the pressure from clients to complete deals or transactions is enormous. A whole series of events may be contingent upon a particular deal closing or a settlement occurring. As a lawyer you may be the one who is required to give the final advice at a critical time in a commercial transaction. The outcome of your advice or your actions may determine whether the deal is made or lost. Your client will be angry and disappointed if a deal is not made and, irrespective of the quality and soundness of your legal advice, may never give you further instructions.

All these factors make it enormously difficult for a lawyer to arrest the progress of a transaction while a proper legal analysis is undertaken and advice given. While you will never find this sort of decision easy, and your desire to please your client will weigh heavily on your mind, you clearly have no other option. The consequences of not properly considering the legal implications of any transaction for your client may be disastrous.

Your client will not thank you and will certainly not understand that you signed off on the deal before you had fully satisfied yourself that your client's interests were protected. The fact that you did so to meet an unrealistic deadline imposed by your client will be quickly forgotten by your client. It will be the final result, which may be less than desirable from your client's point of view, which will be your client's focus.

The solution is simple. You should never give advice which you are not entirely satisfied with even if it means that your client is disappointed that the advice cannot be given within a particular time-frame. If your client imposes unrealistic deadlines which prevent you from carrying out your professional duties, then it is better not to act for that client. To proceed with the matter, even with written disclaimers which point out that you have not had enough time to advise on all relevant matters, is simply too risky.

Being creative

Your duties as a lawyer and the expectations of your client are that you will give sound and timely legal advice. Increasingly, however, particularly in the commercial area, lawyers are often requested by their clients to take a more creative role in suggesting more effective ways of bringing about a particular result.

It will not be sufficient for you simply to regurgitate provisions of statutes or the common law. Your client will want you, quite justifiably, to think of a way to achieve the desired result which is within the law and optimises returns to the client.

Whilst being creative is certainly an essential component of the role of the modern lawyer, it is important that your creativity does not stray beyond the proper boundaries of ethical and professional conduct. Your duties as a practitioner and your client's legitimate expectations are that the client's interests will be protected to the maximum extent possible under the law. If your client expects you to do more than apply your legal skills in an ethical and honourable way to protect his or her interests, then he or she is not worth having as a client.

To be conservative and careful in the advice you give may be considered by some to be old-fashioned but, as a lawyer, it will certainly make you sleep easier at night and reduce the number of negligence suits against you. Some of the lawyers who in the 1980s cut corners or turned a blind eye to ethical considerations in their pursuit of big fees are now either bankrupt, out of practice or in prison. The 1990s will hopefully be the decade where traditional values return to the legal profession.

Chapter 47

Career Options

> "During the first few years at the Bar, every barrister suffers far more trials than he ever conducts in court."
>
> R. E. Megarry, *Lawyer and Litigant in England* (Stevens & Sons Ltd, London, 1962), p. 39.

As a young practitioner, you have several options open to you. Unless your first year as an articled clerk, or whatever has been substituted for articles in your jurisdiction, has completely disillusioned you and has convinced you to get out of the legal profession altogether, you may go to the Bar,[1] you may work as an employee solicitor, you may establish or purchase a sole practice, or you may enter into partnership. Other alternatives include becoming a corporate lawyer, joining the public service, returning to academic life or working as a judge's associate.

Bar

It is fair to say that every lawyer considers the option of going to the Bar, at least once in his or her career. It is a serious step to go to the Bar. For one thing, you must make an immediate cash outlay to lease or buy chambers, buy robes and build up a library. On the other hand, you are unlikely to be earning much income initially.

In the initial years the briefs are likely to be few and far between and most of them will probably be fairly routine and not challenging. You will probably spend a good deal of time reading magazines next to the telephone hoping that it will ring. The magazines will not necessarily be of the learned variety! Not

1. The discussion of this option is more apt for jurisdictions that have a separate Bar.

much money will be coming in and it will be difficult to survive in view of the many overheads involved in keeping chambers.

You may find yourself doing part-time work such as reporting cases for a legal publisher or teaching at a university or college in order to supplement your brief fees. In time, however, the position should improve. The briefs will become more regular and some of them will be interesting.

If it is permissible in your jurisdiction, you should not go to the Bar immediately but should wait until you have worked as a solicitor for a few years.

For one thing, working as a solicitor will give you the opportunity to save some money to see you through the early lean years at the Bar. Also, it will give you a good perspective on how solicitors' offices operate as well as familiarity with the standard documents and procedures that are used by solicitors in various areas of practice. Such familiarity may in some circumstances assist you in advising clients properly.

In addition, the longer you remain a solicitor, the more solicitors you will meet and become friendly with. Such contacts may be a source of briefs when you go to the Bar.

Once you decide to go to the Bar, you should consult established barristers with a view to making the right choices in relation to which master to read with and which chambers and clerk to select. You should ensure that you obtain experience in as many areas as possible in your early years at the Bar so as to make an informed decision on where your talents and interests would be better served if you specialised in a particular area.

As a barrister, your "clients" are the solicitors who brief you. They are not as easy to fool as lay clients and neither are the courts before which you will be arguing cases. Therefore if you set out to be a successful barrister, you will certainly need to work very hard. You will be working for yourself and will not have the same back-up facilities that sizeable solicitors' practices have.

Whether or not you become successful will depend on your efforts. Certainly, successful barristers are so busy that they are forced to reject briefs. But to get to that position, it is odds-on that they have spent many late weeknights and weekends in chambers. Someone once said that lights never go out in Owen Dixon Chambers.[2] The same applies for other chambers all over the world.

2. Owen Dixon Chambers are located in Melbourne.

Apart from the hard work, life at the Bar can be very rewarding. The thrill of winning a case never disappears, nor does pride in the fact that you are central to the administration of justice. Every day you will be talking to judges, court officials, solicitors and other members of the Bar.

Of course, if you have ambitions of becoming a judge, there is no better way of doing it than by going to the Bar.

Employee solicitor

This is the most likely short-term option that you will adopt. If you have completed articles with a particular firm, it is likely you will remain there for a while.

There is a lot to be said for the security and stability associated with being an employee solicitor. The salary is more likely than not to be inadequate and it will probably remain so for several years. However, even though you will be working very hard to enrich someone else, at least you will have the opportunity of widening your experience in more diverse areas of the law and to build up your confidence as a lawyer. It is fair to say that an inexperienced solicitor is not much better than an articled clerk. In many ways it is experience which makes a good lawyer rather than good academic qualifications.

There is a lot to learn when you enter the profession and not all of this can be squeezed into one year of articles or whatever has been substituted for articles in your jurisdiction. Unless you are an extremely fast learner, it is advisable to remain an employee solicitor for a couple of years to acquire basic competence in the running of a legal office before launching into practice on your own.

Sole practitioner

Establishing or purchasing a sole practice is not an easy option. There are many responsibilities on sole practitioners, not all of them of a legal nature. Apart from seeing demanding clients, you will need to manage an office, supervise staff, see to the acquisition of equipment and books, keep up with legal developments and developments in areas such as office efficiency, and make sure that your accounts—and especially your trust accounts—are in order. You will probably need to borrow money to fund your own practice and this will place financial strains on you in your early years.

On the other hand, the emotional rewards of a successful and thriving practice built up by your own efforts are enormous. Of course, there are also the financial rewards—the fruits or profits of your labour (after the tax office takes its share) are yours alone.

If you decide to practise on your own, you should talk to established sole practitioners and seek their guidance on how to manage your practice efficiently and profitably. Your Law Society may well have experts on law office management who may assist you. You may also obtain some assistance by consulting relevant literature, and your Law Society is a good place to refer to for such literature.

Without proper preparation, you will have difficulties in coping with the tremendous pressures of legal practice. Your clients will also suffer because they will not be receiving a high standard of professional service.

Partnership

> "A bad partnership can be financially worse than a bad marriage. Your spouse can only cost you everything you have. Your partner can cost you your future."[3]

The option that solicitors have of entering into a partnership is usually a more long-term one. If you work for a large and prestigious firm, the prospect of being admitted into partnership before your 30th birthday is extremely remote. More likely than not you will have to endure the "overworked and underpaid" lot of an employee solicitor for several years before you have any chance of enjoying the fruits of proprietorship.

If and when you are offered a partnership, don't rush into it. Don't get carried away and fail to make an informed decision. You should seek information about important matters such as the financial position and management arrangements of the firm before committing yourself. Speak to as many partners as possible and do not be content to accept what the spokesperson for the firm tells you because it is possible that there are differences of opinion about the firm held by existing partners.

Make sure that you read carefully any existing partnership agreement before committing yourself and suggest amendments if you are not happy with it. If the firm does not have a partnership agreement then insist that one be drawn up which

3. J. G. Foonberg, *How to Start and Build a Law Practice* (American Bar Association, Chicago, 1976), p. 12.

covers the overall relationship of the partners to each other. A comprehensive partnership agreement is necessary to establish discipline, to define conduct, to reduce friction and to minimise misunderstandings amongst members of the partnership.

While it is impossible to define an ideal partnership, there are some essential ingredients required for a successful one and basically these ingredients are human rather than legal. You must be satisfied that you and your partners will respect and trust one another and will enjoy a workable and profitable association with each other, even if you may not become the closest of friends.

Consider the type of people that you want as partners. There are still all-Catholic, all-Protestant and all-Jewish firms but these prejudices are fading fast and mixed firms are becoming more and more common. It is not necessary to have mutual political or religious views for a partnership to be successful. Mutual trust and respect can flow from the most unlikely and different political, religious, social and economic backgrounds. Remember that a diverse firm is not necessarily a weak one; diversity may promote strength and vitality.

Pay particular attention to the financial arrangements involved in entering a partnership. If you have to contribute any capital in order to enter into partnership, make sure it will not be an excessive burden on your finances and standard of living. Obtain independent financial advice if necessary.

Make sure you are clear about your entitlement to profits. Many partnerships founder because of unequal sharing of income.

Some firms adhere to the notion that the "senior partner" should get a greater piece of the cake than the "junior partner" on the basis that the "senior partner" started the firm, attracted all the "important clients", had to battle in the "early days", made it "the hard way", and that it would cause the immediate collapse of the practice if the "senior partner" suddenly tired of breathing. It is often the case, however, that the "junior partner" works harder and earns more revenue for the firm than the "senior partner" who is less productive. A partnership developed in this way is born with a potential time bomb. The unfortunate long term results may be that a quality practice is destroyed or fragmented. Perhaps the solution is for all the partners to share profits equally but that the senior partner is given non-financial concessions such as additional time off.

Make sure that all partners recognise that good communication between them is fundamental and that they agree that they will have regular and uninterrupted meetings on budgeting, staffing, partners' movements and particular client problems.

You should also consider how the office will be managed. Time spent on administrative matters involves an opportunity cost. In a partnership of any size, it is money well spent to have an office manager who acts as financial controller and staff supervisor. The days when a partner could waste time interviewing junior staff or fixing the office plumbing have long since gone.

The Auckland District Law Society a few years ago published a booklet entitled *A Guide to Legal Partnerships* which set out the following list of matters that you should consider when contemplating entry into partnership:

1. *Incomes*
   (a) Are income levels satisfactory throughout the firm?
   (b) How are relative incomes calculated?
   (c) How long does it take to reach equality with senior partners?
   (d) What expenses or other allowances are paid?
2. *Goodwill/capital*
   (a) Is any payable?
   (b) If so, how much and when? Is any assistance given by way of guarantee?
3. *Democracy*
   (a) How are decisions made within the firm?
   (b) Are there regular partners' meetings?
   (c) Is the firm run on business-like lines?
4. *Restrictive covenant*
   (a) Are you expected to sign one?
   (b) Are its duration and radius reasonable?
   (c) Does it exclude employment in commerce?
   (d) If you agree to it, are you paid goodwill etc. by the firm on retiring?
5. *Retirement*
   (a) What does a retiring or deceased partner receive? And when?

(b) What is the voluntary retirement age?

(c) What is the compulsory retirement age?

6. *Disability*

What happens if you become disabled from practising by reason of accident or ill health?

(a) For a short period (say three months)?

(b) In the long term?

7. *Potential problems*

(a) Are all partners in good health?

(b) Is there a good age mix of partners?

(c) Does any existing partner plan to retire in the medium-term future?

(d) Does the firm plan to admit any new partner in the medium-term future?

(e) Does any partner have a substantial outside interest which might affect his or her contribution to the firm?

(f) How dependent is the firm on any one client or on any small number of clients? Is the loss of such client(s) a serious present concern?

(g) Are any professional negligence claims against the firm pending or anticipated?

(h) Does the firm have adequate insurance against:

(i) Professional negligence?

(ii) Loss of physical assets?

(iii) Consequential loss (for example, cost of moving premises and replacing lost documents)?

(iv) Sudden death of a partner?

(v) Long-term disability?

(i) Is a shift of premises contemplated? Or substantial equipment purchases? If so, what will the cost be and how will it be financed?

8. *Bank arrangements*

(a) What borrowing arrangements does the firm have with its bankers?

(b) Does any partner or group of partners have substantial borrowings from that bank? Is the liability of the other partners excluded?

9. *Partnership investments*
   - (a) Do the partners have any group investments (for example, tax schemes)?
   - (b) Who owns the partnership premises?
10. *Holidays*
    - (a) How often and when?
    - (b) Are you entitled to sabbatical leave? What income will be received whilst on leave?
11. *Superannuation*

    Is there a superannuation scheme for partners?
12. *Documentation*
    - (a) Have you examined the last three years' accounts of the partnership and have you discussed them with the firm?
    - (b) Have you examined the partnership agreement?

Corporate lawyer

A number of large companies employ lawyers in their own internal legal departments. In the past, companies recruited young practitioners with one or two years' experience in a corporate law firm. Now it is becoming increasingly more common to select graduates to start their working life in the company.

The lawyer who works in-house provides advice on a variety of subject areas. These include: contract, financial agreements, tort, consumer protection legislation, advertising, company law, taxation law and property law.[4]

Working as a corporate lawyer can be challenging and rewarding. Apart from career prospects in the law, there are also opportunities to advance your career in non-legal areas within the organisation. Some corporate lawyers, for example, are promoted to senior management positions.

Public service

There are many opportunities for a young lawyer in government departments and statutory authorities.

4. H. H. Price, "What Do Corporations Want From Their Corporate Lawyers?" (1983) 57 *Law Institute Journal* 836.

Lawyers are employed by a variety of public sector organisations, including the Attorney-General's Department, Australian Government Solicitor, Director of Public Prosecutions, Department of Social Security, Australian Taxation Office, the Trade Practices Commission, the Australian Securities Commission and Legal Aid agencies.

In addition to practising in areas such as administrative law, commercial law, personal injuries claims work, bankruptcy and debt recovery (to name but a few of the more prominent areas of law practised by government lawyers), practitioners are also employed in the policy and research areas of public authorities.

There are a number of advantages of working for the government. These include flexible conditions of employment, less pressured working environment and job security.[5]

Judge's associate

As a judge's associate, you will work as the judge's assistant. You will be the judge's spokesperson and will be required to liaise with the registry of the court, the legal profession and sometimes members of the public.

Apart from giving you a sound background in court procedure and exposure to advocacy skills, which is particularly relevant for those who contemplate going to the Bar, life as a judge's associate can provide varied and responsible work.

The precise work that you do will depend on the individual judge. Some judges require their associates to do research for them and assist in the preparation of judgments. Other judges, however, involve their associates in purely administrative tasks. You should make inquiries about the approach taken by a particular judge. It is advisable to speak to the judge's former associates for information.

Academic

A number of practitioners discover after their first year in legal practice that it is not at all what they thought it would be. Some lawyers decide early in their careers that they are best suited to academic life. Opportunities exist as tutors and lecturers in universities or other tertiary colleges.

5. For a discussion on current working life in the government see C. Erskine "Working for the Government" in *Articles on Articles—And Other Important Information For Young Lawyers* (Law Institute of Victoria, 1992), p. 29.

The advantages of academic life include the constant intellectual challenges demanded by the job, the interaction with students and colleagues, opportunities for research and writing, opportunities for travel and further study and generous sabbatical leave.

The main disadvantage of an academic appointment is monetary. Generally speaking, you will earn less as an academic than as a practising barrister or solicitor.

At the end of the day, your career choices will depend on your personal interests, goals, lifestyle and family and other commitments.

Chapter 48

A Survival Kit for New Lawyers

> "Fasten your seat belt, it's going to be a bumpy ride."
>
> Bette Davis.

Most of us have vivid memories of our early days in a legal office. Some lawyers have felt sick in the stomach every morning before going to work. Others have had nightmares throughout their first year in practice and whatever confidence they had begun with, was lost by the end of the year. Most of us have felt desperately insecure, ill-trained and probably unsuited to practise law.

Many new lawyers believe:

1. Partners never make mistakes.
2. They are nigh on illiterate when it comes to drafting correspondence or documents.
3. The most junior worker in the office knows more than they do.
4. If a matter has the potential to go wrong, then it surely will.
5. There are not enough years left in their miserable lives to enable them to find out what legal practice is all about.
6. It is an act of charity that their employers should pay them as they have done nothing to deserve it and they are only adding to the woes and cares of their employers by hanging around.

Well, take heart, all new lawyers, because it is not nearly as bad as you imagine. Here are some reassuring and comforting thoughts for you to read before you go to sleep each night:

1. Partners make mistakes. The perfect lawyer has not yet been invented.

2. While some of your draft documents and letters may be rough and ready, it is much easier to play God and correct settled drafts than approach the initial problem of creation. Bearing in mind that most people draft first and correct later, as a new lawyer you have been forced into the role of the creator of a draft upon which anyone, and we mean anyone, can improve.
3. Close supervision tends to highlight shortcomings in anyone's work. For example, take the case of a partner or employee solicitor leaving a firm. Immediately access is gained to that person's files, it is rare that unblurred hindsight does not reveal at least one skeleton in the legal cupboard.
4. In drafting everyone has their own particular style. Within certain limits there can be many "right" versions of the same thing. However, when it becomes a debate as to whether the word to be used should be "obtained" or "got", "acknowledged" or "received", "taken" or "obtained", "dispatched" or "sent", then the views of the correcting principal will inevitably prevail.
5. Other more senior employees do make mistakes too, but:
   - (a) no-one scrutinises their daily doings;
   - (b) experience gives you the know-how of retrieving many threatening situations;
   - (c) they are not under the searchlight that is directed at new solicitors.
6. Most of the mistakes that you make do not matter because they are part of your "learning curve". Because you are supervised, you are in a situation that the most damage you can do is to your own ego.
7. Remember that any system of training contemplates inexperience and a need for supervision. Presumably that supervision is designed to ensure that any mistakes are caught before the rabbit gets out of the net.
8. Alan Rosenberg, in an article on professional insecurity published originally in the *New York State Bar Association Journal*, said this: "Over the ensuing years these first impressions underwent a gradual metamorphosis. It was not so much that I grew in stature, but that those around me became smaller and less awesome. I gradually learned a basic truth about the law . . . the practice of the law is an intellectually humbling experience."

9. Partners do know more than inexperienced employee solicitors, although they were once inexperienced themselves. This superiority can be attributed to experience which is another way of saying that they made the same mistakes that you do, only they made them some years ago.
10. We know of one lawyer who in his first year of practice was required to write letters to a particular insurance company with a view to making recommendations about both liability and quantum. One of the partners used to re-draft them with such fury that the lawyer used to think that as a culmination of his rage, he would tear them to shreds, throw the pieces on the floor and begin to jump up and down on them. As it was, once the letters had been duly emasculated, they were sent to the partner's typist (because the typist was the only one who could read his writing) and were retyped in their amended form. The young lawyer would shed tears of frustration, until one day, on the suggestion of a senior (and very sympathetic) secretary he went to the partner and said "OK, you have torn all my efforts to bits. Now what about some positive advice on how I should go about it?" The partner looked startled, but to his credit he pulled out half a dozen letters that he thought were of acceptable standard and then he sat down and told the lawyer why letters should be in that particular form. With that positive advice something that had become a source of dread for the lawyer suddenly disappeared.
11. Remember there are few mistakes that cannot be rectified, particularly at the level of responsibility entrusted to you as an inexperienced employee solicitor.

New lawyers defence kit

Set out below are a number of suggestions to assist you in your early days of practice:

1. Ensure that you know precisely what you have been asked to do.
2. Find out how long you have to do it.
3. Know the facts of the file backwards, forwards and sideways.
4. If in doubt about what to do, do not guess.
5. In such a case, try all means of contacting your principal.
6. Anything is better than guessing. Try to get another person to help, telephone a friend if necessary.

7. Keep memos of your instructions from your principal.
8. If a mistake is made and you believe you are being unfairly used as a whipping boy/girl, say so.
9. If your letters are being butchered and you do not know why—find out.
10. New lawyers have been known to be right about some things—if you believe you are right, say so.

The corridors of legal offices are strewn with the egos of new lawyers who did not continually stick up for themselves when the going got tough.

Chapter 49

Women in the Law

> "The peculiar qualities of womanhood, its gentle graces, its quick sensibility, its tender susceptibility, its purity, its delicacy, its emotional impulses, its subordination of hard reason to sympathetic feeling, are surely not qualifications for forensic strife."
>
> *Re Goodell*, 39 Wisc. 232 (Wisconsin S.C., 1875) per Ryan C.J. Quoted in D. Weisbrot, *Australian Lawyers* (1990), p. 84.

A friend of ours who has been practising law for about ten years told us recently that she was sick to death of other practitioners calling her "girlie" and that she would go "right off" at the next male practitioner who asked her to put him through to her principal.

Although the position of female practitioners has improved in recent years, there are still too many practitioners who regard the practice of law as a male preserve and who believe that in order to succeed, women have to be demonstrably better than their male counterparts.

Women no longer professional curiosities

Women lawyers have moved from being professional curiosities, to uncommon creatures, to a marked minority, to a point where today there is a general acceptance of them as a significant and growing proportion of the legal profession.

Women now represent about one half of law school graduates and about one quarter of the practising profession. Women are well represented in academic life (at least in junior ranks), government and corporate sectors. Their numbers in private practice, however, are smaller and their representation at partnership level and in the judiciary is significantly lower.[1]

Areas of practice

Some diehard male practitioners, who are fighting a rearguard action on behalf of their sex, begrudgingly admit that women should be admitted to practise law and immediately add "in family law, conveyancing, probate and the like".

Although these views are not prevalent, the reality is that in many cases the types of work that men and women undertake in the law are different. Women work predominantly in family law, government and administrative law, legal aid and welfare law. Many corporate law areas are dominated by men.[2]

Some reasons that are advanced by conservative practitioners for keeping women out of particular areas of the law are:

1. Women are inexperienced in the relevant area. This argument is dependent upon the same practitioners refusing to give women the basic work to allow them to overcome the inexperience. It is a self-fulfilling prophecy!
2. Women are unacceptable to clients. This argument is no longer credible. Whilst some clients may be chauvinists, by far the great majority of clients judge their lawyers not by their gender but by their ability to provide quality service at a reasonable price.
3. Women have domestic chores and are unable to work the same number of hours as men. In most cases, this is a myth. The ability to work hard is not dependent on gender but rather on one's personality and career aspirations.

1. These figures and statements come from a number of sources: "Women in Law—The Statistical Picture" (1992) 66 *Law Institute Journal* 161; S. Roach Anleu, "Women in the Legal Profession" (1992) 66 *Law Institute Journal* 162; Y. Hilton, "Women in Legal Practice—Changing Pattern Needed" (1992) 27 (December) *Australian Law News* 12; J. A. Scutt, *Women and the Law—Commentary and Materials* (Law Book Company Ltd, 1990), pp. 30-38; C. Falls, "Women at the Top—What Price Partnership?" (1988) 26 (July) *Law Society Journal* 36; D. Weisbrot, *Australian Lawyers* (Longman Cheshire, Malaysia, 1990), pp. 85-90.
2. "Women in the Law—The Statistical Picture" (1992) 66 *Law Institute Journal* 161; S. Roach Anleu, "Women in the Legal Profession" (1992) 66 *Law Institute Journal* 162; D. Weisbrot, *Australian Lawyers* (Longman Cheshire, Malaysia, 1990), pp. 87-88.

4. Women are not as "tough" as men in some areas such as litigation and negotiation of commercial agreements. Again, this is a myth. There are some excellent female litigators and corporate lawyers.

While the practice of law does not require physical strength, there still seems to be a heavy veil of tradition and prejudice which women have to lift in some areas of legal practice.

The best way for you to avoid being stereotyped and confined to so-called "feminine" areas of legal practice, is to make known the area of practice that you are interested in and seek an opportunity to demonstrate your skills in that area.

Prejudices

If a woman is to be successful in the law, does the way she presents herself matter? There is, of course, no empirical evidence on this. Our experience has been that young practitioners, irrespective of their gender, who are well groomed and present themselves well are received more favourably by clients and colleagues.

Our experience has also been that most women lawyers, both barristers and solicitors, present themselves far better than many of their male counterparts. Some male lawyers we know seem to be refugees from church opportunity shops and seem indifferent to how they present themselves to their clients.

Although employers are not permitted to discriminate in staff choices on the basis of gender or marital status, there are less obvious biases that continue to operate against women. Results of a national survey of recent law graduates revealed that about one third of women considered that being a woman was a disadvantage in day-to-day legal work.[3]

Job interviews

In addition to barriers in daily practice, one third of the women in the same survey reported that their gender created difficulties in finding work.[4]

3. D. Weisbrot, *Australian Lawyers* (Longman Cheshire, Malaysia, 1990), p. 89. This is consistent with a survey conducted in the United Kingdom which suggested that discrimination on gender grounds was rampant within the legal profession: M. Martin, "Women Judges—When?" (1992) 66 *Law Institute Journal* 393.
4. D. Weisbrot, *Australian Lawyers* (Longman Cheshire, Malaysia, 1990).

Perhaps the greatest difficulty in finding work is negotiating your way through a job interview. Being interviewed by partners (and often male partners) in legal firms can be a daunting experience. Studies suggest that women (in comparison to men) are more likely to belittle their achievements and are less likely to put themselves forward as confident and successful people.[5] Aim to present an assessment of your skills confidently and realistically.

Some practitioners who conduct interviews still ask women about their marital status and plans for having children. They are either not aware that these types of questions are contrary to equal opportunity legislation or else they choose to ignore this.

It is difficult to know how to react to such questions, particularly when they are prefaced with a seemingly innocuous "just out of interest".

Many women are aware that such questions are improper but choose to answer them anyway for fear of prejudicing their job prospects.

One way of dealing with such questions is to say politely that you have not given any consideration to the matter because it never occurred to you that it might be relevant to your ability to perform your work well.

Be confident

It is important that you present your work and ideas confidently and without apology. Do not focus unnecessarily on what you do wrong at the expense of what you do right. All young practitioners make mistakes. Being a woman does not mean you will make more mistakes than men.

It can, of course, be difficult to present confidently when clients and other practitioners intentionally, or more often unintentionally, are patronising. It can be demoralising to attend your first client meeting and be told by the client that he would like his coffee black. There is no point responding indignantly or rudely. You should explain politely to your client that you are a lawyer and that you will arrange for the firm's catering staff to bring refreshments.

5. R. Hunter, *Indirect Discrimination in the Workplace* (Federation Press, 1992), p. 167.

Children

Probably the greatest difficulty confronting women in the law is the issue of children.[6] Government employers are required by statute to accommodate women's decisions about children. However, in private practice, a decision to have a child can often be construed by your employer as a decision to abandon your career. There are few opportunities for part-time jobs and many firms lack the commitment required to make part-time positions work.

The outlook is, however, changing as more legal firms accept the economic necessity of flexible working policies, maternity leave and part-time work. Firms are developing maternity leave programmes that permit women to work from home, or reorganise their working requirements.

If you are contemplating working for a particular firm after becoming a mother, you should make enquiries about the attitudes of that firm to working mothers by speaking to women already working in that firm. If the corporate culture of the firm is not conducive to child-raising, you should think twice about joining that firm.

Female lawyer's survival kit

For those who are still fighting some of the diehard male prejudices, we have put together some key elements of the female lawyer's survival kit:

1. If you are tired of being called "girlie" or "love", call the person who is referring to you in that manner "boyo" or "sweetie" or something equally offensive!
2. If people refuse to believe you are the solicitor, not the secretary, announce your name and follow it immediately by "solicitor".
3. If you are concerned that clients will not take you seriously, tell them who you are and what you are. A professional manner quickly wins over recalcitrant clients.

6. M. Martin, "Working Nine to Five—Not A Way To Make A Living If You're Bringing Up Young Children" (1992) 66 *Law Institute Journal* 286.

Part 9

Leaving the Law—Common Legal Diseases

Chapter 50

Introduction

"Every calling is great when greatly pursued."

Oliver Wendell Holmes, "The Law", *Speeches*, 1913. Quoted in D. Schrager and E. Frost, *The Quotable Lawyer* (1986), p. 198.

The practice of law has many professional rewards but it is often very stressful.

There will be times where you will be ecstatic with your work, such as when you win a case for a deserving client against an aggressive and unworthy opponent. There will be other times where the pressures of work and the inevitable injustices that occur will depress you and cause you to reflect on alternative ways of making a living.

If you find that you no longer have faith in what you do, you should seriously consider making a career change. Unless you remedy the situation quickly, you may find that not only the quality of your work will suffer, but also your health and your relationship with your clients, colleagues and family.

In Part 9, we discuss some of the common legal diseases that afflict lawyers.

Chapter 51

Professional Paralysis

> "I like work: it fascinates me. I can sit and look at it for hours. I love to keep it by me: the idea of getting rid of it nearly breaks my heart."
>
> Jerome K. Jerome, *Three Men in a Boat*, Ch. 15.

As a young practitioner, you are unlikely to be familiar with the dreaded disease "professional paralysis". This chapter provides an insight into the disease and how to cope with it.

In 1984 there was a case of a solicitor who failed to answer more than thirty letters which had been written to him by his Law Society in relation to a number of complaints. That inability to cope with correspondence was matched by his inability to handle current files. The solicitor said that each time he received an envelope with the Law Society's endorsement on the outside he had begun to shake and he had a special drawer in his desk where he placed the envelope unopened. He received letters from clients which he could identify from the handwriting which he placed in another desk drawer unopened. Irrespective of the horrendous consequences he was physically incapable of facing up to the contents of those letters and he hoped that they would go away. He became a legal ostrich.

The failure of some solicitors to reply to correspondence is due to a disease, a terrible debilitating psychological disease that virtually paralyses the solicitor whenever any pressure situation develops.

The complaint is unrelated to logic and capable of incapacitating any solicitor, young or old. The result is a total inability to cope with work pressure, a growing heap of files in the "too hard basket", a multitude of dissatisfied clients, piles of unanswered correspondence and deep resentment of the telephone.

Indeed, if all the time spent making excuses to clients and other solicitors for inactivity were redirected towards getting on with the job, a partial recovery would be possible.

It is a form of professional breakdown. A bewildering, mind-blurring condition that is illogical, inexplicable and sometimes untreatable.

Symptoms

Because of its insidious nature and because it is frequently a lonely complaint, a very private condition which cannot be shared with other practitioners, it is not always easy to diagnose. Some of the symptoms are:

1. File stagnation. You pick up a file and then put it down again. Then you pick up another file and, without doing anything, put it down. There is a virtual inability to decide which file should receive precedence and in the end, none of them do.
2. The unopened drawer of the filing cabinet. There is a standing joke about a too hard basket, but a symptom of the condition is an actual drawer in the filing cabinet which you prefer not to open or are physically incapable of opening. Some of the files become so pressing that you cannot bear the sight of them and there is an increasing tendency to pretend that they do not exist.
3. The fast lane for the easy files. By doing the easy jobs, those that involve a quick turnover and easy client satisfaction, you delude yourself that you are on top of your practice. A check of the month's earnings is used to satisfy yourself that the practice is really healthy and has no problems. It is a self-induced delusion.
4. Excuses. To explain the inactivity in particular matters, you begin to make weaker and weaker excuses to your clients. It becomes addictive. At first the excuses are difficult, but then they become easier and easier. When at first quick action could give reality to the excuse, the passing of time makes that impossible. You become more reckless. Clients are told that actions are set down for hearing in the full knowledge that within weeks or months the client will be badgering you for a hearing date. Clients are told that conveyancing matters are ready for settlement, when you know full well there are problems associated with the transaction.

5. Procrastination and explanation. You become involved in attendances that do not advance the file at all. You do the easy peripheral things without coming to grips with the real problem. Hours are spent on the telephone, giving weak excuses as to why matters have not been attended to. If that time were redirected into positive action, the difficulties in the file might be overcome.
6. Non-response. You do not telephone back, you do not answer letters. You pull down the shutters and hope that it will all go away.

Causes

The most difficult thing of all is to state definitely the causes of the dread disease. We have seen it at close hand and the following is a list of some of its causes:

1. Genuine overwork. Some solicitors believe that a successful practice can be measured by the number of files in a filing cabinet. That overwork can lead to a convincing flow of easy work on the surface but with a series of more difficult files slowly slipping to the bottom of filing cabinets, where they remain untouched.
2. Incompetence in some areas. Some very competent and effective solicitors have an Achilles' heel. For example, we have known solicitors who have been excellent common lawyers, but utterly incapable of making workers' compensation applications. The result is that they concentrate on the areas of the law in which they are very competent and hope that, by some miracle, the areas in which they are less competent can be attended to by negotiation or compromise, rather than through taking the procedural steps necessary to advance the matter.
3. Fear of losing clients. Whether it is caused by greed or insecurity, some solicitors can never refuse a client. A dog-with-a-bone mentality develops and all clients are accepted, whether the instructions involve a land transfer on the Nullarbor Plain or damage caused by an escaped lion from the Melbourne Zoo.[1]
4. Lack of assistance. This particularly affects young solicitors who have started from scratch, built up a reasonable practice but yet are uncertain at what stage they should

1. See below, Ch. 52.

either take on an employee solicitor or a partner. If the decision is delayed too long, the swell of work becomes overwhelming and the only way the solicitor can cope is by doing the quick, easy and profitable work at the expense of more difficult matters.

5. Failure to come to grips with basic economics. Some solicitors who have suffered from the disease have told us that they could not afford to put on a locum solicitor or engage an employee to handle a backlog of troublesome matters. They seem incapable of appreciating that it is better to pay someone $1,000 per week to complete and cost 50 difficult files worth $100,000 than to allow those files to remain dormant and uncosted.
6. A general emotional and psychological breakdown. Legal practice involves enormous stresses. Those stresses are contributed to by the competition within the profession itself, the demands of clients and the strict requirements of courts and public offices. All those pressures can lead to a solicitor feeling utterly beleaguered.
7. Ego. We asked a solicitor who suffered from the disease why, when he realised that he was in great trouble with his practice, he did not consult other practitioners and seek their assistance in matters which he was incompetent to handle? He told us that such a step would humiliate him and he did not want to become the subject of talk, in his local profession, that he was incompetent or a bungler.

Treatment

Whether the disease is terminal or whether it can be treated depends on the particular case. In the case of a total psychological breakdown, brought about by overwork and work-related stress, some solicitors must clearly wind down their practices and look for something easier to do.

We knew a solicitor once who dreaded coming into the office and who treated one drawer of his filing cabinet as though it contained a number of anti-social vipers. He felt sick in the stomach when he walked into his office and towards the end it became physically impossible for him to open some files or to respond to correspondence about them.

On our advice he went into his office one Sunday morning, took every file out of its cabinet and spread them in rows on the floor and sat down and laboriously went through each matter one by one. Seeing the files and physically handling them in an atmosphere where there was no telephone interruption or client pressure allowed him, for the first time, to identify some of the horrors that he had on his hands. Once he had isolated those files he classified them into those matters which he did not have the expertise to handle, those matters where the delays were so bad that they were incapable of being retrieved by him and those matters which only required something to be done quickly. His actions included all the ingredients of trying to cope with professional paralysis.

1. Physically face up to the problem, make time, open the file and find out just how bad it is.
2. If the problem is lack of expertise, send the file to a solicitor who specialises in the particular area of the law and, irrespective of whether you receive any costs over and above his charges, get the matter moving and completed.
3. Where the file is entangled in a web of deception, get the clients in, explain the situation and let them decide whether they want to take the file away or persevere with you while you straighten out their matters. If you have prejudiced their position, suggest that they obtain independent legal advice. You should also notify your professional indemnity insurer.
4. Where the problem stems from overwork, telephone a legal employment agency and endeavour to engage a locum or an employee solicitor to help you cope with the overall pressure.
5. Share the problem with someone else. Talk to a friend. Legal practice can be desperately lonely.

Chapter 52

"I Can't Say No" Syndrome

"I'm just a lawyer who can't say no
I'm in a terrible fix
I always say come on let's go
Just when I oughta say nix."
(With apologies to Rodgers & Hammerstein, *Oklahoma*.)

When one considers the claims statistics published in respect of professional indemnity insurance covers each year or the number of defalcations which have been committed by lawyers during the past decade, one can only wonder how many of them would have been avoided if the lawyer in question had shaken his or her head and sadly walked away.

The fact is that the inability to refuse instructions or avoid making outlandish promises is a prime cause of trouble, both in the area of professional negligence and defalcations.

Here are some of the scenarios which occur again and again.

1. A badly overworked solicitor is unable to cope with his or her day-to-day practice. He or she has more files than a fruit cake smuggled into prison and still clients come to him or her. Does he or she knock them back and say "I'm sorry but I can't handle the files I've already got."? No, he or she takes them on-board until unknowingly their files join the great morass of inactive matters in his or her filing cabinet. Somehow the solicitor fondly believes that some catastrophe will ensue should he or she turn a client away, or send that client to another solicitor who may either want the work or have the necessary expertise to perform it.
2. The file miser—the solicitor who collects files like some of us collect books, stamps or butterflies. The solicitor receives instructions for a difficult drainage matter. Does the solicitor

say to the clients "Look, I've only ever done one of these and it's not my area of expertise. You should go to see Roach & Roach who are the best in the drainage game."? No, either for reason of ego, avarice or blind stupidity the solicitor takes the clients on. And like most things that are beyond our intellectual capacity, our experience or just our workload, nothing occurs. There is nothing as hard as the too hard basket. And so the matter languishes there, until one day the clients no longer believe the half-baked excuses they have been served up. They become impatient and go to another solicitor who ultimately finds that the matter is hopelessly out of time and so yet another claim is referred to the professional indemnity insurance scheme.

3. When he was in third year, Jimmy Hayho was elected the most popular law student. He loves being popular, he wants to please everyone and so whatever he is asked, he grants. Or at least he agrees to grant. He takes on actions which would have caused Clarence Darrow to have a heart attack. No case is too difficult, no claim too small. His optimism is infectious. He is the most popular lawyer on the block. Ultimately, that is where his head ends, because miracle workers only come along every few thousand years and Jimmy Hayho leaves a trail of optimistic destruction behind him. He is incapable of breaking bad news to clients, or of displeasing them by telling them that they are either wrong or that they have no cause of action. Ultimately they are displeased, but some thousands of dollars later.
4. Some solicitors develop reputations as money managers. When money is almost unobtainable they keep their practices alive through their reputation for obtaining funds at reasonable rates. Sometimes that reputation is justly earned, but sometimes it is a fabrication.

Too many of the defalcations by solicitors are unrelated to any desire for personal gain. Rather they have been associated with a desire to achieve personal popularity or a fear of losing the client to someone who might have the funds available for a particular transaction. Sometimes the fiddling begins on a temporary basis. Peter is robbed to pay Paul and to ensure that important conveyancing transactions go on, clients unknowingly become the generous donors who ensure that this conveyancing web of deception continues.

But as we all know, once you put your toe in the water it becomes easier the next time, and so the deception grows and grows until truthfully, the solicitor has no comprehension of how much has been taken or from whom.

The task of unravelling the mess is left to either the auditors or the relevant Law Society. The public always presumes that when a solicitor steals trust money there has been personal benefit. In our experience that is the exception rather than the rule. In many cases, some clients benefit a great deal, but, of course, when there are winners there are also losers.

Here are some warnings for the solicitors who want to be Mr or Ms Popularity of the year.

1. Remember, it is better to lose clients by giving accurate advice and by properly assessing their chance of success than to lose them eventually by giving incorrect advice. Never be tempted to sugar the pill merely to keep a client in the hope that you might be able to punt the action through.
2. Before you agree to act for a client ask yourself whether you have the expertise to carry out the task entrusted to you.
3. Before you agree to pull that filing cabinet drawer open just once more to force yet another file in, ask yourself whether you are coping with the work that you currently have on hand. If the answer is "no" ask yourself why you are agreeing to take on this additional matter. Are you an egotist, are you greedy or do you just want to be popular? If you suspect that the answer might be one of those three, take out a Lawyer-to-Lawyer Directory and send your clients to someone who can look after them properly.
4. If you are asked for finance which you have not got in order to keep major conveyancing or commercial matters, do not fiddle with it. Immediately send the client away.
5. If in order to keep a client there is a temptation to adjust the trust account a little bit to enable you to provide short-term finance, you are just a whisker away from losing your right to practise.
6. If you are worried about what your clients might think of you if you refuse to act for them, think again and contemplate what they will think of you after you have finished acting for them.
7. Practise making comments such as:

   "I'm sorry Mr Smith, you haven't got a cause of action."; or

   "You're wasting your time Mrs Smith. That matter of principle will cost you a fortune."; or

"Look, I don't know anything about it, you need an expert in this field. Why don't you go and see Bloggs?"; or

"I'm just too busy to take on any more matters. The file will just lie around in my filing cabinet for months. Why don't you go to see Ms Chapel? She's an excellent lawyer who has just opened up a new practice. She'll be pleased to act for you."; or

"Look, I'd like to act for you in this $4 million transaction, but quite frankly I just can't provide the finance. All the trust money that I've had for investment is out and there isn't any more."

All too simple? Perhaps so, but each year there are a multitude of lawyers who do not know any better. Some are the most popular people in prison.

Chapter 53

"Time to Quit" Condition

> "A heart specialist once said: 'I have two questions for you—firstly, what do you spend most of your time doing? and secondly, is your heart in it?'"
>
> T. Norquay, "Burnout" (1985) 59 *Law Institute Journal* 1046 at 1049.

The inability of a lawyer to refuse instructions when unable to cope with work on hand is a symptom of a major problem: the failure of lawyers to recognise when it is time to quit.

Recently, a lawyer sought our advice about some problems he had encountered with his practice. As events turned out the practice itself was the biggest problem of all and in that situation it is difficult to come up with any smart ideas. When we told him that he should dispose of his practice and take a job either as an employee lawyer or in some other capacity, he looked at us goggle-eyed.

Certainly our advice was not what he wanted to hear and he became angry with us. But what else can you say to someone whose practice had not grossed more than $120,000 in each of the past five years and which after payment of salaries, rental and other overheads had netted him an average of $30,000 per annum during that time? We pointed out that his net income for that year promised to be $2,500 more than he was paying his secretary, who was a single woman of 20, while he had three children and a working wife. Still the penny did not drop.

He talked about "things getting better," "cutting overheads," "a crook period". We told him that his income figures indicated that he was not able to make a go of it in the favourable economic climate of the 1980s so heaven help him now that the tide had turned.

He asked us why he could not make a go of it. Well the truth is, some people have it and some people do not. Certainly some people are more secure earning a salary and despite all the advice in the world find it difficult to run a business. But in this case as a lawyer aged 38 years with some 14 years of practice behind him, the important thing was that he should recognise that none of the variables which he mentioned to us were likely to rescue him from the financial squeeze in which he found himself.

It is not that uncommon to meet lawyers who should give up practice. Balance sheets are sometimes relevant, but more often than not there are other danger signs which call for a lawyer to face up to reality. Forty seems to be a dangerous age in this regard, and it seems to be this legal mid-life crisis which catches up with lawyers of both sexes. Do you fit any of these examples?

1. You have been in practice for 15 years and for the last ten you have been practising by yourself. You have an articled clerk and a secretary, who also doubles as your Titles Office clerk. You have a receptionist but she only wants to work part-time because of a growing family. Fifteen years after commencing practice you are earning $5,000 a year more than your secretary. Your wife returned to work two years ago and is now earning twice your gross income working as a school teacher. It surely must be time to think again?

2. You are 45 years of age and have been practising law for 20 years. You have been doing what you are doing now, be it common law, conveyancing, commercial law, whatever, for most of those 20 years and you are pretty good at it. You are earning big money, you own a Mercedes Benz, you sail your yacht at the weekends, you are a member of several of the best clubs and above all else, you are absolutely sick and tired of legal practice.

   If you are a common lawyer, the clients now take three times as long to give you draft answers to interrogatories. Even the simplest question as to whether they sounded the horn of their motor vehicle causes them to reflect, when you know what the answer is. You often feel like shaking them.

   If you are a conveyancer, the clients always seem to want to take possession prior to settlement or lock their furniture in the garage of their new house before they are entitled to.

   In commercial law, clients seldom read what they sign and they often go behind your back in negotiations with the other party without telling you what is going on. Frankly, you are tired of the sight of them.

The receptionist does not get your telephone calls quickly enough, the word processors seem to give priority to every other lawyer in the office, and your own secretary, who has been with you for seven years, has suddenly become absolutely unreasonable.

When you go home at night you want to kick the dog, run over the bicycle that is left in the driveway, and light the incinerator next to your neighbour's lounge room window.

In the mornings you do not want to get up, you are sick to death of the screaming and punching that goes on between the children before they go to school, and you have even taken to listening to talkback radio on the way to the office, and sometimes you find yourself agreeing with the callers! Clearly it is time to quit.

Whether it is economic necessity or sheer professional fatigue, there comes a time when, irrespective of how much money you are making or how good you have become at your craft, you must ask yourself the question, do I want to do this for the rest of my days?

If a small voice inside you cries out "No!", then it is time not only to think about quitting but to turn your mind to what else you would like to do.

No remuneration, no prestige, no professional pride can justify entrapping yourself in a daily environment which has long since ceased to be acceptable. You are clearly in legal mid-life crisis, which may not necessarily involve you in leaving the law. Perhaps rescue can be achieved by a dramatic change in your surroundings or in the type of work that you do.

Is it time that you had a new challenge? Should you turn your back on the malingering plaintiff, the routine medical examinations, the faltering answers to interrogatories and learn new skills? For example, does your firm brief counsel in the local court or an administrative appeals tribunal? Why not volunteer to act as your firm's advocate in any appearances there, rather than briefing out? Perhaps there may be other partners within the firm who feel exactly as you do and who would be prepared to virtually swap professional responsibilities and act as a tutor to provide you with some in-house education in their particular area of practice.

Certainly there are no glib answers, and it is worthwhile sitting down with someone, a senior partner, a colleague, your wife, husband or domestic partner to try to identify what it is that you have tolerated for 15 years but can no longer cope with. Unfortunately, at about 40 the trap is well and truly set. The responsibilities are at a maximum, the schooling is at its most expensive, the family is at its most dependent, the mortgage is at its largest, the social pressures are at their most oppressive. And yet it is at about that age that many practitioners have made brave decisions.

As we have said before in this book, legal practice can be desperately lonely.

Part 10
Miscellaneous

Chapter 54

Questions

> " 'What do you know about this business?' the King said to Alice. 'Nothing' said Alice. 'Nothing whatever?' persisted the King. 'Nothing whatever' said Alice. 'That's very important,' the King said turning to the jury."
>
> Lewis Carroll, *Alice's Adventures in Wonderland*, Ch. 12.

The theme of this book has been that common sense is a necessary prerequisite to the practice of law. If you have been generously endowed with common sense, you will be in a better position to resolve the many problems that arise in practice for which the law does not provide a direct answer.

If you think you have learned anything from reading this book, have a go at the following questions. The questions are based on actual complaints and inquiries received by the Law Institute of Victoria.

Responsibility for sexual predilections of articled clerks

You have been appointed Secretary of the Law Institute of Victoria (God help you!) and you receive a complaint from an irate husband that the solicitor acting for his wife in a matrimonial dispute is having sexual intercourse with her. You cannot believe that a solicitor would do such a thing and you write a letter to the complainant husband telling him that he will have to have proper proof before you will investigate. You think that that is the last of it.

Then comes a letter from the triumphant husband enclosing photographs of the goings-on which he has taken from a hill near the wife's home through a camera with a telescopic lens. You take up the complaint and write to the solicitor acting for the wife who replies indignantly saying that the photographs disclose not him but recognisable portions of his articled clerk.

Would you:

(a) take sick leave?

(b) regard the matter as being none of your business and do nothing?

(c) suggest to the articled clerk that he pull down the blinds in future?

(d) point out to the husband that although the articled clerk's conduct is disgraceful, you have no control over the conduct of articled clerks pursuant to the *Legal Profession Practice Act* 1958 (Vic.) and that they are expected to behave abysmally in any event?

(e) hold the solicitor primarily responsible for the sexual predilections of his articled clerk—after all, he is supposed to be supervising and controlling him isn't he?

(f) slip a note to the Board of Examiners so as to prevent the articled clerk from being admitted as a solicitor?

Defective will

You are consulted by a husband and wife who claim to have been left a large estate pursuant to a will of a friend. The estate is worth approximately $250,000 and there are a number of living nephews and nieces who get nothing. You examine the will and note that there is only one witness. You tell the clients that the will is invalid and unless another can be found, the deceased will have died intestate.

Your clients are very disappointed and suggest that perhaps you could witness the will there and then. You mumble something about the *Crimes Act* and look pompous. They thank you for your advice and ask how much they owe you and then begin to leave. You (stupidly) ask them what they intend to do. They reply that they will probably obtain the signature of another witness to the will and instruct another solicitor to apply for a grant of probate.

Would you:

(a) volunteer to help in that regard for 10% of the estate?

(b) do nothing?

(c) telephone your Law Society and ask what to do?

(d) telephone the Registrar of Probates and tell him what has happened and advise him to keep an eye open?

(e) watch for the advertisement of the grant and contact the solicitor named?

(f) contact the police?

Other side's brief

You act for a plaintiff company in a major commercial case involving $20 million. Your client company has received advice from you and your barrister that there are grave difficulties associated with the proceeding. Your firm frequently uses barrister X in commercial litigation but on this occasion, he has been retained by the solicitors representing the defendant company.

A bundle of briefs is sent back to your office by barrister X's clerk and inside one of the briefs you find a written memorandum which contains advice unrelated to the brief itself but in respect of the commercial case in which you are acting for the plaintiff company.

The memorandum from counsel to the defendant's solicitors occupies five pages but the thrust of it is that barrister X does not like the defendant's case at all. He recites adverse facts to support this view of which you and your client company were previously unaware, and he recommends a settlement offer of $7.5 million but urges the defendant to go to $15 million rather than allow the matter to go to court.

Would you:

(a) block your ears, wash out your mouth with soap and water, put your eyes out with a burning stick and continue to act?

(b) do nothing?

(c) read the opinion a second time and begin to walk around the room with a new spring in your step?

(d) return the memorandum with a "with compliments" card to barrister X and continue to act?

(e) return the opinion to barrister X with an appropriate note and advise your client company that for reasons you cannot disclose you cannot continue to act further?

(f) advise the defendant's solicitors what has happened and continue to act?

Recalcitrant insured

You have been instructed by an insurance company to handle the defence of a Supreme Court writ issued on behalf of a passenger who suffered severe injuries as a consequence of a vehicle running off the road and colliding with a tree. The plaintiff's father, who claimed to have been driving, seems to have been totally to blame for the collision and the tree completely innocent. The passenger has been rendered a paraplegic. The father was uninjured.

An investigator's report was obtained and it reveals that there are two witnesses who saw the father and son leave a restaurant near the scene of the collision just before the accident and it was the son who got behind the steering wheel.

You have to deliver a defence and when the father comes in you put it to him that his story is a pack of lies. You also put to him what the two witnesses have said. The father describes the story of the witnesses as nonsense and reaffirms his instructions that he was the driver of the vehicle. You say that you do not believe him. You tell him that you will deliver a defence denying that he was the driver and that is the way that you propose to handle the case.

The father replies by saying that he will admit being the driver of the car in answer to interrogatories and intends to go to the hearing in person as the defendant on the record and that he will give evidence supporting his son's story, whether you like it or not.

Would you:

(a) obtain a prescription for valium in cake form?

(b) do nothing?

(c) suggest that the defendant seek independent legal advice immediately?

(d) warn the defendant about the criminal law and what happens to people who commit perjury?

(e) make application for a restraining order to prevent the defendant being allowed within the precincts of the Supreme Court?

(f) rely upon the doctrine of derapulative nugency?

(g) advise the defendant that in future you act for the insurer and that he should make his own arrangements?

(h) hide the plaintiff's interrogatories from the defendant?

Mad client

You are consulted by Mrs X, who has been severely injured in a motor accident. You take the usual instructions and obtain copy medical reports from all the hospitals and doctors where she has received treatment. You also have her medically examined by specialists. Although she has been severely injured, there is no reference to concussion, and it does not seem that she lost consciousness as a consequence of the accident.

However, during the course of acting for her, it becomes apparent that Mrs X is somewhat unusual. Her conduct is quite erratic, with the instructions you receive from her varying from meeting to meeting. On one occasion she will tell you that she will not accept less than $20,000, while on the next occasion she will tell you that the figure is really $200,000. Your fears about her are strengthened when she tells you that she believes that the collision was not an accident, but a deliberate attempt to kill her by the driver of the other vehicle.

The defendant pays the sum of $50,000 into court. When you contact Mrs X and ask her to come in to see you, she tells you that the offer of $50,000 is far too much, that it is contrary to her religious beliefs to profit from an accident, that it was clearly God's will, and insists that the maximum she wants is $10,000, and that the balance should be repaid to the insurance company.

Would you:

(a) prepare a detailed memorandum of settlement and have the plaintiff sign it before following her instructions?

(b) give notice of acceptance of money paid into court, give Mrs X $10,000 and keep the rest?

(c) advise the insurance company that the payment into court is rejected by the plaintiff and put a counter offer of $10,000?

(d) contact the relatives of Mrs X and advise them of your doubts about her sanity?

(e) without any instruction from your client, or anyone else, make application for a guardian to be appointed to represent Mrs X?

(f) buy a thumbscrew and re-interview Mrs X?

Crooked client

You see on your appointments pad that a client, whose name rings a bell with you, has made an appointment to see you. You read the morning paper and there you see that a large public company has gone into liquidation and that it is likely that criminal proceedings will be commenced against its former directors. The name of one of the directors is the same as that of the client who is coming to see you.

The client arrives and you satisfy yourself from the photograph in the newspaper that he is one of the directors against whom criminal proceedings are contemplated. The accusation is that the directors have transferred a large proportion of the company's funds into Swiss bank accounts.

The client director seeks your advice on the laws of extradition and, in particular, wishes to know which is the most difficult country from which to be extradited back to Australia.

Would you:

(a) bring the client down with a rugby tackle and bind him hand and foot?

(b) telephone the police from another room while having your secretary serve your client with tea and biscuits?

(c) accept the client's instructions on the basis that you are prepared to advise him where it is difficult to be extradited from, but that you will not tell him where he should escape to?

(d) ask for costs in advance, and then set about the research necessary to advise him properly in accordance with your professional obligations?

(e) refuse to advise him?

(f) quadruple your fees and ask for payment in Swiss francs?

Reneging client

In a long-drawn-out action you have acted on behalf of a plaintiff who, at various times, has been the most unreasonable, rude and difficult client you have ever acted for. At long last the action is listed for hearing and at the door of the court the defendant's solicitors offer an amount of $200,000 in full and final settlement of the plaintiff's case.

You obtain instructions from the plaintiff to accept this amount and, because of the difficulties which you have had with him in the past, you arrange for those instructions to be given in writing. The plaintiff signs a release.

Twenty-eight days later, in accordance with the terms of settlement, a cheque for $200,000 is received which you pay into your trust account and subsequently draw against, to forward a cheque to the plaintiff for his entitlement from the settlement.

The plaintiff returns the cheque to you with a brief note saying that the amount is insufficient, that you misled him and that he is now no longer prepared to settle for that amount. You return the cheque to him with a note telling him not to be silly. He returns the cheque to you.

Would you:

(a) contact the defendant's insurer and tell it that the settlement is off and that it was all just a silly mistake?

(b) tell your client that he is bound by the settlement and that if he does not accept the cheque he should instruct another solicitor to act for him?

(c) keep the sum of $200,000 in trust after writing a letter to the plaintiff telling him that you hold the money on his behalf, and it will remain there without earning interest until he claims it?

(d) telephone your Law Society and seek guidance?

(e) keep returning the cheque to him forever?

(f) send a cheque for the sum of $200,000 to the Receiver of Unclaimed Moneys?

(g) invest the settlement moneys in an authorised trustee investment at call and advise the client it will remain there until he claims it?

Lying client

You are an experienced Magistrates Court advocate and you know that whatever happens, you are not allowed to let your client commit perjury or give evidence that is contrary to the instructions that he or she has given you. But then it happens! In a case involving breaking and entering you put the defendant in the witness box and begin to examine him in accordance with the instructions he has given you.

His responses can only be described as startling. The version of the facts which he now proceeds to give in response to your questions is as different as *Alice in Wonderland* is to *Moby Dick*. You try to re-direct his answers but he seems intent upon perjuring himself. His replies are even more fanciful in cross-examination.

Would you:

(a) stop after a few questions, get the matter stood down, and ask him what the hell he is trying to do?

(b) shrug your shoulders and put it down to experience?

(c) tell the magistrate that it is all news to you, and that your client is clearly lying in the witness box, and suggest that he should be severely punished?

(d) advise the court that you wish to withdraw as the practitioner representing the defendant, but refuse to give reasons for your request?

(e) assume that the defendant is only now telling the truth for the first time, and that previously he was just too shy to come out with it?

(f) telephone your Law Society from a public telephone box with coins borrowed from the prosecutor?

Would your answer be any different if the defendant made an unsworn statement from the body of the court, and the substance of what he said not only differed from his original instructions to you, but should have been included in a volume of the world's great short stories?

Chapter 55

Afterthought

"There ain't nothing more to write about and I'm rotten glad of it, because if I'd a knowd what a trouble it was to make a book, I wouldn't a tackled it."

Mark Twain, *Huckleberry Finn*.

Index